MW01504272

Enthymemes and Topoi in Dialogue

# Current Research in the Semantics/Pragmatics Interface

*Series Editors*

Klaus von Heusinger (*University of Cologne*)
Ken Turner (*University of Brighton*)

*Editorial Board*

VOLUME 41

The titles published in this series are listed at *brill.com/crispi*

# Enthymemes and Topoi in Dialogue

*The Use of Common Sense Reasoning in Conversation*

*By*

Ellen Breitholtz

**BRILL**

LEIDEN | BOSTON

Library of Congress Cataloging-in-Publication Data

Names: Breitholtz, Ellen, author.
Title: Enthymemes and topoi in dialogue : the use of common sense reasoning in conversation / Ellen Breitholtz.
Description: Leiden ; Boston : Brill, 2020. | Series: Current research in the semantics/pragmatics interface, 1472-7870 ; 41 | Includes bibliographical references and index.
Identifiers: LCCN 2020041641 (print) | LCCN 2020041642 (ebook) | ISBN 9789004436787 (hardback) | ISBN 9789004436794 (ebook)
Subjects: LCSH: Reasoning. | Enthymeme (Logic) | Toposes. | Language and logic. | Conversation analysis.
Classification: LCC BC177 .B735 2020 (print) | LCC BC177 (ebook) | DDC 160–dc23
LC record available at https://lccn.loc.gov/2020041641
LC ebook record available at https://lccn.loc.gov/2020041642

Typeface for the Latin, Greek, and Cyrillic scripts: "Brill". See and download: brill.com/brill-typeface.

ISSN 1472-7870
ISBN 978-90-04-43678-7 (hardback)
ISBN 978-90-04-43679-4 (e-book)

# Contents

# Acknowledgements

This book is partly based on my 2014 PhD thesis on enthymemes in conversation, and developing it into a "real" book has been a challenging and lengthy process. However, I have had lots of help and support from a number of people who all have contributed to also make this process stimulating and enjoyable. First, I should mention Robin Cooper and Christine Howes who have tirelessly read and commented on various parts and versions of this book, not to mention helping me develop many of the ideas presented here in our two projects on reasoning in dialogue—"Incremental reasoning in Dialogue" and "Dialogical reasoning in patients with schizophrenia". I also owe a great thanks to Staffan Larsson for relentlessly pointing out TTR errors and being generally helpful and supportive. Other people who have contributed, either by working with me on things related to enthymemes and topoi, or by reading and commenting on parts of this book at various stages of gestation, are Gunnar Björnson, Stergios Chatzikyriakidis, Stina Ericson, Raquel Fernández, Jonathan Ginzburg, Klaus von Heusinger, Per Linell, Peter Ljunglöf, Vlad Maraev, Ana Maria Mora-Márquez, Coco Norén, Bill Noble, David Schlangen and Julian Schlöder. Last but not least I am very grateful to the anonymous reviewer whose input has been extremely valuable, and to the Swedish Research Council for financing the projects "Incremental Reasoning in Dialogue" (VR: 2016-01162) and CLASP, "Centre of Linguistic Theory and Studies in Probability", (VR: 2014–39) which have enabled me to finish this book.

# Figures

# CHAPTER 1

# Micro-Rhetoric in Dialogic Interaction

(1.1)   Oh! I'm invited to a wedding that night. But the bride is pregnant so I might drop by in the wee hours

The piece of discourse in (1.1) is taken from the facebook event page for a birthday party. The person who wrote (1.1) on the wall of the event did so to communicate that she would be busy on the night of the party, but that she might be able to stop by anyway. Many of us might find her communication clear and her reason for possibly being able to stop by quite reasonable. However, if we think of the argumentation in the second part of the example it is not obvious how the discourse coheres:

(1.2)   The bride (of the wedding I am going to) is pregnant, so I might drop by (at the party) in the wee hours.

Because of the conventional implicature generated by "so", we recognise (1.2) as an argument. By "argument" we mean a piece of discourse where some proposition is supported or explained by another proposition. However, for this argument to be successful—in the sense that the host of the birthday party understands and accepts that the bride being pregnant is a good reason for the guest to be able to stop by at the birthday party later on—additional information is required. This additional information might be a chain of inference like "if the bride is pregnant, she will be tired", and "if she is tired the wedding might not go on for that long".

Moreover, it seems to be the case that—faced with a discourse like (1.1), which conveys an argument—a language user may tentatively accommodate some warrant which would underpin the argument. Arguments like these, which require additional world knowledge to be acceptable or understandable, are important in rhetoric where they are called *enthymemes*. Crucial for the use of enthymemes in rhetorical discourse is that they are based on principles or notions which are so obvious to the audience that the argument seems to express necessity, rather than possibility. The basis for this seems to be cognitive—if we have to do less work to understand an argument, the content of it will appear more natural to us.

Walker (1996) suggests that this is also true for dialogue: Presenting a proposition in connection with some support or back up facilitates processing even when the supporting proposition does not add new information. Walker gives numerous examples that can be seen as constituting arguments with implicit premises.

Enthymemes are not uncommon in conversation. They seem to play a role over and above the rhetorical device found in speeches, and enthymeme-like inferences are at the heart of theories of implicature—not least Relevance Theory (Sperber and Wilson, 1995; Wilson and Sperber, 2004). Despite this, very little work has been done on enthymemes as such in dialogue. An exception to this is Jackson and Jacobs (1980) who link the phenomenon to general principles of conversation.

This work aims to remedy this situation by placing the enthymeme in the context of interactional linguistics and pragmatics. We propose an account of how enthymemes in dialogue interact with patterns of reasoning stored in our cognitive resources to provide structure in discourse and communicate implicit information. Such patterns, in rhetorical theory, are referred to as *topoi*. We also suggest how enthymemes and topoi can be included in a dialogue semantic program, extending theories like KoS (Ginzburg, 2012), where TTR, a type theory with records (Cooper 2005a, 2012) is used to capture dialogue phenomena unaccounted for by traditional formal approaches. In this chapter we will first look at some fields of research in linguistics and computational linguistics which provide many of the main ideas of the theory presented in this book. We will then provide some brief background on enthymemes and topoi and their role in interaction, and finally sketch an outline of the book.

## 1.1    Interaction Based Linguistics

Consider the interpretation of *rise* in (1.3):

(1.3)   CHERRILYN:   Yeah I mean ⟨pause⟩ dog hairs rise anyway so
        FIONA:       What do you mean, rise?
        CHERRILYN:   The hair ⟨pause⟩ it rises upstairs.

                                                    (BNC file KBL:4201–4203)

A snippet of dialogue such as (1.3) can be difficult to make sense of, and this difficulty lies in determining the meaning of particular lexical items (such as *rise*), but also—perhaps to a greater degree—in building hypotheses about situational and discursive contexts where the exchange in (1.3) would make sense. If we consider a larger excerpt from the same dialogue (1.4), we get a better idea of what is going on. From an analytical point of view, however, describing in a precise way how a speaker of English makes sense of (1.4) is challenging to say the least.

(1.4)  CHERRILYN:   Most dogs aren't allowed up ⟨pause⟩ upstairs.
                    He's allowed to go wherever he wants ⟨pause⟩ do whatever he likes.
       FIONA:       Too right!
                    So they should!
                    Shouldn't they?
       CHERRILYN:   Yeah I mean ⟨pause⟩ dog hairs rise anyway so
       FIONA:       What do you mean, rise?
       CHERRILYN:   The hair ⟨pause⟩ it rises upstairs.
                    I mean I, you know friends said it was, oh God I wouldn't allow mine upstairs because of all the ⟨pause⟩ dog hairs!
                    Oh well ⟨pause⟩ they go up there anyway.
       FIONA:       So, but I don't know what it is, right, it's only a few bloody hairs!                    (BNC file KBL:4196–4206)

The dialogue in (1.4) is an excerpt from a conversation regarding dogs (which we will consider in more detail in Chapter 6), and whether or not they should be allowed in certain parts of the house, particularly upstairs. This overarching content is something that most people who have a moderate knowledge of English could determine in a few seconds after first seeing the text. However, the interpretation process is complex, and accounting for it involves explaining many diverse phenomena: We need to explain how we manage to interpret the contextual meaning of words, which is sometimes—as in the case of *rise* in (1.4)—ambiguous, and we need a theory for how words are combined to express propositions. However, we also need to account for how utterances make sense in relation to other utterances. This includes things like anaphor resolution—how do we define, for example, to whom "they" in "Oh well ⟨pause⟩ they go up there anyway" refers?

We also need to explain how speakers make inferences that are necessary for the dialogue to cohere. For example, how does Cherrilyn's utterance about what her friend said serve to address Fiona's clarification request *What do you mean, rise?* And how do we relate Fiona's final utterance *So, but I don't know what it is, right, it's only a few bloody hairs!* to the rest of the dialogue?

Traditional semantics tends to ignore the complexity demonstrated above and instead treats language in terms of sentences which are generated via a set of rules pertaining to an ideal speaker, and the context-free truth conditions of these sentences (Montague, 1973; Kratzer and Heim, 1998).

In pragmatics the truth-conditional accounts of meaning are extended to things like presupposition and implicature. In more recent approaches some of these problems are addressed and to some extent resolved, in the sense that context is taken into account when meanings are interpreted. However, typical dialogue features such as non-sentential utterances (Fernández and Ginzburg, 2002), cross-person compound contributions (Howes, 2012), and disfluencies (Clark and Fox Tree, 2002) are still largely ignored. So, if we are going to analyse language as it appears in dialogue, it would entail additional complexity. For example, some dialogue contributions are in fact non-sentential, a fact that has been noted by philosophers such as Wittgenstein (1953) as well as by linguists doing data driven research (Fernández and Ginzburg, 2002; Schlangen and Lascarides, 2003; Fernández et al., 2007).

Moreover, research in psychology as well as Conversation Analysis (CA) has established that dialogue participants easily interpret and produce incomplete utterances, that is, utterances which are interrupted or where the speaker stops mid sentence (Goodwin, 1979; Altmann and Kamide, 1999). Since conversation is such a essential part of language use, trying to understand how language works without taking dialogue phenomena into account means we will not have a complete picture.

### 1.1.1    *Dialogism*

One interesting aspect of the excerpt in (1.4) is that the dialogue does not run completely smoothly. Cherrilyn says something that Fiona obviously does not understand, and so Fiona makes a clarification request. The fact that we as language users sometimes fail to correctly interpret an utterance provides some clues to what it is that we do when our interpretation is actually successful. How we manage to set the conversation straight again, how we correct our mistakes, is revealing.

One of the approaches to linguistics that emphasises the importance of dialogue is the *dialogical* tradition originating in the ideas of Bakhtin (1986). The umbrella of dialogism covers various types of research, philosophical as well as empirical. Common traits in dialogical research are *contextualism* and *interactionism*. Contextualism means that contexts are always viewed as relevant, and in fact a primary factor in communication. Interactionism means that dialogue, considered as a kind of interaction between agents, is central to the understanding of how language works. One aspect of this is a focus on features typical of dialogue like repairs, corrections and co-constructed sentences.

Linell (1998, 2009)—one of the most recent representatives of the dialogistic tradition—contrasts the dialogistic and the *monologistic* view, which (in the case of linguistics and similar fields) is characterised by a conception of interaction as secondary in the understanding of communication. Linell concedes that a certain amount of monologistic analysis is necessary in linguistic research, as in other research. However, he is skeptical of the reductionism in formal theories. The risk, according to Linell, is that theories which do not pay sufficient attention to the interactive aspect of language, tend to give their users a distorted picture of how language actually works.

Since the late nineties, however, a branch of formal semantics has emerged which takes interaction as its point of departure, and in fact shares many assumptions about the nature of language with dialogism. One notable representative of this line of research is Ginzburg, who has been developing his program—notably in his book *The Interactive Stance* (Ginzburg, 2012)—over the last decades.

### 1.1.2 *Dialogue Semantics*

Influenced by insights from philosophy, artificial intelligence and conversation analysis Ginzburg (2012) has developed KoS, a semantic framework which combines insights from Conversation Analysis and dynamic semantic approaches like Discourse Representation Theory (DRT, Kamp, 1981; Kamp and Reyle, 1993) and Segmented Discourse Representation Theory (SDRT, Asher and Lascarides, 2003; Lascarides and Asher, 2008).

KoS offers a way of accounting for misunderstandings and miscommunication using *dialogue gameboards* (DGB) cast in TTR—a type theory with records first introduced by Cooper (2005b,a, 2012)—to represent the development of the dialogue participants' information states through the course of a dialogue.

One of the fundamental assumptions underpinning any type of dialogue semantics is that structure in language is to a great extent created through interaction—a viewpoint which formal dialogue theories like KoS have in common with Conversation Analysis. Many of the phenomena addressed in work in the KoS spirit involve issues that are relevant to this kind of structure, such as questions, interjections and non sentential utterances, repair and context. Out of these issues, the ones that are most obviously related to enthymemes and topoi are dialogical structure-creating phenomena and context.

In theories of rhetorical relations such as Rhetorical Structure Theory (RST, Mann and Thompson, 1986, 1988) and SDRT (Asher and Lascarides, 2003) a fine-grained taxonomy of rhetorical relations has been proposed, of which many are not dialogical per se, even though they do occur in dialogue. Examples of such relations are *background, narration* and *contrast*.

The approach taken in this book can be said to be a version of KoS. However, the formal details are closer to TTR as it appears in the work of Cooper (2012, 2016) and Breitholtz and Cooper (2011). We will take a closer look at some of the relevant similarities and differences in Chapters 3 and 4.

## 1.2      Micro-rhetorical Linguistics

The interest in "imperfect" language use is something that Ginzburg and Linell have in common with Paul Hopper. In his paper *Linguistics and Micro-Rhetoric: A Twenty-First Century Encounter*, (Hopper, 2007), he argues that grammar is essentially an abstraction of the way we string together prefabricated fragments and fixed phrases, and that grammaticality as well as deviations from grammaticality can usually be explained by our tendency towards efficiency in communication—which is emphasised in rhetoric. Hopper argues that the interactive perspective with its focus on language as situated in time and space brings the disciplines of linguistics and rhetoric closer together:

> ... in fact (usage based) linguistics is nothing but the micro-end of rhetoric
> HOPPER (2007) p. 236

Hopper argues that a micro-rhetorical analysis would differ from the type of analysis usually applied in traditional rhetoric—if we want to find out things about words and phrases rather than debates, speeches and their contexts and effects, we have to look at smaller bits of language like utterances or short episodes. The linguistic phenomena which Hopper is interested in are mainly syntactic, like the case of *apo koinou* (or pivot) constructions, sometimes found in natural data. *Apo koinou* is a construction where one constituent serves as the end of one grammatical sentence and the beginning of another, for example "That's what grabs their attention most is adverts" (Hopper, 2007).

However, if we apply a micro-rhetorical perspective to other areas of linguistics, there seem to be other language phenomena which are to some extent addressed in rhetoric, often from a different perspective than that applied to the same phenomena in linguistics. In semantics and pragmatics for example, the notion of inference is essential. In semantics we study inferences like presuppositions, which derive from the meanings of particular words and constructions. For example the word "again" in a sentence such as "I lost the book again", triggers the presupposition that the speaker has lost the book before. This is due to the meaning of "again", and not context dependent.

Other types of inferences, like conversational implicatures, are to a great extent dependent on context and on the assumption of some general expectations we have about communication. Inferences are also central in rhetoric. In fact, the art of rhetoric is much focused on how to lead an audience to make particular inferences, and thereby become convinced of the point which the speaker wishes to communicate.

In rhetorical theory the enthymeme is the type of evidence, or proof, which relates to reasoning and making inferences. In the early eighties, Jackson and Jacobs (1980) suggested that enthymemes are related to conversational practices that we use continuously when we talk and communicate in other ways. They argue that the rhetorical enthymeme is derived from more general principles of communication and interaction. While this seems likely, it is nevertheless the case that the connection between inferences and conversational phenomena such as turn-taking and preference structure has not been a focus in linguistics. Inferences like implicature and presupposition are mainly studied in philosophy of language and pragmatics, while conversational practices and contextualised language use is mainly considered by conversation analysts. However, in rhetoric there is a focus on the inferential quality of language in use as well as on how we should use this quality to our advantage, that is, how we should employ inferences to make the communication run smoothly in a particular context.

It seems to us that the rhetorical perspective has not been considered enough in linguistics although it could contribute to the understanding of inference, coherence and other phenomena in dialogue and other types of linguistic communication. Thus, we aim in this work to look more closely at enthymematic reasoning and how it plays out in dialogue. In Section 1.6 we will state our aim in more detail, but let us first take a closer look at the concepts of enthymeme and topos.

## 1.3    The Aristotelian Enthymeme

### 1.3.1    *Aristotelian Rhetoric*
Aristotle's *Rhetoric* was intended as instruction on the art of public speaking, but in fact it is also a comprehensive introduction to a number of aspects of linguistics which are relevant to the study of linguistic interaction. It does not deal with logic, but with the logic-like type of reasoning which frequently occurs in dialogue and other types of discourse. Aristotle's *Rhetoric* also discusses emotions and their causes and effects, as well as cognitive aspects of language and style. Thus Aristotelian rhetorical theory actually combines ele-

ments of what we would today call the pragmatics, psycholinguistics and sociolinguistics of dialogue.

For a modern day researcher who looks to the classics, it is important to know whether one is motivated by an interest in historical reconstruction, i.e. in trying to understand a text in its historical context and interpreting its original meaning, or in attempting to seek inspiration from the insights of classical theorists. Since our aim here is to use our interpretation of some Aristotelian notions to contribute to contemporary theories of dialogue semantics and pragmatics, this work is clearly a case of the latter. Therefore we will just give a brief account of the social and cultural context of the *Rhetoric*, and of the concepts of enthymeme and topos as they occur in renditions of Aristotle's text.[1]

Aristotle's *Rhetoric* was written as a guide for students of rhetoric in a context where the ability to speak well in public was important to any free citizen. There were no professional lawyers or prosecutors, so anyone who wanted to take a case to court or who was summoned to court to meet an accusation had to stand up and speak for himself (for a more detailed account, see Corbett and Connors, 1999). Also, in a democracy like Athens where ordinary people without much insight into public matters and state affairs were allowed to vote, it was essential for anyone aspiring to a political career to master the art of persuasion by referring to the likelihood of possibilities rather than to knowledge and facts alone. In the *Rhetoric*, book one, chapter one, section eleven, Aristotle explicitly states the importance of tapping into common beliefs and opinions when dealing with a crowd, rather than presenting the audience with facts and strictly logical reasoning:

> Speech based on knowledge is teaching, but teaching is impossible with some audiences; rather, it is necessary for *pisteis* (proof) and speeches as a whole to be formed on the basis of common beliefs.
>
> *Rhet I 1.11*

### 1.3.2    *The Syllogism and the Enthymeme*

Apart from the importance of adjusting the arguments to the audience, Aristotle claims that rhetoric should not (as it had in previous rhetorical handbooks) focus on external matters such as the different parts of a speech and in which order they should appear in the discourse, but rather on *logos*, reasoning (*Rhet. I 1.9*), which is also the aspect of rhetoric which is most relevant to our discussion.

---

1    All citations of the *Rhetoric* refer to Kennedy's translation (Aristotle, ca. 340 B.C.E./2007).

Before we look further at Aristotle's view of rhetorical reasoning, let's say something about his view of the related field of logic. First, it is important to remember that Aristotelian logic is not equivalent to modern, formal logic, although it has been pointed out that the differences are perhaps less pronounced than what was thought to be the case in the early 20th century (Smith, 2012). One essential difference, however, is that while modern logic is formulated by means of artificial languages, Aristotle dealt only with natural language. A central concept in the Aristotelian theory of deduction is the *syllogism*. In the *Prior Analytics* Aristotle defines it as

> An argument (*logos*) in which, certain things having been supposed, something different from the things supposed results of necessity because these things are so
>
> *Pr An I I.24b 18–20*

The phrase "certain things having been supposed" refers to the set of premises, and, being in the plural, "the things supposed" indicates, according to Keyt (2009), that there must be more than one premise. In rhetoric, the correlate of the deductive type of proof, the syllogism, is the enthymeme. The conclusion of an enthymeme does not—in contrast to that of a syllogism—need to follow of necessity. Nor is there a need for the set of premises to consist of more than one premise. These are formal requirements, but there are also some other ways in which syllogisms and enthymemes differ, mainly having to do with subject matter. While logical arguments should deal with general statements, enthymemes deal with particular cases. Thus, while in logic you argue for or against a general claim about the world, in rhetoric you seek to persuade someone of something regarding a particular case.

In (1.5) we see an example of a syllogism, where the conclusion necessarily follows from the premises. In (1.6) on the other hand, the conclusion depends on a notion that if someone has done something which is considered bad, then that person is likely to also have done less bad things. As Aristotle puts it: "if the greater thing is true, then the lesser is also, for people strike their fathers less than their neighbours" (*Rhet. II 23.4*).

(1.5)  Socrates is a man
       All men are mortal
       ―――――――――――――
       Socrates is mortal

(1.6)      $x$ had beaten his father
       ―――――――――――――――――
       $x$ has also beaten his neighbour

Presenting an argument based on implicit premises is possible since the members of an audience—just like people who partake in a conversation—have knowledge and beliefs regarding the world around them. In this case Aristotle expected the audience to recognise, based on experience and previous input, that it is more common and a lesser crime to beat your neighbour than your father, so when they hear that someone is known to have beaten his father, they may find it quite reasonable that he is also guilty of beating his neighbour, if such charge has been made against him.

## 1.4     Topoi—the Warrants of Enthymemes

In order to be efficient, an enthymeme needs to draw on some commonly recognised notion that "fills in" the information that is lacking in the set of premises. This notion Aristotle refers to as the *topos* of the enthymeme. Some topoi may be applied to various subjects, while others are specific to a particular subject. An example of a general topos is the *topos of the more and the less,* of which Aristotle says

> ... to form syllogisms or speak enthymemes from this about justice is just as possible as about physics or anything else, although these subjects differ in species.
>
> *Rhet I 2.21*

An example of a general type of topos is that of *opposites*, on which the enthymeme in (1.7) is based.

(1.7)   a. ... to be temperate is a good thing, for lack of self-control is harmful
           (*Rhet II 23.1.*)

         b.  lack of self-control is harmful
            to be temperate is a good thing

The enthymeme in (1.7) draws on the idea that since self-control and lack of self-control are opposites, the opposite of what is true of self-control is true of lack of self-control. Alternatively, and more generally, if two things are opposites, the opposite of what is true of the first must (or is usually) true of the second. This example shows that the common notion of Aristotelian enthymemes as syllogisms with one hidden or silent premise, is not always correct. Strictly speaking, enthymemes based on the topos of opposites seem to require a set of additional premises to constitute a reasonable argument to an audience.

### 1.4.1   Topoi in Linguistics

The concept of topos is essential in the theory of argumentation presented by Ducrot (1980, 1988), to an extent in collaboration with Anscombre (1995). The theory is based on the idea that between two utterances $U$ and $V$ where one of them is an assertion or a suggestion, exhortation, etc. and the other an assertion which functions as a support for the first, there is always a link which sanctions the interpretation of $U$ and $V$ as an argument. For example, imagine a situation where two people are at the cinema trying to decide which film to see. One of them utters (1.8), where (1.8b) is clearly a reason for the suggestion made in (1.8a).

(1.8)    a.  *A*: Let's not see a drama
         b.  *A*: I'm too tired

According to Ducrot a dialogue contribution like (1.8) exploits a link which sanctions the interpretation that the drama genre should be avoided by tired people. This link could be the idea that dramas are complex and cognitively challenging compared to other genres. This seems reasonable and something that most adults would recognise, if not agree with. A link like this is referred to by Ducrot and Anscombre as a *topos*.

Ducrot (1988) argues that topoi are notions which are *common*, that is they are assumed or taken for granted in a community, even before the conversation in which they are employed takes place. Topoi are also *gradual*, that is if I say "it's warm today, let's go to the beach", the topos—that warm weather makes the beach an attractive destination—is more true the warmer it is, and less true the less warm it is. A consequence of this would be that an enthymeme evoking a topos may be more or less convincing, depending on the context of utterance.

Topoi are also *general* in the sense that one topos can be employed in various arguments, in various situations. The opposite, that different topoi may be employed in similar situations, is also true. Anscombre (1995) argues that when we say *Give a coin to the porter, he carried the bags all the way here*, there is an obvious connection between the first and second proposition expressed in the utterance. However, the connection between "carrying luggage" and "getting a tip" is not linguistic, it's the common place principle that work should be rewarded, which is generally recognised, if not agreed upon in all situations. Interestingly, argues Anscombre, there are other, equally acceptable, principles which would lead to an opposite conclusion, such as principles that porters get paid to carry luggage already, and you should not get a tip for doing your job.

Anscombre also makes the important observation that topoi, contrary to logical rules, do not constitute a monolithic system. Instead the system of topoi consists of principles which may be combined in different ways, like logical rules, but which may be inconsistent if combined in a specific situation. Anscombre (1995) suggests that this is because topoi are part of ideology, ways in which we perceive the world, and ideologies are not monolithic. Therefore, a principle like *opposites attract* and *birds of a feather flock together* may co-exist not only in one community, but in the set of topoi of one individual, and be applicable in different contexts.

### 1.4.2    *Topoi as Cultural Indicators*

The idea of a dichotomy of beliefs in *episteme* and *doxa* goes back to Plato. On the Platonic view, episteme is knowledge about the world of forms (world of ideas), while doxa represents our beliefs about the world of perception.

The concept of doxa has been connected to rhetoric in an interesting way. Rosengren (2002) argues that doxa is in some respects a more relevant concept than episteme: The difference, as Rosengren sees it, between traditional epistemology and the doxology he argues in favour of, is that while epistemology is concerned with (universally) true beliefs, doxology is concerned with what is *held* to be true, appropriate or right in a certain context—in other words— which topoi are applicable in that context. To be aware of what is consistent with the doxa—the topoi—of a certain community could thus be more relevant for a speaker constructing arguments than the beliefs which are *actually* true—it is possible to construct convincing arguments from false beliefs just as well as from true ones.

The technique of adapting your arguments to the beliefs of the audience is well established in rhetorical theory, and Rosengren argues that rhetoric can be seen not only as a tool for *forming* arguments which are persuasive to a certain audience in a certain context, but also as a tool for *finding out* what the speaker and the audience of a discourse believe to be true (or, in the case of the audience, what the speaker believes they believe to be true), right and just.

Rosengren follows Perelman and Olbrechts-Tyteca (1969) in declaring that the topoi which a speaker's arguments draw on to some extent define the world view of the speaker and the addressee. Rosengren (2002, p. 87), argues that in this terminology, it is possible to describe different societies by describing the topoi which are dominant within these societies. In the context of dialogue modelling, this would mean that modelling the topoi available to an agent is a way of modelling that agent's take on (a limited part of) the agent's sociocultural context.

## 1.5      Linking Enthymeme and Topos

To conclude the discussion about the view of enthymemes and topoi in previous literature, we should say something about the role they play in discourse and in relation to each other.

Enthymemes are units of discourse that may simultaneously serve many purposes. Enthymemes convey propositions that are not explicit in the discourse. They do this by requiring underpinning by topoi for an acceptable interpretation. The pragmatic meaning conveyed by an enthymeme in relation to a listener depends on which topos the listener accesses in the interpretation process.

In (1.9) President Bush, in his "State of the Union" address 2005, argues that Americans must join together to save social security, since the system is headed towards bankruptcy (the enthymeme $\varepsilon$ below). This argument is underpinned by a topos ($\tau$ below) that if a certain state of affairs is beneficial or good, it should be safeguarded. The argument also depends on a premise that social security is a good thing.

(1.9)    a. "... we must join together to strengthen and save Social Security"
            (Bush, 2005 State of the Union par. 16).
            "[Because] Social Security will be paying out more than it takes
            in ... by the year 2042, the entire system would be exhausted and
            bankrupt." (Bush, 2005 State of the Union par. 19).

    b. $\varepsilon = \dfrac{\text{the social security system is heading towards bankruptcy}}{\text{we must save social security}}$

    c. $\tau = \dfrac{\text{something worth keeping is heading towards destruction}}{\text{it must be saved}}$

If we accept the validity of $\tau$ in (1.9c), and (at least) the premise that social security is something worth keeping, the conclusion of $\varepsilon$ in (1.9b) follows by necessity. It is thus possible to accept the topos, but not the premises that make the enthymeme an instantiation of the topos, and thus reject the enthymeme.

## 1.6    Aim and Outline of This Book

In this chapter we have described a number of dialogue features where enthymematic structure seems to play a role. Examples of such features are sense-making and coherence in language use. These questions are at the heart of pragmatics, and much of what we refer to here as "enthymematic reasoning" is discussed in theories of implicature, such as Gricean and neo-Gricean approaches (Horn, 1984; Levinson, 2000) and Relevance Theory (Sperber and Wilson, 1995; Carston and Hall, 2012). Some of the processes described in this book are also accounted for in other theories. However, while theories of implicature account for many of the principles of pragmatic reasoning, they still rely heavily on inferential processes which are not defined in the theory. Drawing on principles such as the principle of relevance and Gricean maxims we can make predictions about the existence of implicated conclusions, but we cannot make any precise predictions about the nature of these conclusions given a certain situational context and background. The theory presented here can make such predictions, which makes it possible to use in implementations of pragmatic inference.

We also considered a number of approaches to linguistics which we believe share many theoretical and methodological assumptions. All of these—dialogism, KoS and the micro-rhetorical perspective—focus on accounting for phenomena which are common in dialogue. Coherence in conversation cannot always be accounted for by theories of anaphora and other phenomena treated in dynamic semantics. We often express ourselves elliptically, engage in clarification, and repair our utterances. Adopting a theoretical standpoint where these features are relevant parts of language rather than non-standard features, means among other things that context and pragmatic processes must be integrated, or at least possible to integrate, in any linguistic theory.

Enthymematic reasoning relies heavily on context, and often interacts with dialogue features such as clarification and ellipsis. Our aim is thus to formulate a theory for how enthymemes and topoi play a role in dialogue, in a framework that allows for a rich account of context as well as integration of dialogue features such as repair and clarification.

In the remainder of this book we will first, in Chapter 2, look at a number of linguistic phenomena discussed in the literature which are in various ways related to enthymemes. In Chapter 3 we will give a brief introduction to TTR and information states modelled as gameboards, and sketch a gameboard analysis of some simple dialogue examples involving enthymematic reasoning. In Chapter 4 we will go into the types of information states in more detail and extend the model by introducing update rules to account for interpretation of dialogue contributions involving enthymemes and topoi. In Chapter 5 we will consider how dialogue participants draw on topoi in inventing enthymemes and how the production and interpretation of enthymemes are related to particular conversational games. In Chapter 6 we will look at some applications of our theory, considering issues like non-monotonic reasoning and lexical disambiguation. Finally, in Chapter 7, we will present our conclusions and discuss remaining problems and future work.

# CHAPTER 2

# Enthymematic Reasoning and Pragmatics

## 2.1    Introduction

There is an obvious connection between on the one hand enthymematic reasoning and topoi, and on the other pragmatic phenomena like implicature, presupposition and different types of discourse relations. In this chapter we will briefly discuss the relation between rhetorical reasoning drawing on topoi and such phenomena.

First, in Section 2.2 we will look at presupposition (Strawson, 1950; Stalnaker, 1974; Karttunen, 1974), moving on to Grice's account of conversational implicature (Grice, 1975) in Section 2.3. In Sections 2.4 and 2.5 we are still concerned with inference, considering the approach to implicature taken in Relevance Theory (Sperber and Wilson, 1995), and the anti-inferentialist view of inference presented in Recanati (2004). In Section 2.6 we will consider sense-making of longer strands of discourse and how we assign rhetorical relations between sentences or utterances.

We do not claim that this account of topics related to enthymemes and topoi is exhaustive. It would probably be possible to fill a book with a relevant discussion on the relation between enthymemes and implicature alone. However, we hope that this chapter will give an overview and answer some questions, while also raising many new ones.

## 2.2    Presupposition

The classic, semantic, definition of presupposition is that it is an inference which survives embedding under negation (see for example Strawson, 1950). Stalnaker (1974) argued against the notion of semantic presupposition and diagnostics such as the negation test, in favour of a pragmatic analysis. In (2.1a) and (2.1b) we see Stalnaker's definition of semantic and pragmatic presupposition respectively.

(2.1)   a.   ... a proposition that $P$ presupposes that $Q$ iff $Q$ must be true in order that $P$ have a truth-value at all (Stalnaker, 1974 p. 48).
        b.   ... something like the background beliefs of the speaker—propositions whose truth he takes for granted, or seems to take for granted, in making his statement (Stalnaker, 1974 p. 48).

An example of an utterance that would carry a presupposition according to the definition in (2.1a) is (2.2), which presupposes that there is a queen of England; this needs to be true for the sentence to be true or false.

(2.2)    A: The queen of England is bald.

The presupposition of (2.2) would be the same regardless of which of the definitions in (2.1) we use. However, the pragmatic definition would include other types of inferences too, which would not fall under presupposition according to the semantic definition in (2.1b). Let us consider one of the examples from Chapter 1, repeated in (2.3):

(2.3)    The bride is pregnant, so I might drop by in the wee hours!

The example in (2.3) conveys the enthymeme in (2.4).

(2.4)    $$\frac{\text{the bride is pregnant}}{\text{I might drop by in the wee hours}}$$

According to Stalnaker's definition in (2.1b), (2.4) carries a (pragmatic) presupposition that a pregnant bride is a reason for a wedding party to end early. This indicates that topoi sometimes are pragmatic presuppositions. However, this is not very specific, since pragmatic presupposition seems to encompass a whole array of ways of communicating implicit meaning. The example in (2.4), for example, is similar to that given by Grice (1975) to illustrate the notion of *conventional implicature*:

(2.5)    a. S: He is an Englishman. He is, therefore, brave (Grice, 1975).
         b. Conventional implicature: If someone is an Englishman, he is brave.

Grice claims that the word *therefore* in (2.5a) gives rise to the conventional implicature in (2.5b). From a micro-rhetorical point of view, we can see (2.5a) as an enthymematic argument that a particular person will be brave since he is an Englishman, based on a topos that if someone is an Englishman then that someone will be brave.

So, we have established that topoi may function as pragmatic presuppositions, and that some topoi could also be categorised as conventional implicatures. However, a topos cannot be the exact same thing as a conventional implicature, since some enthymemes lack a lexical item that conventionally implicates a particular structure between its constituents. Let us consider, for example, (2.6), an authentic dialogue example originally used by Walker (1996). The turn in the excerpt consists of two utterances produced by the same speaker[1] *A*—the speaker—and *B*—the addressee—are two colleagues on their way to work. They meet up somewhere along the way and continue their walk together. This is something they often do, and they are thus both familiar with the surroundings as well as with the physical goal of the walk.

(2.6)   A: Let's walk along Walnut Street. It's shorter.

For this turn to make sense to an addressee, they would have to assume that the speaker presupposes some kind of link between Walnut Street being shorter and the suggestion to walk along Walnut Street. However, since there is no specific word in (2.6) which warrants this assumption, this link cannot be a conventional implicature. Instead it seems to be the case that the rhetorical structure of (2.6)—and thereby part of its meaning—depends on the dialogue participants already having access to a notion that a route being short is a reason for choosing that route. In micro-rhetorical terms we would say that this notion is a topos, which may also be a subtype of a more abstract topos having to do with convenience, efficiency, etc.

### 2.2.1   *Accommodation*

The process of adding a presupposition (semantic or pragmatic) to the discourse model is usually referred to as *accommodation*. This phenomenon was discussed by Stalnaker (1974) and Karttunen (1974), but the term was coined by Lewis (1979).

Lewis illustrates the notion of presupposition accommodation with the example (2.7), where (2.7a) is ok but (2.7b) seems odd.

(2.7)   a. Fred has children, all Fred's children are asleep.
        b. All Fred's children are asleep, and Fred has children

The reason for this, argues Lewis, is that the proposition *All Fred's children are asleep* presupposes that Fred has children. Thus, the belief that Fred has children is already integrated in the discourse model for speaker and addressee alike, and adding it a second time is redundant.

---

1   The term *utterance* is sometimes defined as a string of words produced by a speaker while said speaker is holding the floor. We will use the term *turn* to refer to such a unit, and reserve *utterance* for units that convey an atomic proposition, something like what Schlangen (2005) refers to as *intentional units*.

The presupposition in (2.7) is a semantic presupposition triggered by the possessive *Fred's children*, but Lewis' definition of presupposition accommodation in (2.8) seems to include any type of pragmatic presupposition.

(2.8)    If at time $t$ something is said that requires a presupposition $P$ to be acceptable, and if $P$ is not presupposed just before $t$, then—*ceteris paribus* and within certain limits—presupposition $P$ comes into existence at $t$ (Lewis, 1979 p. 340).

This means, for example, that if nobody in the discourse context objects when a speaker utters (2.6), the assumption of a link between the route being short and the advantage of choosing it will be accommodated in the conversation. However, if someone says something like *"What do you mean shorter—why would we want to choose the shortest route?"*, this is evidence that the pragmatic presupposition—or topos—has not been accommodated in that speaker's discourse model. Stalnaker (1998) points out that in order for accommodation to work a speaker cannot expect controversial assumptions to be accommodated, and quotes Heim (1992):

> One may explicitly assert controversial and surprising things (in fact one should) but to expect one's audience to accept them by way of accommodation is not good conversational practice.

In rhetorical terms we could say that it is not wise to choose an enthymeme which is not already associated with a suitable topos that the addressee has access to, or that evokes a topos which is acceptable to the audience.

Lewis shows that the principle of accommodation applies to several linguistic phenomena, such as definiteness, modal expressions, etc. To that list we would like to add topoi—when a topos which is necessary for an enthymematic argument to make sense is added to the discourse model—and enthymemes—when a topos in the resources of an agent causes her to assign an enthymematic structure to the discourse.

In this section we have shown that topoi are included in Stalnaker's wide definition of pragmatic presupposition. In addition to this, in some cases topoi are to be considered conventional implicatures, in the sense of Grice (1975). Whether a topos is conventionally implicated or not depends on whether the enthymematic structure is established by means of lexical items signaling that the speaker assumes a causal relation between the premise and conclusion of the enthymeme.

There is a distinctly rhetorical dimension to accommodation of presuppositions as well as accommodation of other phenomena, in that it may allow content to be smuggled into the discourse and trick hearers into accepting—or at least not objecting to—things they would reject if they were said explicitly. We suggest that we could talk about accommodation of both topoi (as types of pragmatic presuppositions) and enthymemes (argumentative structure). We also suggest that the notion of "surprising" or "controversial" presuppositions which Stalnaker (1998) and Heim (1992) argue should not be left to accommodation according to good conversational practices, are presuppositions which cannot be identified as belonging to a topos that is acceptable by the agent in question.

## 2.3    Conversational Implicature

Grice's theory of conversational implicature is an attempt to systematically describe how it is possible for language users to convey (and mean) more— or something different—than the truth-conditional content of an utterance. Grice (1975) distinguishes between *what is said* and *what is implicated. What is said* corresponds to the truth-conditional meaning of an utterance and *what is implicated* to what a speaker conveys by uttering a certain string of words in a certain context, assuming (though perhaps not aware of) the *principle of cooperation* elaborated as four *maxims* of rational and efficient communication. In the exchange in (2.9) below, from Grice (1975), $B$'s reply that there is a garage around the corner would not be very helpful if $B$ knew the garage to be closed, not to sell petrol, etc.

(2.9)    a. *A*: I am out of petrol
          b. *B*: There is a garage around the corner

$A$ expects $B$'s utterance to be a relevant, truthful and complete reply, based on background knowledge and an assumption that $B$ is being cooperative. As mentioned, Grice specifies the assumptions of the Cooperative Principle further in the four *maxims of conversation* (paraphrased):

1    Quantity: Make your contribution informative enough, but do not say more than is required.
2    Quality: Be truthful, or at least only say what you believe to be true.
3    Relation: Be relevant.
4    Manner: Be orderly, avoid ambiguity, etc.

By adhering to, or blatantly ignoring (*flouting*) the maxims and the cooperative principle, a speaker may express a lot more than the truth-conditional content of his/her utterance. So, Grice would say that we would interpret (2.9b) as implicating that the garage is open (or at least that the speaker believes this) due to the maxim of relation, since the information that there is a garage around the corner would otherwise be irrelevant. Let us now consider (2.10), which we looked at in the previous section. In Gricean terms it could be analysed like this:

(2.10)  a.  *A*: Let's walk along Walnut Street.
        b.  *A*: It's shorter.
        c.  Implicature: Walnut Street being shorter is a good reason for choosing Walnut Street.

Due to the maxim of relation, we as language users want to interpret (2.10b) as a relevant contribution. One way of doing this would be to interpret it as a relevant reason for choosing Walnut Street. However, it seems to us that we need something more than the Cooperative Principle and the maxims to get at the correct implicature in (2.10). We can illustrate this by comparing (2.10) with the similar dialogue (2.11):

(2.11)  a.  *A*: Let's walk along Walnut Street.
        b.  *A*: It's longer.
        c.  Implicature: ??

Now, by simply applying the cooperative principle and the maxims *A*'s conversational partner *B* might be able to infer that (2.11b) is relevant in relation to (2.11a). However, if *B*'s resources do not include a topos underpinning (2.11b) as a premise in an argument for choosing Walnut Street—such as *longer routes are better* or *it is preferable to spend longer time doing things*—it would be hard for *B* to arrive at a relevant interpretation. This is of course context dependent— there are some things that we like spending as long time as possible doing, and if walking is one of them, it is natural that a longer route is preferred. If *B* knew that *A* is always interested in getting exercise, which of course a longer route would provide in greater measure, *B* might also be able to derive the relevant interpretation of (2.11). However, considering the notions most of us have about comfort, efficiency, etc. (2.10) seems like less of a stretch unless the context is set up in a specific way. So, even if the maxims tell us that we should try to interpret contributions as relevant, true, etc., in order to do this we need some underpinning in the form of a pattern of reasoning—a topos—that fits in with the contribution we are trying to make sense of. If we consider yet another manipulation of our original example, this is even more clear:

(2.12)   a. *A*: Let's walk along Walnut Street.
         b. *A*: In the European Union, labour market conditions showed no
            signs of improvement during 2013.

The contribution in (2.12b) is very difficult to make sense of in the context of
(2.12a), and would probably be taken as relating to an earlier utterance or as *A*
abruptly changing the subject (however, it cannot be excluded that it *could* be
interpreted as relevant under particular circumstances).

So, even though it appears that we use some notions corresponding to Grice's
principle of cooperation and related maxims to interpet enthymemes, we need
access to some underpinning pattern or topos to actually arrive at an interpretation. If we do not have access to relevant topoi, or if the contribution does not
contain enough information to point us in the direction of a relevant topos, we
have difficulty making a relevant interpretation. In cases like these we may get
additional information by making a clarification request. Imagine for example
a context of (2.9) where *B* would be totally unaware that you can buy petrol in
a garage. The dialogue in (2.9) could then play out as in (2.13):

(2.13)   a. *A*: I am out of petrol
         b. *B*: There is a garage around the corner
         c. *A*: What do you mean garage—I need to buy petrol?
         d. *B*: They sell petrol
         e. *A*: Ah—ok!

To conclude, it seems that the principles suggested by Grice lead us in some
cases to infer that a speaker means something more than what is said. However,
if we have access to relevant topoi we can understand not only *that* something
is implicated but *what* is implicated. If we, on the contrary, do not have access to
a topos that fits the discourse, it is difficult for us to make sense of an utterance
where part of the meaning is conversationally implicated. Some conversational
implicatures can be accounted for by other means, for example scalar implicatures (Horn, 1984). However, in the case of relevance implicature for example,
we need something like a topos to produce and interpret contributions.

## 2.4    Relevance Theory

While the neo-Gricean developments of implicature theory have reduced the
maxims to a smaller set of communicative principles, Relevance Theory (Sperber and Wilson, 1995; Wilson and Sperber, 2004; Carston, 2006) has replaced

them with just one *principle of relevance*. Unlike the maxims, this principle is not perceived as a communicative norm based on assumptions of cooperation and rationality, but rather as a fundamental feature of human cognition.

Unlike Gricean pragmatics, which distinguishes between *what is said*—the truth-conditional content of an expression—and *what is implicated*, Relevance theory distinguishes between *explicature* and implicature, where explicature refers to the explicit content of an utterance in a particular context. For example, we would generally interpret (2.14a) as Jack and Jill being married to each other rather than to other people. According to Relevance theory this is the explicit, truth-evaluable content—the explicture—of the utterance, which is arrived at through disambiguation, reference resolution and other pragmatic processes.

(2.14)   a. Utterance: Jack and Jill are married
         b. Explicature: Jack and Jill are married to each other.

Meaning interpretation in Relevance Theory is not perceived as something that happens in steps where one step is executed after the other (primary and secondary processes). Instead, the interpretation process is seen as incremental, and hypotheses about explicatures, implicated premises and implicated conclusions are developed in parallel. According to Sperber and Wilson (2004) this is an inferential process, i.e. if certain explicatures are assumed, certain implicated premises (intended contextual assumptions) and implicated conclusions (implicatures) follow by necessity. This is illustrated very well by the example in (2.15) (Sperber and Wilson, 1995):

(2.15)   a. Peter: Would you drive a Saab?
         b. Mary: I wouldn't drive ANY Swedish car.
         c. Implicated premise: A Saab is a Swedish car
         d. Implicated conclusion: Mary wouldn't drive a Saab

In (2.15) the implicated conclusion (implicature) is that Mary would not drive a Saab, based on the implicated premise that a Saab is a Swedish car. According to Relevance Theory, this premise presents itself automatically due to the relevance assumption—if a Saab were not a Swedish car, why would Mary answer the way she did? However, if Peter thought that a Saab is a German car, the implicated premise and conclusion might not be obvious to him, despite the relevance assumption. And if a Saab were not, in fact, a Swedish car, and Peter knew this, the relevance assumption alone would probably not be enough for the interaction to run smoothly.

The example in (2.15) is neat, since the relevance assumption seems to do the work unless one of the agents involved in the dialogue lacks necessary background knowledge. However, in (2.16), an example taken from Carston and Hall (2012), the situation is not as straightforward:

(2.16)   a. Max: How was the party?
         b. Amy: There wasn't enough to drink and everybody left early

Here we would probably infer the implicated conclusion that the party was not a success, based on implicated premises that "people leaving early" and "lack of drink" are associated with "dull party". As previously discussed, given the implicated premise in (2.15), the implicated conclusion follows by necessity. However, in (2.16), this is not the case. For the implicated premises to necessarily lead to the conclusion that the party was unsuccessful, they would have to be universal rules. For example, the implicated premise "every party at which there is not enough drink is unsuccessful" would, in any context, lead to the conclusion that a *particular* party at which there was not enough drink was unsuccessful. However, this seems unsatisfactory. Many would agree that a low drink supply is acceptable as an explanation for why a party is unsuccessful, but there might also be exceptions to this.

### 2.4.1   *Relevance, Enthymemes and Topoi*
Like Gricean and neo-Gricean theories of implicature, Relevance Theory provides an account for why we interpret utterances like (2.16b) as conveying more than the truth-conditional content. However, both Gricean and Relevance Theoretical accounts require some underpinning for the implicated inferences. The theory that we propose accounts for the nature of the implicated premises, and also for how implicated conclusions are generated. For example, let us consider (2.16) in terms of enthymematic reasoning.

(2.17)   there wasn't enough drink at the party and everyone left early
         ———————————————————————————————————————————
                      the party was not a success

Rather than viewing this enthymeme as an incomplete argument requiring a set of implicated premises which *necessarily* lead to the implicated conclusion, we suggest that the enthymeme is underpinned by more general topoi, licensing the proposition of the antecedent as an acceptable reason for the proposition of the conclusion. The topos that parties at which there is too little to drink are unsuccessful does not hold in all cases, but, if we agree with it, we would probably also agree that it is more acceptable the more it fits in with the situation at hand. That is, if there is almost nothing to drink at a party, it is very likely for the party to be unsuccessful. This is a good example of what Ducrot (1988) refers to as the graduality of topoi (see Section 1.4.1).

The second topos invoked here is one linking "bad party" to "guests leaving early". This might not be a rule that specifically concerns parties and guests, but rather one whose gist is that if people do not like something, they tend to leave—people vote with their feet. We agree with the view that there are implicit premises in dialogues such as (2.16), and that these to some degree have to be anticipated by the speaker and accommodated by the listener. However, we believe that these implicit premises are not precise, but rather an instantiation in the dialogue situation of one or more general topoi.

## 2.5     Anti-inferentialism

Unlike the Relevance Theoretical view, the *anti-inferentialist* (Recanati, 2001, 2004) view of pragmatic meaning in context attributes many aspects of utterance meaning to non-inferential processes. On this view interpretation of an utterance happens in two steps—via *primary pragmatic processes* and *secondary pragmatic processes*, where the primary processes correspond roughly to Relevance Theory's concept of explicature. However, the distinguishing characteristic of primary pragmatic processes is that they do not require the prior identification of some proposition. They are not conscious, since a "normal" language user is unaware of the processes through which the context-free meaning is enriched to fit the situation. Primary pragmatic processes may be bottom up, i.e. they are linguistically mandated, or top down, i.e. they are contextually driven. Recanati (2004) lists four different types of primary pragmatic processes:

- *Saturation*: Mandatory, linguistically motivated disambiguation e.g. anaphor resolution. (Bottom up)
- *Free enrichment*: The sentence *She took out the key and opened the door* would generally be interpreted in a way such that the key that was taken out was the key used to open the door. Usually, free enrichment corresponds to the *specification* of some expression in the utterance by making it contextually more specific.
- *Loosening*: When a concept is used more generally than the literal interpretation allows, for example, in the utterance *the ATM swallowed my credit card*, the aspects of swallowing that the speaker refers to are more general than what we connect with actual swallowing by a living creature.
- *Semantic transfer*: In the utterance *The ham-sandwich left without paying*, *the ham-sandwich* refers to the person who ordered the ham-sandwich—

not to the dish itself. *I'm parked out back* does not mean that the person who performs the utterance is parked out back but that his or her car (or other vehicle) is.

The anti-inferentialist take on interpretation is characterised by the belief that all pragmatic processes which are necessary to arrive at a truth conditional interpretation are perceived as being non-inferential. Of the different types of primary processes mentioned above, all except saturation are contextually mandated (top-down), and these are the ones that interest us most. Recanati proposes that "interpretation is as direct as perception" in these cases, and instead of looking to logic to explain for example enrichment, he turns to *association* between suitable *schemata* (Rumelhart, 1980) or *frames* (Fillmore, 1982) and context free utterance meaning in order to explain how we interpret contextual meaning.

The concept of schema has been around in cognitive science since the seventies at least, and can be described as a system for organising knowledge (or beliefs). Recanati (2004) sketches a picture of how schemata play a role in interpretation: An expression activates a cognitive schema, which is basically a connection between two (or more) semantic values that says that these values fit together. As an example, Recanati considers (2.18).

(2.18)   John was arrested. He had stolen a wallet

Recanati attributes the reference resolution in (2.18) to the fact that (most of us) have access to a schema where "stealing" and "being arrested" are linked. Rumelhart (1980) describes the internal structure of a schema as the script of a play where actors who can fill the different roles of a play in different renditions correspond to variables which can be associated with different aspects of the schema on different instantiations.

### 2.5.1   *A Rhetorical View of Anti-inferentialism*

We consider (2.18) as an enthymematic argument where the conclusion is that John was arrested, and the premise that he stole a wallet, as seen in (2.19).

(2.19)   John had stolen a wallet
$\overline{\text{John was arrested}}$

This enthymeme is underpinned by a topos linking stealing to getting arrested, as seen in (2.20).

(2.20)   If someone steals something, they get arrested

The topos in (2.20) is a warrant for the enthymeme in (2.19), since (2.19) is easily recognisable as an instantiation of (2.20).

In many ways a theory of topoi such as the one in (2.20) is compatible with the anti-inferentialist view that knowledge and beliefs are organised in terms of schemata and frames, making up the cognitive resources available to a language user, based on the experiences of that individual. Like the theory we propose, anti-inferentialism emphasises the importance of context and cognitive resources for meaning interpretation. However, topoi—as they are traditionally perceived in rhetoric—tend to be less domain specific than schemata. This means that one topos could be relevant to one particular association within a schema but irrelevant to—or even inconsistent with—another association within the same schema. Also, one topos may be relevant to, or fit into, several schemata in different domains.

Recanati makes a point of primary pragmatic processes being associative rather than inferential. He defines these processes as being as automatic as perception and non-conscious for the "normal" language user engaged in interaction, while inference to Recanati is something that the normal language user consciously reasons about. However, there seems to be some evidence that a process which is conscious for an individual at one point in time can be non-conscious at some later point in time. For example, Swedish speaking students of French may at first have to think carefully every time they choose which form of a verb to use, due to the fact that Swedish verbs, unlike French, are not conjugated by person. After a while this process will be quicker and less conscious, and eventually, as the students learn to master the language, it becomes more or less automatic.

Dreyfus and Dreyfus (1980) describe the acquisition of skills in terms of five stages, where stage five (highly competent) involves a lot of tacit knowledge and routinised behaviour, while stage one (beginner) involves almost exclusively conscious reasoning. From this view point, if it were true that all enrichment which is necessary to reach the contextualised, fully enriched, truth-conditional content of any sentence, were associative (automatic) it would be difficult to explain language learning.

It would be possible to argue that anti-inferentialist theory is not about language learning, it is an account of the interpretation processes of a fully competent speaker of a language, so this objection is not relevant. However, we would like to argue that even a fully competent language user continues to incorporate new interpretations of expressions and is frequently faced with new types of contexts in which old (and new) expressions are to be interpreted—language change does not only happen between generations—it happens continuously, and the language of an individual develops and changes during the course of the individual's life. While we remain agnostic regarding the cognitive processes underlying different types of pragmatic interpretation, we want to be able to account for associative as well as inferential reasoning. Both convey enthymematic structures in discourse, and both must be warranted by something like topoi.

## 2.6     Discourse Coherence

We are interested in pieces of discourse where two propositions are related in the sense that they convey an enthymematic argument underpinned by a topos or a set of topoi. We argue that this type of relation contributes to coherence. In this section, we look at enthymemes and topoi in the context of coherence in dialogue and rhetorical relations.

Before we look at specific theories accounting for coherence, we will say something about the phenomenon as such. Generally, coherence is taken to mean how a discourse, text or conversation, "sticks together", and *coherent* refers to the property of being interpreted as belonging to the same unit. Leth (2011) suggests that the minimal requirement for coherence is *relation*. This means that when a number of discourse units are put in the same context, or considered in the same context, relations between these units are automatically generated in the minds of the agents involved.

On a general level, the reason for this would be that we try to relate utterances or other linguistic units to each other in some meaningful way as soon as we encounter them. Thereby we also assign a possible discourse relation between these units. The view that our cognition is constantly seeking to create coherence, and that virtually any two constituents in discourse *could* be interpreted as coherent under the right circumstances, seems reasonable and is supported by experimental evidence showing that dialogue participants tend to interpret non-authentic insertions in online dialogue as meaningful contributions (Healey et al., 2018). However, this does not tell us *how* an agent creates coherence between linguistic units, nor does it predict to what degree a linguistic contribution would be seen as relevant in a particular context. In the next two subsections, we will briefly consider two approaches to coherence, which in different ways try to elucidate these problems.

### 2.6.1     *Conversation Analysis*
In Conversation Analysis (CA, Sacks et al., 1974), organisation of discourse is defined in terms of *adjacency pairs*—pairs of functionally related dialogue contributions by two different speakers—and *sequences*. Each sequence revolves

around a *base adjacency pair* conveying the basic action performed in the sequence. A minimal sequence consists of one adjacency pair, for example a greeting followed by another greeting by an interlocutor. However, sequences are often longer than one adjacency pair. By means of the example below, Schegloff (2007) illustrates how a sequence may be expanded with one or more inserted sequences. The context of the dialogue is a girl asking her boyfriend if she can borrow a gun for an assignment in drama class. The first part of the base adjacency pair is *B*'s utterance in lines 9–10, which is not resolved until *J* utters the second part of the base adjacency pair in line 93.

(2.21)  9    *B*: 'n I was wondering if you'd let me borrow
        10       your gun.
        11       (1.2)
        12    *J*: My gun?
        13    *B*: Yeah.
        ...
        93    *J*: Yeah, you can use't.
        94       (0.4)
        95    *B*: .hh Ca:n?
        96    *J*: Yeh-

In between these turns at talk, there are several *sequence expansions* (Couper-Kuhlen and Selting, 2017) consisting of adjacency pairs. Some of these expansions are themselves nested. In addition to the functional relation within adjacency pairs, such as question-answer, request-acceptance, etc., *topic* is also seen as contributing to coherence. Typically, the topic does not shift between the first and second part of a base adjacency pair, and conversely, there is often a topic shift between sequences.

### 2.6.1.1    A Micro Rhetorical Perspective on CA

Even though there is often correspondence between the beginning and end of sequences and topic shift in conversation, there are cases where the connection is less clear (Schegloff, 2007). For example, the topic of an adjacency pair within a sequence expansion might not be the same as the overall topic of the sequence, that is, of the base adjacency pair. Take for example (2.22), an exchange within the long sequence expansion between line 9–10 and 93 in (2.21):

(2.22)  82    *J*: You a good- (.) uh::: (1.8) a- actress?
        83       (1.0)

84    *B*: No: heheheh?
85        (0.5)
86    *J*:  Th'n how d'ju come out to be A:nnie.

It is not obvious how the topic of (2.22) is related to the overall topic of (2.21), the base adjacency pair. This is true of many sequence expansions. There is often a topical link to the previous adjacency pair, but it is not always obvious. In some cases, in order to identify an utterance as the second part of an adjacency pair or the first part of a sequence expansion, rather than as an actual change of topic, a topos is required warranting the interpretation. In (2.22) the question whether *B* is a good actress or not is on topic in virtue of a topos connecting playing the leading role and being a good actor. However, for this adjacency pair to be on topic in relation to the base adjacency pair, more topoi are required.

Even in cases where two turns at talk are clearly related, they often involve the assumption of topoi either to be present in the minds of the interlocutors, or be possible to infer from the context. Due to the ethnomethodological approach to interaction taken by CA, which discourages assumptions of things that are not explicit in the discourse, this is to a great extent ignored in CA. One example where a topos is needed to explain coherence, is the excerpt in (2.22). The functional coherence between lines 82 and 84 is obvious. However, the topical connection to the rest of the dialogue is not clear until we see the follow-up question in line 86. The subsection in (2.22) conveys an enthymeme like the one in (2.23):

(2.23)      <u>*B* is not a good actress</u>
          it is surprising that *B* is playing Annie

This enthymeme is underpinned by a topos saying that if someone plays the lead, they are a good actor. Without this assumption, the relevance of the first part of the adjacency pair in line 82, to the first part of the subsequent adjacency pair in line 86, is not clear. Most of the time, the topoi underpinning a dialogue, by warranting its enthymemes, are so obvious to a conversational participant that they do not require conscious reasoning. However, they still contribute to coherence. Adding enthymemes and topoi provides a more general theory of coherence in dialogue than one only drawing on adjacency pairs and sequence organisation.

### 2.6.2    *Rhetorical Relations*
Work within CA offers many insights to how individual utterances in dialogue relate to each other, thereby contributing to coherence. However, there are

few attempts at generalising these insights to a theory of coherence that could be used to make predictions regarding interpretation and production of language.

CA is typically devoted to conversation, and is not concerned with coherence in other types of discourse. In contrast, theories of rhetorical relations aim at a generalisable theory of coherence which applies to many types of discourse, and is based on content rather than turn taking patterns.

We are particularly interested in Segmented Discourse Representation Theory (SDRT, Asher and Lascarides, 2003), since it—in comparison to e.g. Rhetorical Structure Theory (RST, Mann and Thompson, 1986, 1988)—does not only focus on written text but also considers dialogue data.

A basic premise of SDRT is that rhetorical relations between sentences or utterances are sometimes necessary in addition to compositional or dynamic semantics to fully interpret discourse. According to Asher and Lascarides (2003), traditional dynamic semantics (Kamp and Reyle, 1993; Groenendijk and Stokhof, 1991)—although capable of handling many coherence phenomena—does not adequately handle rhetorical relations, nor the phenomena accounted for by rhetorical relations alone. Some of these phenomena are bridging inference, lexical ambiguity and conversational implicature. In this section we will look at some of the rhetorical relations postulated in SDRT, and consider how they relate to enthymemes and topoi.

The different types of rhetorical relations or discourse relations in SDRT are not based on rhetorical—or functional—criteria alone, but on a combination of rhetorical quality and other properties like tense, mood and discourse order. Apart from the division into main rhetorical relation types—such as *elaboration, narration* and *explanation*—there is also a separate division of relation types into content-level relations, text-structuring relations, cognitive-level relations, divergent relations, and meta-talk relations. Some relation types have subtypes, and these subtypes may also belong to different groups. However, this fine-grained division is not relevant to us at this point, and we will settle for distinguishing between relatively coarse-grained categories. Above all, we are interested in the two types of relation which are most easily associated with enthymemes—*result* and its counterpart *explanation*.

In (2.24) we see an example given by Asher and Lascarides (2003, p. 463), where two utterances are linked by the rhetorical relation *result*.

(2.24)   a. John pushed Max.
         b. He fell.

The relation between (2.24a) and (2.24b) is based on a notion of causation, and the order of discourse matches the temporal order in which the events take place. In (2.25) (Asher and Lascarides, 2003, p. 463) the situation is reversed. As in (2.24), the reasoning relies on a notion of causation. However, in this case the order of events does not match the discourse order, and the relation between (2.25a) and (2.25b) is thus explanation, not result.

(2.25)   a. Max fell.
         b. John pushed him.

The underlying reasoning in the two cases is similarly warranted, and the difference between the relations is the order of the constituents. This is reflected in the logical forms of the axioms postulated in SDRT as underpinning the interpretations of the rhetorical relation result between the constituents of (2.24), and explanation between those of (2.25).

In (2.26), the underlying reasoning is different from that warranting (2.24) and (2.25).

(2.26)   a. Max fell.
         b. John helped him up.

The discourse order and temporal order match, and (2.26a) and (2.26b) are clearly related in the sense that helping someone up is something you might do if they have fallen, but Max falling is not causing John to help him up, it is merely a reason for Max being in need of being helped. This discourse is an example of the rhetorical relation *narration*, which relates two propositions only if the event described by the first proposition temporally precedes that of the second (see also (2.29), below).

As language users, our intuition about (2.26) is that that Max's falling precedes John's helping him up. In the case of (2.25), on the other hand, the intuition is that the falling happens after, and is caused by, the pushing.

Asher and Lascarides argue that rhetorical relations are necessary to capture the disctinct temporal content of (2.26a) and (2.26b), and that these relations are not derived from domain knowledge alone. They say, with regard to the example in (2.26):

> If "pushings typically cause fallings" were part of domain knowledge, one might use it to construct the right logical form, but *this* proposition seems quite implausible and hence not part of domain knowledge.
>
> ASHER and LASCARIDES, 2003 p. 7

Instead, Asher and Lascarides suggest that we infer a causal link in virtue of the presence of a rhetorical link between the two propositions. This raises a few questions: Firstly, is it really implausible that some notion that pushings cause, typically cause, or may cause fallings, is part of domain knowledge? Secondly, how do we as agents interpreting (2.25b) know that we are supposed to infer a *causal* link and not, for example, a narrative link?

### 2.6.2.1    Enthymemes, Topoi and Rhetorical Relations

With regard to (2.24) and (2.25), we may say that while the classification of the discourse relation as either result or explanation depends on the order of the sentences, the two examples convey the same enthymeme. If we accept the relations between the sentences in (2.24) and (2.25) as result and explanation respectively, we also have to accept that it was John who caused Max to fall by pushing him. We can see this discourse as expressing an enthymematic argument where Max's falling is the conclusion and the pushing of him the premise, as in (2.27).

(2.27)  $\dfrac{\text{push(j,m)}}{\text{fall(m)}}$

In order for a proposition to work as an explanation, there there must be an acceptable warrant. In the case of (2.27), we have access to some cognitive resources concerning pushings and fallings, among them a rule of thumb saying that a common/possible/potential relation between pushings and fallings is that pushings cause fallings.

Now, this is not necessarily a rule based on probabilistic reasoning about the real world, but rather a salient notion that speakers may relate to the activity of pushing. Basically, it says that when falling occurs in the context of pushing, we are licensed to assume that the pushing caused the falling. We would say that the discourse in (2.27) evokes a topos like the one in (2.28):

(2.28)  $\dfrac{\text{push(x,y)}}{\text{fall(y)}}$

This topos underpins the enthymeme in (2.27), and helps us accommodate the appropriate discourse relation.

We argue that some discourse relations are clearly related to enthymemes, as they contain some kind of claim or conclusion, as well as a constituent which serves as support for that claim or conclusion. But what about those relations that lack a causal link between utterances—are they unrelated to enthymemes and topoi? Consider the discourse in (2.29) Asher and Lascarides (2003, p. 462):

(2.29)   a. Max came into the room
         b. He sat down
         c. He lit a cigarette

Asher and Lascarides present (2.29) as another example of *narration*. This discourse relation is defined in terms that distinguishes it from, for example, *continuation*. Narration holds between (2.29a) and (2.29b), and between (2.29b) and (2.29c). These relations do not seem to be enthymematic—that someone enters a room is not a *reason* for that person sitting down, neither is sitting down an explanation for lighting a cigarette. There is no enthymematic argument in this discourse in need of a warrant. However, there is still some kind of expected progression in (2.29). We would probably have a harder time interpreting a discourse like (2.30) as coherent:

(2.30)   a. Max sat down
         b. He came into the room
         c. He lit a cigarette

Another problem arises when the content of a sentence is difficult to place in the same space and time as that of another sentence for world-knowledge reasons. For example, if (2.29b) had been *He dived into the Caribbean sea*, rather than *He sat down*, the interpretation of the discourse as linked by narration would be less obvious. This indicates that some principles of world knowledge are underpinning narration, elaboration, continuation, etc. as well as explanation and result. We believe that this knowledge could be modelled in terms of topoi.

We fully agree with the perspective presented in SDRT in that a rhetorical element is necessary to fully capture the content of causal discourse relations, like *explanation* and *result*. Asher and Lascarides reject domain knowledge as a direct means of deciding which rhetorical relation we are dealing with in a particular discourse, since the principles which we draw on can often not be considered defaults which are true for the most part. For example, it is not the case that pushings normally result in fallings. However, we would like to argue that domain related resources in the form of topoi can supply an appropriate logical form to underpin a causal or consequential relation in discourse.

Discussing evidence for cognitive foundations for rhetorical relations, Asher and Lascarides refer to research according to which at least causal relations seem to help interpreters understand texts better (Flower and Hayes, 1980; Meyer and Freedle, 1984—referred to in Asher and Lascarides, 2003, p. 450). Since causal relations are what enthymemes are based on, this seems to support the view that enthymemes help us structure discourse in a coherent way. Asher and Lascarides claim that the discourse relations in SDRT have semantic contents that relate to "fundamental conceptual categories by means of which we organise our beliefs", for example causation, sequencing, and part/whole. These categories could be seen as supertypes of more specific topoi, somewhat reminiscent of Aristotle's "common topoi"—topoi that may be used to underpin arguments within all domains.

## 2.7    Summary

In this chapter we have explored how enthymemes and topoi relate to a number of theories within pragmatics and philosophy of language. We noted that although pragmatic inferences are consistent with general principles like the maxim of relevance and assumptions of rationality and cooperation, these principles are not always enough to predict the actual inferences a language user makes in a given situation. Nor do they explain how a dialogue participant determines what contribution to make in order for an interlocutor to arrive at a particular conclusion. In response to this, we have sketched a picture of how enthymemes and topoi contribute to pragmatic processes by providing structure (enthymemes) and warrants (topoi) for reasoning.

We suggested that we could talk about accommodation of both topoi and enthymemes. Interpreting a discourse where the rhetorical structure is not explicit, a salient topos—one which by the language user is easily associated with the discourse situation—may be adopted as an underpinning for the discourse. Drawing on this topos the language user can accommodate an appropriate enthymeme, or some other type of rhetorical relation, which provides structure to the discourse. The discourse in (2.25) is an example of this.

Secondly, we may have an explicit enthymematic structure actually present in the discourse, as in Grice's example of a sentence giving rise to conventional implicature, (2.5a). In cases like this the structure already points to a topos, or at least at some instantiation of a topos, and the topos is thus more easily accommodated. However, in cases like this we can still expect the dialogue to be disrupted if we force a dialogue participant to accommodate a topos which is alien to him, or not salient in the situation.

We agreed with the anti-inferentialist view of cognitive resources underpinning pragmatic processes. However, we opposed the idea that these processes are either entirely associative, automatic and unconscious (as Recanati claims of primary pragmatic processes) or entirely inferential (as is claimed in Relevance Theory). Instead we argue that when dialogue participants make use of topoi which are established in the cognitive resources of the other dialogue participants, the pragmatic interpretations are more associative in nature, and when the dialogue participants are forced to accommodate novel or unexpected topoi, the process is mainly inferential. We suggested that topoi might be a good way of warranting not only enthymematic discourse relations, but also non-causal relations such as narration.

# CHAPTER 3

# Enthymemes in Dialogue

## 3.1 Introduction

In the previous chapters we have looked at enthymematic arguments and topoi in the context of pragmatics and interactional linguistics. We have seen that rhetorical reasoning is intimately related to the kind of inferences that are the focus in pragmatics, and that the usage of enthymemes exploits foundational principles of interactional linguistics such as dialogicity and grounding. However, although we have demonstrated the relevance of the enthymeme in interactive linguistics, we have not yet presented a theoretical framework which may be used for precise analyses of enthymematic reasoning.

In this chapter we will work our way towards a more detailed account of enthymemes and topoi and the role they play in interaction. First, we will discuss some concepts which are important for the subsequent analysis, and then we will move on to look at some examples. We will take as our point of departure an information state update approach as described by Larsson and Traum (2000) and Larsson (2002), including questions under discussion (QUD), as developed by Ginzburg (1994, 1996, 1998), Cooper et al. (2000) and Ginzburg (2012). We will look at how we can account for various types of examples involving enthymemes and topoi. Our analysis will especially focus on the different types of accommodation which are necessary for dialogue participants to be able to draw on rhetorical resources made up of sets of topoi.

The formal framework we will use is TTR, a type theory with records Cooper (2005a, 2012, 2016).[1] TTR is a rich type theory, which has been successfully employed to account for a range of linguistic phenomena, including ones particular to dialogue (Cooper, 2005b; Ginzburg, 2012; Cooper and Ginzburg, 2015; Lücking, 2016).

---

1  The reference Cooper (2016) refers to an unpublished stable draft, dated 2016-11-30. When needed, we will refer to a later draft, accessed 2020-06-29, as Cooper (2020). See bibliography for URLS.

## 3.2    Using TTR to Analyse Interaction

There are several reasons for choosing TTR for dialogue modelling. Cooper (2005b) shows how important aspects of semantic theories such as DRT (Kamp and Reyle, 1993), situation semantics (Barwise and Perry, 1983), and work in the Montague tradition (Montague, 1973) may be cast in TTR. This means that the various problems that these theories were designed to solve may be solved within a single framework. Thus, choosing TTR for the account presented here means we can relate enthymemes and topoi to the issues addressed in these important semantic theories.

Ginzburg (2012) points out that TTR (like other rich type theories) has the advantage of being able to handle utterances as well as utterance types, which is crucial for analysing meta-communicative aspects of interaction. This is a great advantage for us as we are sometimes simultaneously interested in the meaning conveyed by a particular utterance and the role which that type of utterance plays in an enthymematic argument. The TTR notion of *subtyping* is also important for our account of how we employ topoi in different kinds of enthymemes through operations like restriction, generalisation and composition. In TTR we have a convenient way of doing this since we have record types—structured types where we can easily add and remove fields.

Another advantage of TTR is that it offers a way to formally account for natural language without employing the concept of possible worlds. Ranta (1994), Cooper (2005a), Larsson (2011), Cooper and Ginzburg (2012), Fine (2012), Lappin (2013, 2015) and Chatzikyriakidis (2014), among others, point out problems with possible-worlds accounts of meaning. These objections are of a philosophical and semantic as well as a computational nature. The computational issues might not be immediately relevant to us, but they would be relevant if we wanted to take our analysis further and implement aspects of it in a dialogue model, for example.

### 3.2.1    *Some Basic Concepts of TTR*
TTR is based on the fact that humans (and animals) perceive the world in terms of categories or *types*. Not only do we have the ability to classify things in the world as *individuals* (corresponding to *entities*)—which could in itself be seen as typing—but also to categorise them as being of particular types. The identifying of individuals as individuals (individuation) as well as the typing is relative to the physical and cognitive prerequisites of the perceiving agent as well as environmental factors. For example, a human watching a tree from a distance might have no problem identifying it as an entity and recognising it

as being of the type *Tree*, while an ant never gets the macro-perspective that enables the human to perceive the tree as one entity. The ant might instead be able to identify ridges in the bark of the tree as obstacles that need to be overcome in order to reach the anthill. Thus it is not only the conditions of the agent that limits its ability to identify entities and type them, it is also the properties of the objects themselves. The likelihood of an agent typing something in a particular way is related to factors such as what the agent can do in relation to the object. These relations between agents and objects are often referred to as *affordances* (Gibson, 1977). For a detailed discussion about the way perception and the world is seen as connected to types in TTR, see Cooper (2016).

In formal terms, we can describe the judgement that a particular object, *a*, is of a certain type *T*, as *a* : *T*. In TTR the basic type of objects such as humans, animals and things, corresponding to *entity* or *e* in Montague semantics (Montague, 1973), is *Ind*, the type of individuals.

Basic types in TTR are types which are not constructed from other objects in the theory. Examples are *Ind* for individuals and *Real* for real numbers. One way to construct more complex types is to use *predicates*. From predicates we can construct *ptypes*. A ptype consists of a predicate and its arguments, for example *see(a,b)*, "*a* sees *b*". Objects which belong to ptypes are for example *events* and *states*. If a type, for example $T_1$, is realised, there is something of type $T_1$. We say that this object is a *proof* or *witness* of $T_1$. The existence of some particular object *a* of type $T_1$ is a proof that there exists something of type $T_1$.

In order to represent complex situations which potentially involve many ptypes and individuals, as well as other more general types, we use *record types*. A record type is a structure of pairs of labels and types. The same letters that are often used as individual variables in other systems—x, y, etc.—are used as labels associated with the type *Ind*, and the label c with different subscripts is used for *constraints* on the type of situation represented by the record type. In (3.1) we see an example of a record type representing a type of situation where a dog runs.

$$(3.1) \quad \begin{bmatrix} \text{x} : Ind \\ c_{\text{dog}} : \text{dog(x)} \\ c_{\text{run}} : \text{run(x)} \end{bmatrix}$$

The object to which the label 'x' points in (3.1) is of type *Ind*, and there are two constraints on the type of situation, that this individual is a dog ($c_{\text{dog}} : \text{dog(x)}$) and that it runs ($c_{\text{run}} : \text{run(x)}$). In addition to record types we also want to be able to talk about situations that are witnesses of record types. We represent such objects as *records*. A record is a structure where the labels are associated with *values* rather than types. The label and the value are separated by an equals sign. In (3.2) we see a record representing one particular situation. This situation is of the type in (3.1) if all the values are of the appropriate types (a : *Ind*, $s_1$ : *dog*(a), $s_2$ : *run*(a)). If these conditions are fulfilled, the record in (3.2) is a *witness* of (3.1).

$$(3.2) \quad \begin{bmatrix} x & = a \\ c_{dog} = s_1 \\ c_{run} = s_2 \end{bmatrix}$$

Let us assume that we want to talk about a type of situation where a particular dog—Spot—runs. We can do that by making a field in our record type *manifest*. This means that we let a label be associated with both a value and a type, as illustrated in (3.3).

$$(3.3) \quad \begin{bmatrix} x = Spot : Ind \\ c_{dog} : dog(x) \\ c_{run} : run(x) \end{bmatrix}$$

### 3.2.2 *Subtyping in TTR*

Record types in TTR offer a structured way of representing subtyping, which can be used—among other things—to account for how speech situations relate to each other. A type $T_1$ is a subtype of $T_2$ ($T_1 \sqsubseteq T_2$) just in case for any $a$, $a : T_1$ implies $a : T_2$, no matter what is assigned to the basic types and ptypes (Cooper, in prep, p. 39). For a record type $T_1$ to be a subtype of another record type $T_2$, there cannot be any label-type pairs in $T_2$ which do not exist in $T_1$, and there can be no manifest field in $T_2$ that is absent in $T_1$. For example, the record types in (3.4b), (3.4c) and (3.4d) are all subtypes of the record type in (3.4a). The record type in (3.4d) is also a subtype of the record types in (3.4b) and (3.4c). The record types in (3.4b) and (3.4c) are not in a subtype relation to one another, since (3.4c) involves a manifest field which is not present in (3.4b), and (3.4b) involves a label-type pair that is absent in (3.4c).

$$(3.4) \quad a. \quad \begin{bmatrix} x : Ind \\ c_{dog} : dog(x) \end{bmatrix}$$

$$b. \quad \begin{bmatrix} x : Ind \\ c_{dog} : dog(x) \\ c_{run} : run(x) \end{bmatrix}$$

c. $\begin{bmatrix} x = \text{Spot} : Ind \\ c_{\text{dog}} : \text{dog}(x) \end{bmatrix}$

d. $\begin{bmatrix} x = \text{Spot} : Ind \\ c_{\text{dog}} : \text{dog}(x) \\ c_{\text{run}} : \text{run}(x) \end{bmatrix}$

For an in-depth introduction to records and record types including formal definitions, see Cooper (2005b), Cooper (2012), Cooper and Ginzburg (2015) and Cooper (2016).

### 3.2.3 The Dialogue Gameboard

Now that we have introduced basic types like *Ind*, ptypes, record types and records, we will move on to how we do dialogue semantics in TTR. We will start out as simply as possible and add new features along the the way. To model the information states of dialogue participants, we will employ the concept of *dialogue gameboards* (DGB). Following others—most famously Wittgenstein (1953)—Lewis (1979) used the metaphor of language use, particularly conversation, as a game. Lewis claimed that the development of a conversation can be seen in terms of a score analogous to that of a game like baseball. In baseball the score consists of numbers, the number of strikes, runs, etc. In a language game the score is made up of sets of moves, questions, presuppositions, commitments, and other linguistic features which are relevant in the discourse. Lewis also introduced the idea of a scoreboard which keeps track of the progress of the dialogue.

The DGB is Ginzburg's take on the scoreboard approach to dialogue analysis (Ginzburg, 1996, 1998, 2012; Ginzburg et al., 2010; Cooper and Ginzburg, 2012) and an important feature of his theory of dialogue semantics—KoS—which has been developed over the last couple of decades.

However, in this body of work there are no suggestions regarding how to handle enthymematic arguments or topoi. Since our main objective is to account for the role enthymemes and topoi play in dialogue, we do not commit to any particular setup of the DGB from previous literature. However, the model we present here is influenced by previous work in terms of the layout of the DGB. We suggest a version of the DGB which includes enthymemes and topoi, and accounts for how they may interact with each other and with various contextual and co-textual factors. For background on gameboard semantics in TTR we recommend the literature referred to above, particularly Ginzburg (2012) and Cooper (2016).

Following Cooper (2016) we will treat the information state of a conversational participant as a record, and the dialogue gameboard that represents the type of this information state as a record type. This means that the structures we will deal with usually represent the *types* of particular information states rather than the information states themselves. Thus the dialogue gameboard of an agent $A$ is a type of agent $A$'s information state.

We are interested in how conversational and contextual features are introduced and integrated in the discourse model. Our focus is particularly on how individual agents draw on individual (and sometimes distinct) resources. The examples in this section will therefore be described and analysed using separate gameboards for each agent, representing the types of their respective information states. Ginzburg (1998), Larsson (2002), Ericsson (2005), and Ginzburg (2012) all choose this approach.

Larsson and Traum (2000) suggest the possibility of one gameboard depicting an objective take on the development of the dialogue, corresponding to a God's eye perspective on the state of the dialogue, rather than the context as perceived by the speakers themselves. However, such a notion of context does not help us handle dialogue features like misunderstanding, repetition, clarification, etc. To capture such phenomena we must have separate representations for the respective information states of individual dialogue participants, capturing something that more resembles the *common ground* assumed by each dialogue participant.

The concept of common ground (Stalnaker, 1978; Clark et al., 1991; Clark, 1996) is usually taken to mean the things that are taken for granted by an agent as being shared with the other agents involved in conversation, or, to be more precise, the things which this agent *behaves* as if he took for granted, and which are in some way relevant in the interaction. Thus, the concept of common ground is similar to the information we display on the shared part of the dialogue gameboard.

We see the information state of a dialogue participant as comprising two types of information—the kind that the dialogue participant takes to be shared in the context of the conversation, and the kind that he takes to be private. Therefore we keep the basic divide between *private* and *shared* which we find in Larsson (2002), Ericsson (2005) and Ginzburg (2012). Let us say for example that the type of an agent's private information state is $T_p$ and the type of the same agent's shared information state is $T_s$, then, in (3.5), we have the type of that agent's information state.

$$(3.5) \quad \begin{bmatrix} \text{private} : T_p \\ \text{shared} : T_s \end{bmatrix}$$

### 3.2.3.1    Agenda

The type associated with the label 'shared' is a record type representing the agent's take on what is shared information in the dialogue situation. That is, what has in some way been referred to in the dialogue, or what is necessary to integrate in the information state for a dialogue contribution to be interpreted in a relevant way. For example, although a topos may be of central relevance in the dialogue, it does not appear on the gameboard as part of an agent's shared information state until it has been made explicit, or until something has been said which has caused it to be accommodated. Similarly, the type associated with the label 'private' is a record type representing the agent's take on what he himself believes but might not be known by other dialogue participants.

We start out by introducing the most basic features of the gameboard and their functions, starting with the fields that belong to the private section of the gameboard. We represent the intention of an agent to make a specific move in terms of a private *agenda*. The kind of objects that would be on an agenda in the information state of a dialogue participant are dialogue moves that the dialogue participant intends to make in the dialogue. Since we want to be able to account for an agenda involving more than one move, we will eventually model the type of the agenda as a list of move types. For now however, it suffices to let the agenda be of a, as yet unspecified, type $T_{ag}$.

$$(3.6) \quad \begin{bmatrix} \text{private} : \begin{bmatrix} \text{agenda} : T_{ag} \end{bmatrix} \\ \text{shared} : T_s \end{bmatrix}$$

### 3.2.3.2    Project

The agenda is related to the field 'project', which we introduce under 'shared'. The term is inspired by Linell's (2009) concept of *communicative project*, which is reminiscent of Wittgenstein's *language game*. On Linell's account, a communicative project is a jointly accomplished communicative action, typically carried out over several utterances. Linell relates it to the notion of *communicative activity*, as described in Allwood (2000), in that a communicative activity is a comprehensive communicative project tied to a socio-cultural situation type.

Another related concept is that of conversational *genre*, used for example by Ginzburg (2010), to, among other things, account for relevance in dialogue. The concepts of genre and activity are similar, but differ in the perspective from which they are defined. For Ginzburg, a genre is defined by issues that are typically raised in a conversation of that genre. In Allwood's theory an activity type is characterised by the goals and roles that are associated with it. Thus, genre seems to be more of a linguistic category according to which conversations may be analysed, while activity is not necessarily a linguistic category—

even though most social activities involve linguistic behaviour. The concept of activity can thus be used to predict events that give rise to particular types of conversations.

We perceive activity types as part of agents' resources, where they are represented as types of re-occurring sequences of events.[2] which aim to fulfil the same type of goal. Each instance of an activity also often follows a recognisable pattern. Examples of distinguishable activities are *board meeting, dinner conversation, medical consultation,* etc. The event types that make up the sequences which constitute an activity can be more or less obligatory, both in terms of the type of events and in terms of the order in which the events occur. These events may themselves be described in terms of sequences of sub-events, that is, communicative projects. For now we will not get into details about the formal representation of the project, but simply represent it as a type $T_{pr}$.

When we think of a project that is to be jointly carried out, we do not necessarily specify which dialogue participant is supposed to be responsible for carrying out specific parts of the project. For example, if Kay and Sam are decorating their new house, the project of agreeing on where to place a specific armchair does not necessarily contain information about who is supposed to make what move. Correspondingly, the project is associated with one or more *conversational games* specifying the type of moves that different agents involved in the game are allowed to make in relation to each other (provided they keep playing the game), regardless who the agents are. For example, if one dialogue participant makes a suggestion, the other should evaluate and respond. We will leave these games aside for the moment, and return to them when we consider updates of the dialogue gameboard in Chapter 5.

For the purpose of accounting for our data it is sufficient to consider the communicative project as something which is perceived as shared information by all dialogue participants. However, there is no reason in principle why we could not expand the 'private'-field to include private communicative projects to represent "hidden agendas", etc.

### 3.2.3.3    Questions under Discussion, Latest Move, and Commitments

Apart from 'project', we will consider three additional fields under 'shared' on the dialogue gameboard—*Questions under Discussion* ('qud'), *Latest Move* ('l-m') and *Commitments* ('com') The items on 'qud' represent questions which

---

2   Following Fernando (2006) and Cooper (2016), we will formalise sequences of communicative events as *strings of events*. We will return to this in Section 5.3.

have been raised in the dialogue, explicitly or implicitly. We will give a detailed account for how we model questions later on. For now we will use the short-hand $T_q$ to represent the type associated with the label 'qud'.

The term *facts* used by Ginzburg is associated with truth and falsity, which might not necessarily be desirable in the context of accounting for the progress of a dialogue—dialogue participants may believe something to be true which is false, and they may knowingly accept untrue things "for the sake of the argu-ment". Larsson (2002) and Ericsson (2005) emphasise the aspect of mutual agreement by introducing *commitments* instead of facts. We will use *commit-ments* ('com') for propositions that have been grounded in the dialogue. For the time being we refer to the type associated with 'com' as $T_{com}$. The type associated with 'l-m' is a record type featuring information such as speaker, move type, utterance content, etc. However, for now we refer to this as a type $T_{l\text{-}m}$.

The figure in (3.7) shows a dialogue gameboard where the shared field has been further specified as described above. In the next section, we will define the types of the various fields in the DGB in the course of analysing a simple dialogue.

$$(3.7) \quad \begin{bmatrix} \text{private} : \begin{bmatrix} \text{agenda} : T_{ag} \end{bmatrix} \\ \text{shared} : \begin{bmatrix} \text{project} : T_{pr} \\ \text{qud} : T_q \\ \text{l-m} : T_{l\text{-}m} \\ \text{com} : T_{com} \end{bmatrix} \end{bmatrix}$$

## 3.3   Analysing a Simple Dialogue

Let us now explore the possibilities of the gameboard by considering the sim-ple dialogue between agents $A$ and $B$ in (3.8).

(3.8)    a. *A*: Do you have the time?
          b. *B*: It's three thirty.

This dialogue is made up of a standard question-answer sequence without repairs, clarifications or the like. Let us first consider *A*'s initial information state. *A* wishes to find out what time it is, which causes an agenda item to be added to her DGB.

As we have previously seen, manifest fields allow us to let a label be asso-ciated not only with a type but with an object of a type. For example, $\begin{bmatrix} a : T_1 \end{bmatrix}$

means that objects associated with the label "a" are of type $T_1$. If we have such an object, for example the child Sam, we may say that $[a = \text{Sam} : T_1]$. However, if we want the object associated with the label to be a type, for example a record type which includes some information about Sam, the type of this type is *Rec-Type*, the type of record types. We will represent projects and commitments as record types, and hence we take $T_{pr}$ and $T_{com}$ to be *RecType*.

The objects that could go on the agenda are types of moves that an agent is intending to make in an interaction, and we represent these as record types. However, since a dialogue participant may well plan more than one move in advance, we want the object on the agenda to be a *list* of record types where each type corresponds to one type of move. We call the type of a list a *list type* (Cooper, 2016, p. 267). If an object is a list of record types—for example $T_1$ and $T_2$—it is of the type list(*RecType*). We write this as $[T_1, T_2]$ : list(*Rec-Type*).

The type of $A$'s initial information state can be seen in (3.9). The type on the agenda is a record type representing the type of move that is employed when asking about the time. We refer to this type using $T$ with a subscript providing a rough description of the function of such move.

(3.9)   IS 1 $(A)$

$$\begin{bmatrix} \text{private} : \left[ \text{agenda} = \left[ T_{ask\_time} \right] : \text{list}(RecType) \right] \\ \text{shared} : \begin{bmatrix} \text{project} : RecType \\ \text{qud} : \text{list}(Question) \\ \text{l-m} : T_{l\text{-}m} \\ \text{com} : RecType \end{bmatrix} \end{bmatrix}$$

When $A$ has uttered (3.8a), the move realised by this utterance is added to the 'l-m' field of the DGB, and the first item on the list on the agenda is taken off (which in this case means that we have an empty list on the agenda). We see the type of $A$'s information state after the utterance of (3.8a) in (3.10):

(3.10)   IS 2 $(A)$

$$\begin{bmatrix} \text{private} : \left[ \text{agenda} = [\,] : \text{list}(RecType) \right] \\ \text{shared} : \begin{bmatrix} \text{project} : RecType \\ \text{qud} : \text{list}(Question) \\ \text{l-m} : T_{ask\text{-}time} \\ \text{com} : RecType \end{bmatrix} \end{bmatrix}$$

We assume that the updates directly following the uttering of (3.8a) are identical for agents $A$ and $B$. Integrating the lates move of type $T_{ask\text{-}time}$ results in updates of 'project' and 'qud'. *A* and *B* both expect their interlocutor to recognise that an utterance like (3.8a) aims at initiating a project to find out the time. Agent *A* is obviously aware of this project at an earlier stage, but does not expect it to be shared until a move of type $T_{ask\text{-}time}$ is made. Likewise for the update of 'qud'—the question $T_{time?}$ that is pushed onto 'qud' can be expected to be similar for any speaker of English, given the content of (3.8a). To make it possible to track more than one question under discussion, 'qud' is set up as a list in a similar way to the agenda, so $T_q = \text{list}(Question)$. Thus, at the point when 'l-m', 'project' and 'qud' have been updated, the DGB of agent *B* is identical to that of *A*. We see this gameboard in (3.11):

(3.11)  IS 3 (*B*)

$$
\begin{bmatrix}
\text{private} : \begin{bmatrix} \text{agenda} = [\,] : \text{list}(RecType) \end{bmatrix} \\
\text{shared} : \begin{bmatrix}
\text{project} = T_{find\_out\_time} : RecType \\
\text{qud} = [\,T_{time?}\,] : \text{list}(Question) \\
\text{l-m} : T_{ask\text{-}time} \\
\text{com} : RecType
\end{bmatrix}
\end{bmatrix}
$$

Next, *B*'s information state is updated with an item on the agenda representing the next move he intends to make in the dialogue, that is answering the question under discussion by telling *A* what time it is, and thereby also carrying out the communicative project at hand.

(3.12)  IS 4 (*B*)

$$
\begin{bmatrix}
\text{private} : \begin{bmatrix} \text{agenda} = [\,T_{tell\_time}\,] : \text{list}(RecType) \end{bmatrix} \\
\text{shared} : \begin{bmatrix}
\text{project} = T_{find\_out\_time} : RecType \\
\text{qud} = [\,T_{time?}\,] : \text{list}(Question) \\
\text{l-m} : T_{ask\text{-}time} \\
\text{com} : RecType
\end{bmatrix}
\end{bmatrix}
$$

A move of the type on *B*'s agenda ($T_{tell\_time}$) is carried out by his saying (3.8b). At this point, a commitment that the time is three thirty is integrated on the DGBs of both dialogue participants. The interlocutors now expect it to be common ground that the time is three thirty (unless, of course, there is reason to believe that *B* is not telling the truth).

The agenda item is therefore taken off his DGB and 'l-m' is updated for both agents. In addition, the question on 'qud' is resolved, and thus popped off, and the project is carried out. The final information state in this mini-dialogue (for both participants) would thus be of the type in (3.13):

(3.13)   IS 5 ($A$ and $B$)

$$\begin{bmatrix} \text{private} : \begin{bmatrix} \text{agenda} = [\,] : \text{list}(RecType) \end{bmatrix} \\ \text{shared} : \begin{bmatrix} \text{project} : RecType \\ \text{qud} = [] : \text{list}(Question) \\ \text{l-m} : T_{tell\text{-}time} \\ \text{com} = T_{three\_thirty} : RecType \end{bmatrix} \end{bmatrix}$$

## 3.4    Introducing Enthymematic Reasoning on the DGB

A simple question-answer exchange like the one in (3.8) can be handled with the gameboard features we have introduced so far. Let us now turn to a slightly more complex sequence and see if these features are still enough, or if there are some aspects of the interaction that we cannot capture if we stick to the current set up of the dialogue gameboard. The example in (3.14) depicts a situation where a person $A$ asks another person $B$ where he wants to go and then informs him of a suitable route. However, $B$ does not seem convinced this is the optimal route and so asks for a reason why this particular route is preferable. $A$ provides a reason, and $B$ explicitly accepts.

(3.14)   a. *A*: Where do you want to go?
         b. *B*: I want to go home
         c. *A*: Let's take the bypass!
         d. *B*: Why the bypass?
         e. *A*: It's shorter
         f. *B*: OK.

This dialogue, though made up, contains many characteristics of conversation, such as questions (*Where do you want to go?*, *Why the bypass?*) and feedback (*OK*).

Let us imagine a situation where $A$ is $B$'s designated driver (or a dialogue agent in a speech interface for a GPS). Thus, we assume that some communicative project aiming at deciding where to go and how to get there is initially on dialogue participant $A$'s DGB. We refer to the type of this project as $T_{plan\_route}$ and represent it as a record type, but as in the previous section we will not worry about exactly what that record type looks like just yet. Let us assume that this project has caused an update of $A$'s agenda so that it contains an item specifying the next type of move which $A$ intends to make in the dialogue. We will refer to this move type as $T_{ask\_destination}$. In (3.15) we see $A$'s gameboard before any utterance has been made.

$(3.15)$   IS 1 $(A)$

$$\begin{bmatrix} \text{private} : \begin{bmatrix} \text{agenda} = [T_{ask\_destination}] : \text{list}(RecType) \end{bmatrix} \\ \text{shared} : \begin{bmatrix} \text{project} = T_{plan\_route} : RecType \\ \text{qud} : \text{list}(Question) \\ \text{l-m} : T_{l\text{-}m} \\ \text{com} : RecType \end{bmatrix} \end{bmatrix}$$

In $(3.16)$ we see $B$'s DGB before any utterance has been made. We assume that $B$ has a similar idea about the communicative project at hand. $B$'s communicative project is thus of the same type as $A$'s. Let us also assume that $B$ expects $A$ to make the first move in the dialogue, for which reason $B$'s agenda is initially empty.

$(3.16)$   IS 2 $(B)$

$$\begin{bmatrix} \text{private} : \begin{bmatrix} \text{agenda} = [] : \text{list}(RecType) \end{bmatrix} \\ \text{shared} : \begin{bmatrix} \text{project} = T_{plan\_route} : RecType \\ \text{qud} : \text{list}(Question) \\ \text{l-m} : T_{l\text{-}m} \\ \text{com} : RecType \end{bmatrix} \end{bmatrix}$$

In $(3.17)$ we see $A$'s information state just after having asked the question "where do you want to go?", $(3.14a)$. The move type $T_{ask\_destination}$ is taken off the agenda, and a corresponding move appears on 'l-m'. A question, which we refer to as $T_{where\_to?}$ is pushed onto 'qud'.

$(3.17)$   IS 3 $(A)$

$$\begin{bmatrix} \text{private} : \begin{bmatrix} \text{agenda} = [] : \text{list}(RecType) \end{bmatrix} \\ \text{shared} : \begin{bmatrix} \text{project} = T_{plan\_route} : RecType \\ \text{qud} = [T_{where\_to?}] : \text{list}(Question) \\ \text{l-m} : T_{ask\_destination} \\ \text{com} : RecType \end{bmatrix} \end{bmatrix}$$

After $A$'s first utterance $B$'s information state is also updated similarly to $A$'s information state above. After this update, the question on 'qud' results in a move type $T_{reply\_go\_home}$ to appear on the agenda. In $(3.18)$ we see the type of $B$'s information state at this point.

(3.18)  IS 4 (B)

$$\begin{bmatrix} \text{private} : \begin{bmatrix} \text{agenda} = [T_{reply\_go\_home}] : \text{list}(RecType) \end{bmatrix} \\ \text{shared} : \begin{bmatrix} \text{project} = T_{plan\_route} : RecType \\ \text{qud} = [T_{where\_to?}] : \text{list}(Question) \\ \text{l-m} : T_{ask\_destination} \\ \text{com} : RecType \end{bmatrix} \end{bmatrix}$$

When $B$ makes the utterance "I want to go home", (3.14b), $T_{reply\_go\_home}$ is taken off the agenda, along with the question on 'qud'. The field 'l-m' is updated with $T_{reply\_go\_home}$, and the commitment that $B$ wants to go home, $T_{B\_wants\_home}$ is integrated. In (3.19) we see $B$'s DGB at this stage in the conversation.

(3.19)  IS 5 (B)

$$\begin{bmatrix} \text{private} : \begin{bmatrix} \text{agenda} = [] : \text{list}(RecType) \end{bmatrix} \\ \text{shared} : \begin{bmatrix} \text{project} = T_{plan\_route} : RecType \\ \text{qud} = [] : \text{list}(Question) \\ \text{l-m} : T_{reply\_go\_home} \\ \text{com} = T_{B\_wants\_home} : RecType \end{bmatrix} \end{bmatrix}$$

### 3.4.1    *Topoi as Resources for Inventing Arguments*

Thus far the dialogue proceeds according to the principles we introduced in the previous question-answer exchange. Now we want a move type with the content *propose route* or similar to appear on $A$'s agenda. If we imagine the situation being such that there is only one available route which leads "home", this exchange would be similar to the previous ask-for-time exchange. However, as the dialogue in (3.14) is set up, we can assume that there are a number of possible routes and that the choice made is largely dependent on preferences.

Since preferences vary between agents and contexts, we may think of the principle supporting a particular preference not as an absolute rule but as a topos. Let us say, for instance, that there are three possible routes in the scenario in (3.14). We may refer to them as *the bypass*, *the bridge route* and *park lane*. The bypass is the shortest route, park lane is the cheapest (since it is not a toll road), and the bridge route is most scenic. We assume that an individual engaged in the conversation has access to three topoi that may be drawn on in arguments regarding which of the three routes to choose, as seen in (3.20):[3]

---

3  In classical rhetoric there is usually a division between deliberative rhetoric, that is arguing for what should be done, and forensic rhetoric, where arguments concern what has happened

(3.20)   $\tau_{shorter}$:   "If you choose between routes, choose the shortest one"
         $\tau_{scenic}$:   "If you choose between routes, choose the most scenic one"
         $\tau_{cheap}$:   "If you choose between routes, choose the cheapest one"

A dialogue participant who has access to these three topoi about preferences for routes, and (unlike the situation in (3.14)) wishes to make the argument that the bridge route is the preferable route, may thus suggest the bridge route, provide the premise that it is most scenic, and expect this enthymeme to be accepted based on the topos $\tau_{scenic}$, as seen in (3.21):

(3.21)   the bridge route is the most scenic   $(\tau_{scenic})$
         ——————————————————————————
              let's take the bridge route

### 3.4.1.1     Private and Shared Topoi

Topoi may thus be drawn upon to invent arguments. The invention of an argument based on a topos can happen before a suggestion is made. In the dialogue in (3.14) this would involve dialogue participant $A$, perceiving that agent $B$ wants to go home, evaluating the possible routes and their qualities in relation to available topoi. $A$ then suggests the route that is most advantageous in relation to the most salient topos. On this scenario, the topos underpinning the argument is already clear to the speaker before the suggestion of route is made, and the agent may choose to explicitly include a reason for the suggestion, for example "Let's take the bridge route, it's the most scenic", in her utterance. It is also possible, of course, that the suggestion made was selected by chance, or for a reason the speaker does not want to be known. In such case the reasoning about salient topoi may come after the suggestion.

   In short, it may be the case that the topos on which the argument is based is the one the speaker believes most persuasive to an interlocutor—not the topos that the speaker herself finds most convincing. In our present scenario, for example, if $A$ were to suggest a scenic—but longer—route without justifying it, $B$ might think that she has no idea what she is talking about and that she is suggesting a route at random. If she, on the other hand, were to say -*Let's take the bridge-route—it's more scenic!*, $B$ might accept the proposal

———————

in a particular case Corbett and Connors (1999). In the former of these, the conclusion of the enthymematic argument is typically an imperative, in the second it is a declarative. The same topos can be drawn on to underpin any argument, and the mode of the consequent is a matter of the enthymeme, not the underpinning topos. However, at this point we will assume that the consequents of these topoi themselves involve imperatives.

even if he himself would have preferred the bypass on the grounds of it being the shortest possible route.

Because of this double use of topoi—on the one hand they influence our suggestions and givings of reasons, on the other we count on them being shared in discourse—we introduce *private topoi*, for producing and evaluating claims, proposals, suggestions, etc., and *shared topoi* for keeping track of the topoi a dialogue participant counts on being jointly accessible in a conversation.

*B*'s statement that he wants to go home (3.14b) adds a move type $T_{propose\_route}$ to *A*'s agenda. To know which route to suggest, *A* must match one of the available routes with the most convincing reason for proposing a route. The relevant topoi in *A*'s resources tell her that a good reason for proposing a particular route is that it is faster than other available routes. Her resources make it apparent that this reason for proposing a route is in fact many times more likely to be accepted than other possible reasons. For example, she might find a topos saying "if you are choosing between routes, choose the shortest one" ($\tau_{shorter}$ in (3.4.1)). Intuitively, we may think of topoi as functions from one situation to a new type of situation. For example, if we have a situation where a choice is to be made regarding routes, we can predict a type of situation where we should choose the shortest one.

Eventually, we will model topoi as functions which return types. For now we will use variables based on the letter $\tau$. We also say for now that the type of topoi is *Topos*. Being the most salient topos for *A*, $\tau_{shorter}$ is integrated on *A*'s private DGB, and she proposes a route accordingly: (3.22) represents *A*'s information state just before she utters (3.14c), "Let's take the bypass".

(3.22)  IS 6 $(A)$

$$
\begin{bmatrix}
\text{private}: \begin{bmatrix} \text{agenda} = [\,T_{propose\_bypass}\,] : \text{list}(RecType) \\ \text{topoi} = \tau_{shorter} : \text{list}(Topos) \end{bmatrix} \\[2em]
\text{shared}: \begin{bmatrix} \text{project} = T_{plan\_route} : RecType \\ \text{qud} = [\,] : \text{list}(Question) \\ \text{topoi} : \text{list}(Topos) \\ \text{l-m} : T_{reply\_go\_home} \\ \text{com} = T_{B\_wants\_home} : RecType \end{bmatrix}
\end{bmatrix}
$$

When *A* has suggested the bypass, *B*'s gameboard is updated as in (3.23).

(3.23)  IS 7 (B)

$$
\begin{bmatrix}
\text{private}: \begin{bmatrix} \text{agenda} = [] : \text{list}(RecType) \\ \text{topoi} : \text{list}(Topos) \end{bmatrix} \\
\text{shared}: \begin{bmatrix} \text{project} = T_{plan\_route} : RecType \\ \text{qud} = [] : \text{list}(Question) \\ \text{topoi} : \text{list}(Topos) \\ \text{l-m} : T_{propose\_bypass} \\ \text{com} = T_{B\_wants\_home} : RecType \end{bmatrix}
\end{bmatrix}
$$

B does not know anything about the bypass, and thus he does not know which of the accessible topoi that may be used to evaluate the proposal. He decides to elicit a reason by asking a *Why?*-question $T_{ask\_why\_bypass}$, and a question for the reason to choose the bypass is added to the agenda, asked, and pushed onto 'qud'. In (3.24) we see B's IS when he has just asked the question, but it has not yet been resolved.

(3.24)  IS 8 (B)

$$
\begin{bmatrix}
\text{private}: \begin{bmatrix} \text{agenda} = [] : \text{list}(RecType) \\ \text{topoi} : \text{list}(Topos) \end{bmatrix} \\
\text{shared}: \begin{bmatrix} \text{project} = T_{plan\_route} : RecType \\ \text{qud} = [T_{why\_bypass?}] : \text{list}(Question) \\ \text{topoi} : \text{list}(Topos) \\ \text{l-m} : T_{ask\_why\_bypass} \\ \text{com} = T_{B\_wants\_home} : RecType \end{bmatrix}
\end{bmatrix}
$$

### 3.4.2  *Introducing the Enthymeme under Discussion*

After B has asked A for a reason for choosing the bypass, A has to consider a reason which would make proposing a route acceptable. In principle, this reason may or may not match the private topos she herself had for proposing the bypass. However, if we assume that A adheres to the maxim of quality, the topos underpinning the reason she presents in support of her suggestion is identical to the topos used for inventing it. Drawing on this topos, a move type *reply* is added to the agenda.

(3.25)  IS 9 (A)

$$
\begin{bmatrix}
\text{private}: \begin{bmatrix} \text{agenda} = [T_{reply\_bp\_shorter}] : \text{list}(RecType) \\ \text{topoi} = [\tau_{shorter}] : \text{list}(Topos) \end{bmatrix} \\[2em]
\text{shared}: \begin{bmatrix} \text{project} = T_{plan\_route} : RecType \\ \text{qud} = [T_{why\_bypass?}] : Question \\ \text{topoi} : \text{list}(Topos) \\ \text{l-m} : T_{ask\_why\_bypass} \\ \text{com} = T_{B\_wants\_home} : RecType \end{bmatrix}
\end{bmatrix}
$$

To keep track of the enthymemes which are explicit in or can be construed from the dialogue, we introduce an *enthymeme under discussion* (eud) field. In some ways the concept of EUD is parallel to that of QUD. However, where questions tend to be resolved during the course of a dialogue, enthymemes are rather collected, compared and evaluated. For example, you might accept an enthymeme in principle, but present another enthymeme which you for some reason consider more important in the context.

After the utterance *It's shorter* (3.14e), the response is taken off $A$'s agenda and a corresponding move appears on 'l-m'. The question is resolved and an enthymeme stating $A$'s suggestion and her justification for that suggestion is pushed on 'eud'. Also, since $A$ presents the argument "We should choose the bypass since it is shorter", she expects a topos underpinning that argument to be shared after her utterance. Topoi warranting enthymemes in the dialogue appear on the 'shared' part on the DGB under 'topoi'. (3.26) represents $A$'s information state after she has uttered (3.14e). Note that the field 'com' is also updated. The notation $T_1 + T_2$ is used to indicate that the record type representing the commitments in the dialogue includes the commitments $T_1$ and $T_2$.

(3.26)  IS 10 (A)

$$
\begin{bmatrix}
\text{private}: \begin{bmatrix} \text{agenda} = [\,] : \text{list}(RecType) \\ \text{topoi} : \text{list}(Topos) \end{bmatrix} \\[2em]
\text{shared}: \begin{bmatrix} \text{project} = T_{plan\_route} : RecType \\ \text{qud} = [\,] : \text{list}(Question) \\ \text{eud} = [\varepsilon_{bypass\_shorter \to take\_bypass}] : \text{list}(Enthymeme) \\ \text{topoi} = [\tau_{shorter}] : \text{list}(Topos) \\ \text{l-m} : T_{reply\_bp\_shorter} \\ \text{com} = T_{bypass\_shorter} + T_{B\_wants\_home,} : RecType \end{bmatrix}
\end{bmatrix}
$$

We now want to look at how $A$'s reply is integrated in $B$'s gameboard. $B$ happens to have the same rhetorical resources as $A$ regarding short routes, and he therefore recognises $\tau_{shorter}$ as underpinning the enthymeme suggesting the bypass, and this appears in his information state as well. If we assume that $B$ accepts the suggestion if he accepts the reason for making the suggestion, the plan to take the bypass is also added to commitments.

(3.27) IS 11 $(B)$

$$
\begin{bmatrix}
\text{private}: \begin{bmatrix} \text{agenda} = [\,] : \text{list}(RecType) \\ \text{topoi} : \text{list}(Topos) \end{bmatrix} \\[4em]
\text{shared}: \begin{bmatrix} \text{project} = T_{plan\_route} : RecType \\ \text{qud} = [\,] : \text{list}(Question) \\ \text{eud} = \left[\varepsilon_{bypass\_shorter \,\to\, take\_bypass}\right] : \text{list}(Enthymeme) \\ \text{topoi} = \left[\tau_{shorter}\right] : \text{list}(Topos) \\ \text{l-m} : T_{assert\_bp\_shorter} \\ \text{com} = \begin{matrix} T_{B\_wants\_home} \; + \\ T_{bypass\_shorter} \; + \\ T_{A\_and\_B\_will\_take\_bypass} \end{matrix} \quad : RecType \end{bmatrix}
\end{bmatrix}
$$

## 3.5 Summary

In this chapter we have sketched an account of dialogue involving enthymematic reasoning. We described the information state update approach to dialogue and introduced a basic version of TTR, a rich type theory that conveniently let us include contextual features in update rules for dialogue. We also looked at how subtyping in TTR can be used to account for relations between concepts and speech situations. We then described the general architecture of the DGB, and introduced a number of features which enable us to include enthymemes and topoi in a gameboard analysis of dialogue. We returned to the idea of accommodation of enthymemes and topoi introduced in Chapter 2, and presented an informal gameboard analysis of these phenomena.

We showed the progression of the information state update of the participants in our example dialogues, but not the actual update rules. The purpose of this is to introduce the idea of information state update in connection to enthymematic reasoning. In Chapter 4 we will present a more developed formal account including update rules. In Chapter 5 we will return to the issue of communicative projects and conversational games and provide an account of how these features contribute to the development of the dialogue and how they interact with enthymemes and topoi.

# Analysing Enthymematic Dialogue

In the previous chapter we sketched a picture of the role enthymemes and topoi play for dialogue updates. In this chapter we will move on to consider how the DGB is updated. In a dialogue model, situations where enthymematic reasoning occurs are characterised by the sequence of update rules that is required to bring about the progression of the dialogue. In addition to update rules, we also assume an update algorithm that controls in which order rules may be applied. However, we will not go into this in detail, but instead in the rules define the conditions for when an agent is licensed to apply that rule.

We will look at some examples and analyse them gradually introducing new concepts and describing for each update how the relevant features of the gameboard and the necessary update rules work. This way we hope to make clear how we perceive the various features of the gameboard in terms of types, while elucidating some points regarding the dynamics of enthymemes and topoi in this kind of interaction.

## 4.1 Enthymeme Elicited by *Why?*

On a rhetorical view of dialogue, the topoi in the resources of an agent may be drawn on to invent and interpret different kinds of enthymemes. When we talk about how things are, we sometimes use arguments to back up our claims or to give sufficient explanations for the state of affairs reported in our assertions.

In (4.1) we have an example of an interaction where an assertion is backed up with a premise so that the two moves by speaker *A* make up an enthymematic argument. The premise of the enthymeme is elicited by the why-question in (4.1b). In this way the argumentative structure is made explicit—Sam is in hospital *because* he is sick. (4.1) is a slightly altered version of an example from the British National Corpus discussed and analysed by Schlöder et al. (2016), who argue that a *why*-question following an assertion is likely to elicit a reason for the *content* expressed in the first utterance being the case, rather than a reason for making the statement. In many contexts, if the relevance of an utterance is not clear, it is more intuitive to ask "why are you saying that?", "what do you mean?" or similar, rather than a bare "why?". However, there are exceptions

© ELLEN BREITHOLTZ, 2021 | DOI:10.1163/9789004436794_005

to this, see for example Gregoromichelaki and Kempson (2015). Regardless of whether a *why*-question is factive (addresses the facts of a proposition made) or meta-communicative (addresses an interlocutor's reason for saying something), the reply to the *why*-question must evoke a recognisable topos. If it does not, there is no warrant for the response as a support or explanation of the statement preceding the *why*-question.

(4.1)   a. *A*: Sam's in hospital.
      b. *B*: Why?
      c. *A*: He's sick.

In our analysis of (4.1) we omit several steps that would be necessary if we were modelling this dialogue for example for the purpose of implementation. Since we are mostly concerned with the rhetorical aspects of the dialogue, we ignore at this point the machinery adding new move types to the agenda and other updates pertaining to the private field of the DGB. We will start at the point just after *A* has uttered (4.1a), and the utterance "Sam's in hospital" is thus already integrated as the latest move on the DGB. We will refer to the type of the shared information state when (4.1a) has just been integrated as $T_{initial}$.

$$(4.2) \quad T_{initial} \sqsubseteq \left[ \text{sh} : \left[ \begin{array}{l} \text{l-m} : \left[ \begin{array}{l} \text{prev} : Rec \\ e : \left[ \begin{array}{l} e : \text{assert}(x,y,\text{ctnt}) \\ x = A : Ind \\ y = B : Ind \\ \text{ctnt} = \left[ \begin{array}{l} x = \text{Sam} : Ind \\ c_h : \text{in\_hospital}(x) \end{array} \right] : RecType \end{array} \right] \\ \end{array} \right] \\ \text{qud} : \text{list}(Question) \end{array} \right] \right]$$

Since an information state potentially involves a wide range of information, and the types that we manipulate do not necessarily include all of this information, types of actual information states such as $T_{initial}$ involves at least as many constraints as the record types we take as our point of departure when updating the DGB. Thus $T_{initial}$ is a subtype of the record type to the right in (4.3). It is underspecified in terms of the fields present, for example, it lacks all private features of the DGB. Also, the previous move made in the interaction is not specified in terms of the content of that move, and the 'qud'-field does not provide any information about any questions already under discussion in the dialogue. We will use a dot notation to refer to paths in record types. For example, if $s : T_{initial}$, we can refer to "Sam" in (4.3) using the notation 's.sh.l-m.e.ctnt.x'.

In (4.2) the label 'sh' (for 'shared') is associated with a record type including the labels 'l-m', representing the latest moves, and 'qud', representing questions under discussion. (For reasons of space we will replace the label 'shared' with 'sh' and 'private' with 'pr' where necessary.)

Since we do not know anything about the conversation prior to this excerpt, we are, at this initial state, agnostic about any previous moves. We say that the label 'qud' is associated with the type "list of questions", and the label 'l-m' with a record type with the fields 'prev' and 'e', where 'prev' contains information about previous moves. How many previous moves should be included on the DGB, that is, how many turns are in fact accessible to a dialogue participant is an empirical question. However, for the short dialogues we are considering here there is no need to limit the number of previous moves. In each type representing an information state, 'shared.l-m.e' contains information about the very latest move made.

### 4.1.1    *Integrate* Why?

Our first update rule thus concerns the update of *B*'s information state where a *why*-question is pushed onto 'qud' given the assertion "Sam's in hospital" in (4.1a).

Now *B* may choose to move on in the conversation accepting that Sam is in hospital or to address *A*'s assertion for example by questioning it or by asking a follow up question. Let us assume now that *B* intends to make a factive *why*-question investigating the reason for Sam being in hospital (the reasoning behind this intention we will leave aside for the time being). Following Schlöder et al. (2016), we will think of *why*-question as *requests for reasons*.

On a rhetorical view, an acceptable reason for Sam being in hospital would be one warranted by a recognisable topos. This is the case even if the why-question is not meant to inquire into the validity of the claim, but rather to find out the reason for Sam being in hospital. If the reply to the question would be something like "He is such a nice guy", we may speculate that the answer would not be accepted. The reason for this is that there is probably no topos readily available to any of the participants in this dialogue to be recognised as underpinning for the enthymeme "Sam is in hospital because he is such a nice guy". However, we could imagine contexts where the utterance would make perfect sense; there might be a story about Sam having intervened in a fight, since he is a nice guy, and therefore ended up having to undergo hospital treatment. However, on this scenario, the reply to the first question would probably be followed up by yet another question inquiring into why Sam being a nice guy is a reason for his being in hospital.

It is important to emphasise that it is certainly not possible for a linguistic theory to predict which topoi are acknowledged or acceptable within a community or to a specific individual. However, it is possible to predict how reasoning in a particular situation may play out given the agents' access to a particular set of topoi.

In more technical terms, an enthymeme can be regarded as a function from a record of a particular type (corresponding to the antecedent of the enthymeme, in this case "Sam is sick") to a type corresponding to the consequent of the enthymeme, in this case "Sam is in hospital". A *why*-question is obtained by abstracting over $T_{antecedent}$ yielding a function from an antecedent type to an enthymeme. We see such a function in (4.3).

(4.3)    $\lambda t : Type \cdot \lambda r : t \cdot T_{consequent}$

When provided with an answer to the question, we may apply this function to a type $T_{antecedent}$ (corresponding to the answer to the *why*-question):

(4.4)    $\lambda t : Type \cdot \lambda r : t \cdot T_{consequent} (T_{antecedent}) = \lambda r : T_{antecedent} \cdot T_{consequent}$

At the point in the dialogue when $B$ has uttered the *why*-question, we need an update function which allows $A$ to integrate the question on her DGB. This includes interpreting the question, that is, forming a hypothesis of what aspect of the previous utterance the "why?" relates to. This function must take an information state which, like (4.2), meets the requirement of having an assertion on 'shared.l-m.e', and update it so that the updated latest move is the *why*-question, while also pushing the same question on 'qud'. We refer to this function as $f_{why\_assert}$.

(4.5)    $f_{why\_assert} =$

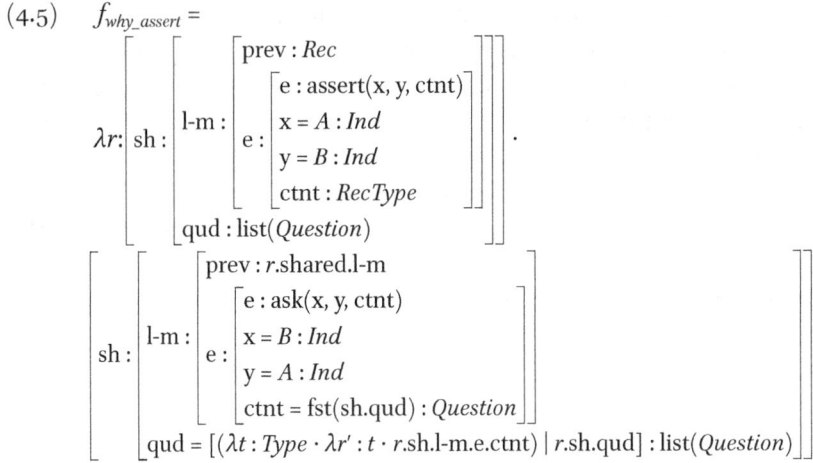

In (4.5) we see the function $f_{why\_assert}$. It can be applied to an information state of the type where the very latest move, 'sh.l-m.e', is associated with a move of a type where an individual $A$ asserts something to an individual $B$.

In the result type of the function the label 'l-m' is associated with a type where the move type that was on 'l-m.e' in the previous information state is now on 'lm.prev', and the label 'e' is associated with a *why*-question regarding the content of the previous move.

In (4.5) we also observe some list operators, namely '|' and 'fst', which is a function from a list to the first element of that list. Thus 'fst(sh.qud)' represents the first element on the list of questions on 'sh.qud'. The "pipe" (or "cons") operator, '|', takes an element and a list and puts that element first in the list.

$f_{why\_assert}$ can be applied to a record of the type in (4.2). However, the result of this operation includes the relevant updates brought about by the function application, but not any information about other dialogue features that might be present in the original information state (in this case of type $T_{initial}$). For example, $T_{initial}$ could include information about previous moves, other questions that have not yet been resolved, commitments, etc. In order to incorporate the new information with the old we need to *asymmetrically merge* $T_{initial}$ and the type obtained through the application of $f_{why\_assert}$ to an information state of type $T_{initial}$.

### 4.1.1.1    Asymmetric Merge

As explained above, in order to obtain the type of the updated information state, the result of applying an update rule will have to be combined with the type of the initial information state. Cooper (2016) refers to this operation as *asymmetric merge*. For types which are not record types, for example ptypes, the asymmetric merge of two types $T_1 \;\boxed{\wedge}\; T_2$ results in $T_2$. This means that for record types, any label that occurs in both $T_1$ and $T_2$ will after an asymmetric merge be associated with the type which that label is associated with in $T_2$. Labels which occur only in one of the record types will be associated with the same type in $T_1 \;\boxed{\wedge}\; T_2$ as in one of the original types $T_1$ or $T_2$. If we look at our example, the type we get when we apply the function $f_{why\_assert}$ to the initial information state, $s_{initial}$, is a type $T'$, which has the same fields as the result (range) type of the function $f_{why\_assert}$. However, this type is not necessarily the type of the updated information state since the type of $s_{initial}$ may have had more information in it.

To obtain the type of our updated information state, we must combine the type of the information state at the start of the update, $T_{initial}$, and the result type of the function application, $T'$, so that everything that is on the gameboard before the update carries over to the new information state. In (4.6) we see the asymmetric merge of $T_{initial}$ and $T'$, resulting in the type of $A$'s information state after the application of rule $f_{why\_assert}$ to $s_{initial}$ (where $s_{initial}$.sh.qud=$rest$), that is, the type of $A$'s information state when she has integrated the *why*-question.

(4.6)

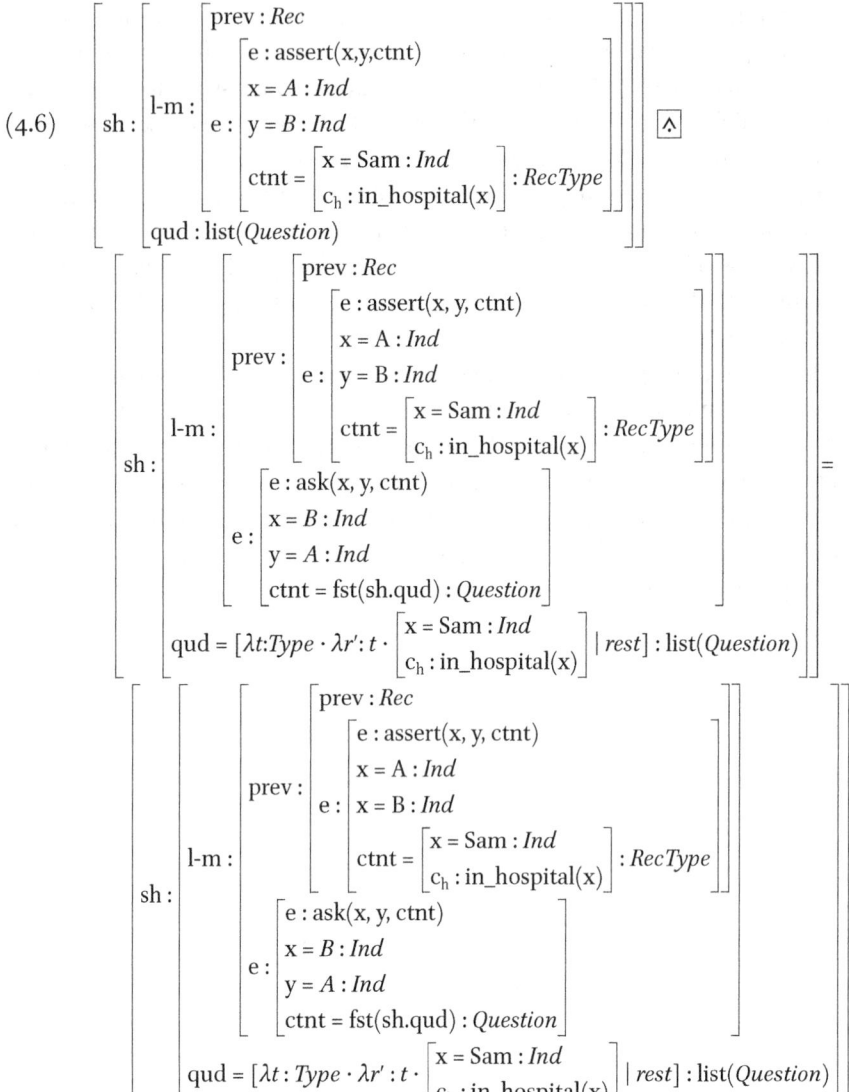

### 4.1.2    Integrate Enthymeme_{Why?}

After having interpreted *B*'s utterance "why?" in (4.1b), in order to reply, *A* must decide what kind of answer to give. For now we will not discuss the reasoning behind this answer, and skip straight to the point where *B* is interpreting and evaluating it. We will do this in steps starting at a point when *A*'s reply in (4.1c) is integrated on 'l-m.e' on the DGB. Since the rhetorical structure of the reply in relation to the initial assertion is made explicit by the *why*-question, an enthymeme under discussion is also integrated on the shared DGB. *B* then checks his resources for a topos warranting the enthymeme, and accommodates this topos. We will discuss accommodation of topoi further in section 4.2.5.

Let us now consider the type of $B$'s information state just after $A$ has uttered (4.1c), as seen in (4.7). Let us call this type $T_3$.

$$
(4.7) \quad T_3 = \left[ \text{sh}: \left[ \text{l-m}: \left[ \begin{array}{l} \text{prev}: \left[ \text{prev}: \left[ \text{prev}: \left[ \begin{array}{l} \text{prev}: Rec \\ e: \left[ \begin{array}{l} e: \text{assert(x,y,ctnt)} \\ x = A: Ind \\ y = B: Ind \\ ctnt = \left[ \begin{array}{l} x = Sam: Ind \\ c_h: \text{in\_hospital(x)} \end{array} \right] : RecType \end{array} \right] \end{array} \right] \right] \\ e: \left[ \begin{array}{l} e: \text{ask(x,y,ctnt)} \\ x = B: Ind \\ y = A: Ind \\ ctnt = \text{fst(sh.qud)}: Question \end{array} \right] \end{array} \right] \\ e: \left[ \begin{array}{l} e: \text{assert(x,y,ctnt)} \\ x = A: Ind \\ y = B: Ind \\ ctnt = \left[ \begin{array}{l} x = Sam: Ind \\ c_s: \text{sick(x)} \end{array} \right] : RecType \end{array} \right] \\ \text{qud} = [\lambda t:Type \cdot \lambda r:t \cdot \left[ \begin{array}{l} x = Sam: Ind \\ c_h: \text{in\_hospital(x)} \end{array} \right] \mid rest]: \text{list(Question)} \end{array} \right] \right]
$$

Now, as we discussed in the context of (4.4), an enthymeme elicited by a *why*-question can be considered as the result of applying the question to its answer. In this case the enthymeme under discussion is the *why*-question applied to the assertion "Sam is sick", as seen in (4.8).

$$
(4.8) \quad \lambda t: Type \cdot \lambda r:t \cdot \left[ \begin{array}{l} x = Sam: Ind \\ c_h: \text{in\_hospital(x)} \end{array} \right] ( \left[ \begin{array}{l} x = Sam: Ind \\ c_s: \text{sick(x)} \end{array} \right] ) =
$$
$$
\lambda r: \left[ \begin{array}{l} x = Sam: Ind \\ c_s: \text{sick(x)} \end{array} \right] \cdot \left[ \begin{array}{l} x = Sam: Ind \\ c_h: \text{in\_hospital(x)} \end{array} \right]
$$

A function for integrating an enthymeme after a factive *why*-question takes an information state where the third-to-latest move ('sh.l-m.prev.prev') and the latest move ('sh.l-m.prev') are assertions, and the question under discussion is a *why*-question, and returns a type of state where there is an enthymeme on 'eud' related to the question under discussion. We see this rule below in (4.9).

(4.9)   $f_{integrate\_enthymeme\_why}$ =

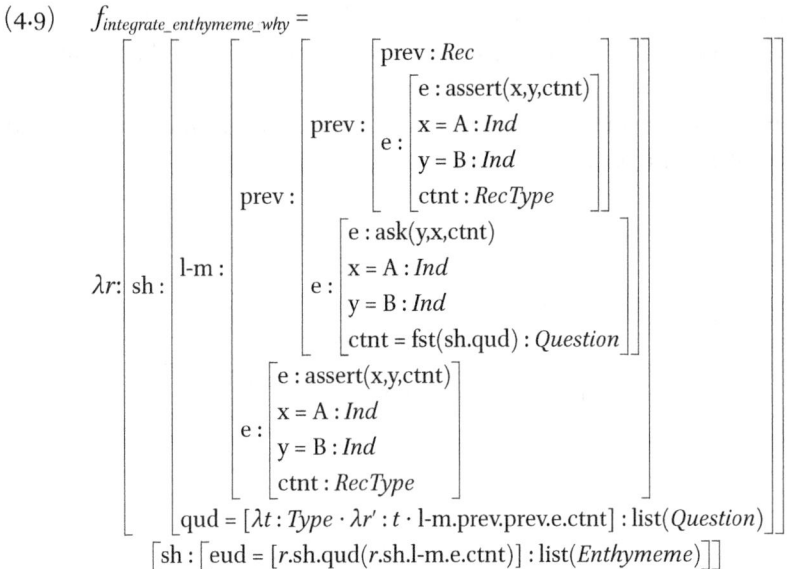

$$\left[ \lambda r: \left[ sh: \left[ \begin{array}{l} l\text{-m}: \left[ prev: \left[ prev: \left[ \begin{array}{l} prev: \left[ \begin{array}{l} prev: Rec \\ e: \left[ \begin{array}{l} e: assert(x,y,ctnt) \\ x = A: Ind \\ y = B: Ind \\ ctnt: RecType \end{array} \right] \end{array} \right] \\ e: \left[ \begin{array}{l} e: ask(y,x,ctnt) \\ x = A: Ind \\ y = B: Ind \\ ctnt = fst(sh.qud): Question \end{array} \right] \end{array} \right] \right] \\ e: \left[ \begin{array}{l} e: assert(x,y,ctnt) \\ x = A: Ind \\ y = B: Ind \\ ctnt: RecType \end{array} \right] \\ qud = [\lambda t: Type \cdot \lambda r': t \cdot l\text{-m.prev.prev.e.ctnt}]: list(Question) \end{array} \right] \right] \\ \left[ sh: \left[ eud = [r.sh.qud(r.sh.l\text{-m.e.ctnt})]: list(Enthymeme) \right] \right] \end{array} \right].$$

We will now consider the result of applying $f_{integrate\_enthymeme\_why}$ to a record $s_3$ of type $T_3$ (shown in 4.10).

(4.10)   $f_{integrate\_enthymeme\_why}(s_3)$ =
$$\left[ sh: \left[ eud = [\ \lambda r: \left[ \begin{array}{l} x = Sam: Ind \\ c_s: sick(x) \end{array} \right] \cdot \left[ \begin{array}{l} x = Sam: Ind \\ c_h: in\_hospital(x) \end{array} \right]\ ]: list(Enthymeme) \right] \right]$$

In (4.11) we see the type of $B$'s information state after the application of $f_{integrate\_enthymeme\_why}$ and an asymmetric merge with $T_3$.

$$(4.11) \quad \text{sh} : \left[ \text{l-m} : \left[ \begin{array}{l} \text{prev} : \left[ \text{prev} : \left[ \begin{array}{l} \text{prev} : Rec \\ e : \left[ \begin{array}{l} e : \text{assert(x,y,ctnt)} \\ x = A : Ind \\ y = B : Ind \\ \text{ctnt} = \begin{bmatrix} x = \text{Sam} : Ind \\ c_h : \text{in\_hospital(x)} \end{bmatrix} : RecType \end{array} \right] \end{array} \right] \\ e : \left[ \begin{array}{l} e : \text{ask(x,y,ctnt)} \\ x = B : Ind \\ y = A : Ind \\ \text{ctnt} = \text{fst(sh.qud)} : Question \end{array} \right] \end{array} \right] \right.$$

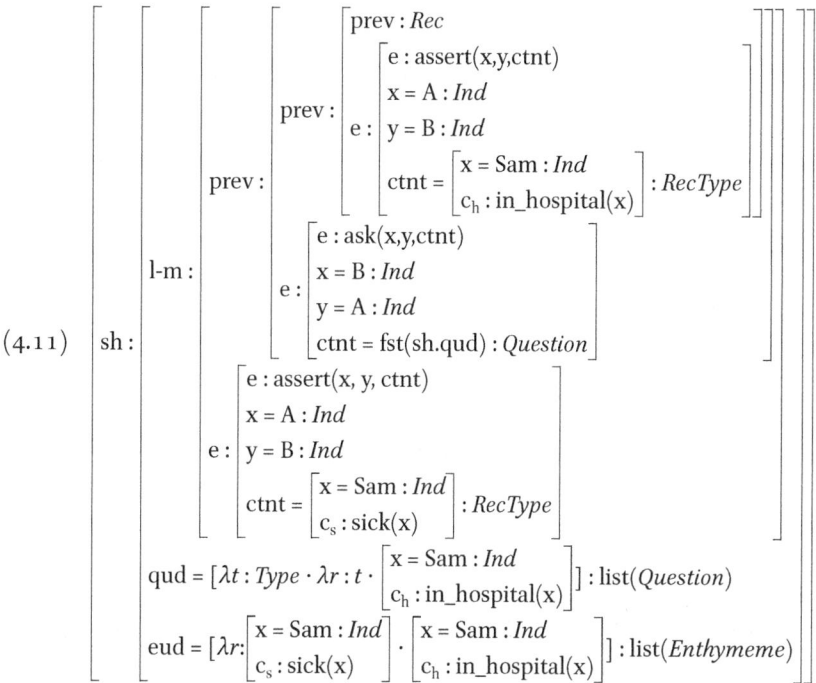

The full nested record type structure reads:

- **l-m:**
  - **prev:**
    - **prev:**
      - prev : *Rec*
      - e : [ e : assert(x,y,ctnt); x = A : *Ind*; y = B : *Ind*; ctnt = [ x = Sam : *Ind*; c_h : in_hospital(x) ] : *RecType* ]
    - e : [ e : ask(x,y,ctnt); x = B : *Ind*; y = A : *Ind*; ctnt = fst(sh.qud) : *Question* ]
  - e : [ e : assert(x, y, ctnt); x = A : *Ind*; y = B : *Ind*; ctnt = [ x = Sam : *Ind*; c_s : sick(x) ] : *RecType* ]
  - qud = [$\lambda t : Type \cdot \lambda r : t \cdot$ [ x = Sam : *Ind*; c_h : in_hospital(x) ]] : list(*Question*)
  - eud = [$\lambda r$:[ x = Sam : *Ind*; c_s : sick(x) ] $\cdot$ [ x = Sam : *Ind*; c_h : in_hospital(x) ]] : list(*Enthymeme*)

## 4.2 Coordinating on Topoi

In the previous section (4.1), we have looked at how an enthymeme under discussion is integrated on the dialogue gameboard as the result of a *Why*-question. In this section, we will look at various ways in which dialogue participants can coordinate on the topoi underpinning enthymemes in dialogue.

### 4.2.1 *Integrating Topos*
Let us return to our example (repeated here for convenience).

(4.12)  a. *A*: Sam's in hospital.
        b. *B*: Why?
        c. *A*: He's sick.

The enthymeme "Sam is in the hospital since he is sick" is now part of *B*'s information state, meaning that he has interpreted (4.12c) as given by *A* as a reason for the content of utterance (4.12a). There are (at least) two goals associated with the utterance (4.12c): First, *A* wants *B* to recognise the reason given as something which is *relevant* in relation to (4.12a). Second, she wants *B* to accept it as an explanation or support of the assertion (4.12a). For the first goal to be achieved, $B$ must have access to a topos warranting the enthymeme. In other words: The interpretation of an enthymeme by an agent is much facilitated if the agent has access to a warranting principle which is more generally applicable than the enthymeme conveyed in the discourse. Consider the following example:

(4.13)   a.  *A*: I am hungry.
         b.  *B*: Have a piece of fruit!

The type of situation where the speaker is hungry is a subtype of a type of situation where *someone* is hungry. Also, a situation where the speaker is having a piece of fruit is a subtype of a type of situation where *someone* eats *something*. Thus, a topos that provides a warrant for the dialogue in (4.13) could be somethig like "if you are hungry, you should eat something".

Likewise, the enthymeme "Sam is sick, therefore he is in hospital" is underpinned by a topos associating being sick with being in or going to hospital. In (4.14a) we see the enthymeme "Since Sam is sick, he is in hospital". In (4.14b) we see the topos drawn on to interpret the enthymeme ("If someone is sick, they are in hospital").

$$(4.14) \quad \text{a.} \quad \lambda r: \begin{bmatrix} x = Sam : Ind \\ c_s : sick(x) \end{bmatrix} \cdot \left[ c_h : in\_hospital(r.x) \right]$$

$$\text{b.} \quad \lambda r: \begin{bmatrix} x : Ind \\ c_s : sick(x) \end{bmatrix} \cdot \left[ c_h : in\_hospital(r.x) \right]$$

A key idea in our theory is that enthymemes conveyed in discourse are often *specifications* of more generally applicable topoi. For example, the utterance "Kitty likes milk, she is a cat" conveys the enthymeme "Kitty is a cat, therefore she likes milk". This enthymeme is a specification of a topos saying that if $x$ is a cat, then $x$ likes milk. In this case the specification amounts to the topos being restricted to concern just the individual Kitty, but a specification could also involve adding constraints to the type of situation to which an enthymeme or a topos applies, the antecedent- or domain type of the function.

In the formal account, the notion of specification is linked to subtyping (see Section 3.2.2). The requirements for an enthymeme $\varepsilon$ to be a specification of a topos $\tau$, is that the antecedent type of $\varepsilon$ must be a subtype of the antecedent type of $\tau$, and the result of applying $\varepsilon$ to any record (representing, for example, a situation) must be a subtype of the result of applying $\tau$ to the same record.

(4.15) Assuming topos $\tau = \lambda r{:}T_1 \cdot T_2$ and enthymeme $\varepsilon = \lambda r{:}T_3 \cdot T_4$, $\varepsilon$ is a specification of $\tau$, i.e., specification($\varepsilon,\tau$) is witnessed, iff $T_3 \sqsubseteq T_1$ and for any $r$, $\varepsilon(r) \sqsubseteq \tau(r)$.

It should be emphasised that the perceived relation between enthymemes and topoi is relative to the agents involved in dialogue—dialogue participants can disagree about whether a given enthymeme is a specification of a particular topos. For an enthymematic dialogue contribution to be interpreted correctly, it is important that the enthymeme is *recognisable* as a specification of a topos for that topos to be evoked in the discourse. From a rhetorical point of view, to maximise persuasion, the topos must also be acceptable to the audience in the context where it is being evoked.

When interpreting an enthymeme, an agent compares the topos they have on private on the DGB to the enthymeme. If the agent recognises the enthymeme as a specification of the private topos, the topos is loaded onto the shared DGB as the topos believed by the interpreting agent to underpin the enthymeme. In (4.16), we see the update rule $f_{integrate\_topos}$. When applied to an information state including both a private topos and an enthymeme which is a specification of that topos,[1] it returns a type where the private topos has been integrated in the shared DGB.

(4.16) $f_{integrate\_topos} =$
$$\lambda r{:}\begin{bmatrix} \text{private} : [\,\text{topoi} : \text{list}(\textit{Topos})\,] \\ \text{shared} : \begin{bmatrix} \text{eud} : \text{list}(\textit{Enthymeme}) \\ \text{topoi} : \text{list}(\textit{Topos}) \end{bmatrix} \end{bmatrix} \cdot$$
$$\lambda e{:}\begin{bmatrix} t : \textit{Topos} \\ c_1 : \text{in}(t, r.\text{private.topoi}) \\ c_2 : \text{specification}(\text{fst}(r.\text{shared.eud}), t) \end{bmatrix} \cdot$$
$$[\,\text{shared} : [\,\text{topoi} = [e.t \mid r.\text{shared.topoi}] : \text{list}(\textit{Topos})\,]\,]$$

We will call the type of $B$'s information state before the update of shared topos $T_4$.

(4.17) $T_4 \sqsubseteq \begin{bmatrix} \text{pr} : \begin{bmatrix} \text{topoi} = [\lambda r{:}\begin{bmatrix} x : \textit{Ind} \\ c_s : \text{sick}(x) \end{bmatrix} \cdot [\,c_h : \text{in\_hospital}(r.x)\,]\,] : \text{list}(\textit{Topos}) \end{bmatrix} \end{bmatrix}$

---

1   We use abstraction over $e$ to introduce conditions on information states whose witnesses are not part of the information state proper.

The shared part of $T_4$ is identical to that in (4.11). To update 'shared topos', we apply $f_{integrate\_topos}$ to an information state $s_4$ of type $T_4$, and a record that witnesses that the first enthymeme in 'shared.eud' is a specification of a topos in 'private.topoi', resulting in a type $T_5$ shown in (4.18).

$$(4.18) \quad T_5 = \left[ sh : \left[ topoi = [\lambda r : \begin{bmatrix} x : Ind \\ c_s : sick(x) \end{bmatrix} \cdot [c_h : in\_hospital(r.x)]] : list(Topos) \right] \right]$$

After having asymmetrically merged $T_4$ with $T_5$ we get the type of the updated information state, seen in (4.19).

(4.19)

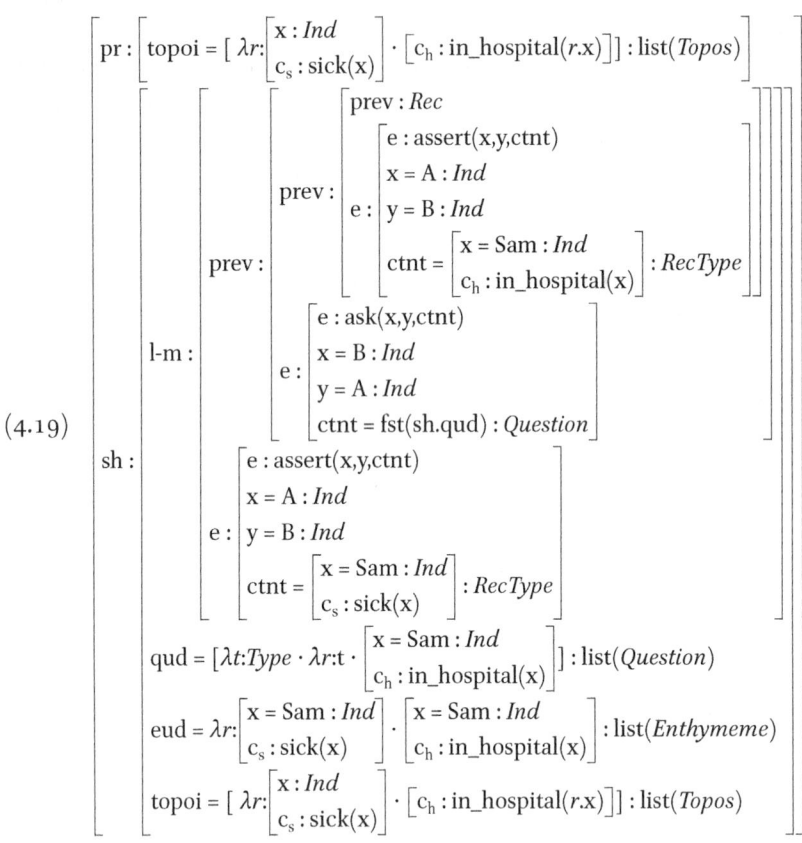

4.2.1.1     Understanding and Accepting Arguments

The update rule just presented, $f_{integrate\_topos}$, represents the process of an agent recognising a topos and assuming that it is indeed this topos on which the speaker is basing her argument. It should be emphasised that this does not necessarily mean that the agent agrees with or accepts the assertion made (the conclusion of the argument), but merely that she recognises it as underpinning the enthymeme.

There is a difference between interpreting an enthymeme in a coherent way and agreeing to the claim or proposition made, as illustrated by the example in (4.20):

(4.20)   a.  Child:  Can I go swimming?
         b.  Father: No, we just had lunch.
         c.  Child:  But dad, swimming after meals is actually not harmful!

The child in the previous example accommodates a topos presumably underpinning the father's argument, namely the notion that it is dangerous to swim after meals (which research has shown to be false). In order to correctly interpret the enthymeme the child must be familiar with this notion. However, this does not mean that she agrees with it. The two levels of interpretation of enthymemes we will focus on here are understanding and acceptance. By the former we mean that the agent in question has access to a relevant topos, by the latter that the interlocutor accepts the enthymeme and tentatively accommodates a topos based on the enthymeme. However, none of these actually mean that the interpreting agent agrees with the conclusion or that she agrees that the topos holds and is relevant in the context. Still, as is the case with presupposition accommodation, if the dialogue continues after the accommodation of a topos without any questioning from the interlocutor, we can only assume that the interlocutor agrees, at least for the time being. Obviously, issues, questions, enthymemes and topoi may be raised and reraised at any time. Those points in discourse where reraising occurs are often interesting, as topoi are often made explicit in such contexts. This also gives the interlocutors an opportunity to coordinate to make sure that they draw on the same topos when interpreting an enthymeme. In the next section we will look further at what happens when interlocutors draw on different topoi to underpin enthymemes in the discourse, and how they resolve such situations.

### 4.2.2   Topoi from Underspecified Enthymemes

In the previous section we considered how a *why*-question can be seen as eliciting an enthymeme. If this enthymeme matches a topos available to and accepted by the agent posing the question, chances are that he or she will be satisfied with the reply. Arguably, the assumption in such cases is that the underpinning of the argument, the topos, is similar in the information states of the conversational participants. However, it is also possible that two agents involved in dialogue accommodate different topoi which both satisfy the criteria for underpinning a particular enthymeme. This kind of mismatch of topoi may go unnoticed in cases where consensus is reached. After all, if interlocutors agree, there is often no reason to argue about the rationale for agreeing.

In this section, we will look at a dialogue example where it is made explicit that the speaker and the listener interpret an enthymeme drawing on different topoi. This snippet of dialogue is taken from a radio program where discussion alternates with music. The interviewee is Swedish hip hop artist Petter, and much of the dialogue relates to the songs being played in the music sections. Just before the dialogue in (4.21) a tune by a metal band has been played. Petter is being asked for his opinion of the song.

(4.21)   a. *P*: Metal was actually the reason I started doing hip hop
         b. *P*: ... because I hated metal
         c. *J*: Oh, I thought you were going to say something completely different!

This example is interesting since it provides evidence that dialogue participant *J* reasons incrementally about the enthymeme *P* is producing. In fact, *P*'s utterance can be seen as an incomplete enthymeme—there is *something* about metal that made Petter start doing hip hop. We think of this as the antecedent type of the enthymeme being *underspecified*. Intuitively, this means that there is no readily available topos warranting this enthymeme.[2] We can think of the utterance in (4.21a) as describing a situation where the music genre metal occurs, leading to a situation where the speaker starts practicing music of the hip hop genre. Thus, the enthymeme is a function of the type seen in (4.22). We refer to this enthymeme as $\varepsilon_{reason}$.

$$(4.22) \quad \varepsilon_{reason} = \lambda r: \begin{bmatrix} T = Music : Type \\ x = metal : T \\ z = Petter : Ind \\ c_1 : relevant(T) \end{bmatrix} \cdot \begin{bmatrix} y = hiphop : r.T \\ c_2 : do(r.z, y) \end{bmatrix}$$

---

2   As pointed out previously regarding the relation between enthymeme and topos, underspecification is context relative. It is not inconceivable that there would be a topos warranting this enthymeme in a particular context.

There might be several topoi accessible to $J$ which could be drawn on to underpin the enthymeme in (4.22). Judging from $J$'s utterance she is surprised by $P$'s assertion that he hated metal. We cannot say exactly in which way Petter hating metal is "completely different" from what $J$ expected. However, it seems reasonable to assume that she expected metal being the reason for $P$ starting to "do" hiphop being due to some positive quality of metal or some positive relation between him and metal. Thus, a possible topos could be one saying that if two things are of the same type, and something positive is associated with one of them, that thing may cause someone to "do" the other thing. From a logical point of view this principle is, of course, shaky at best. However, it still seems to be fairly productive in everyday argumentation. Think of examples like "Karate got me interested in Kung Fu", etc. We see a formalisation of this topos, $\tau_{similar}$ in (4.23).

$$(4.23) \quad \tau_{similar} = \lambda r: \begin{bmatrix} T : Type \\ x : T \\ z : Ind \\ c_1 : relevant(T) \\ c_2 : like(z, x) \end{bmatrix} \cdot \begin{bmatrix} y : r.T \\ c_3 : do(r.z, y) \end{bmatrix}$$

In the previous section we introduced the rule *integrate topos*, (4.16), for adding topoi to the shared field of the DGB. According to this update rule, a particular enthymeme justifies the loading of a topos onto the DGB if the enthymeme is a *specification* of the topos. We defined that as meeting two conditions. First, the domain- or antecedent part of the enthymeme must be a subtype of (i.e., more specific or identical to) the corresponding part of the topos. Secondly, the result of applying the enthymeme to a record $r$ must be a subtype of the result of applying the topos to the same record.

If we compare $\tau_{similar}$ and $\varepsilon_{reason}$, we see that the domain type of $\varepsilon_{reason}$ is *not* a subtype of the domain type of $\tau_{similar}$, since it lacks the constraint $c_2$: like(z, x). The first requirement for applying the update function $f_{integrate\_topos}$ (see (4.16)) is thus not met.

However, since dialogue participants sometimes do accommodate topoi based on underspecified enthymemes, we want to be able to model how topoi may be integrated based on less strict requirements. In order to do this we introduce an additional update rule $f_{integrate\_topos'}$. This rule says that we may integrate a topos on the shared gameboard if the application of the first enthymeme on the list of enthymemes under discussion (we may call this max-EUD, parallel to Ginzburg's (2012) terminology for QUD) to any $r$, is a subtype of the application of the topos to $r$, and there is no accessible topos where the rule $f_{integrate\_topos}$

applies. In other words: if there is no accessible topos that is a more general version of the enthymeme, look for a topos of which the enthymeme is a more general version. We talk about this kind of enthymeme as *underspecified* in relation to the topos. In (4.24) is a more precise definition of the concept of an underspecified enthymeme.

(4.24)   Assuming topos $\tau = \lambda r{:}T_1 \cdot T_2$ and enthymeme $\varepsilon = \lambda r{:}T_3 \cdot T_4$, $\varepsilon$ is an underspecification of $\tau$, i.e., underspecification$(\varepsilon,\tau)$ is witnessed, iff $T_1 \sqsubseteq T_3$ and for any $r$, $\varepsilon(r) \sqsubseteq \tau(r)$.

Since the domain type of $\varepsilon_{reason}$ includes manifest fields which are not manifest in the domain type of $\tau_{similar}$, $\varepsilon_{reason}$ is not underspecified with regard to $\tau_{similar}$. However, we are always allowed to *generalise* enthymemes by removing the values of manifest fields (making manifest fields non-manifest) in the domain type. We may also remove entire fields of the domain type as long as nothing in the result type depends on the removed field.

If we generalise $\varepsilon_{reason}$ by removing the values of x and z, we obtain the enthymeme in (4.25):

$$(4.25) \quad \varepsilon_{reason_{gen}} = \lambda r{:} \begin{bmatrix} T : Type \\ x : T \\ z : Ind \\ c_1 : relevant(T) \end{bmatrix} \cdot \begin{bmatrix} y = \text{hiphop} : r.T \\ c_2 : do(r.z, y) \end{bmatrix}$$

We may now finally apply the rule for integrating topoi on the shared DGB based on an underspecified enthymeme—$f_{integrate\_topos'}$.

$$(4.26) \quad f_{integrate\_topos'} =$$
$$\lambda r{:} \begin{bmatrix} private : [topoi : list(topos)] \\ shared : \begin{bmatrix} eud : list(Enthymeme) \\ topoi : list(Topos) \end{bmatrix} \end{bmatrix} \cdot$$
$$\lambda e{:} \begin{bmatrix} t : Topos \\ c_1 : in(t, r.private.topoi) \\ c_2 : underspec.(fst(r.shared.eud), t)) \end{bmatrix} \cdot$$
$$[shared : [topoi = [e.t \mid r.private.topoi] : list(Topos)]]$$

$\tau_{similar}$ is on J's private gameboard at the start of the operation to integrate it on her shared gameboard. For now, let us not care about exactly how this topos got selected to the private gameboard, let us just assume that the private gameboard holds a depository of topoi that the speaker finds salient in the context.

Furthermore, we assume that we have $s_1$ representing $J$'s information state, and $e_1$ imposing conditions as in (4.27):

(4.27) a. $s_1$ :
$$
\begin{bmatrix}
\text{pr} : \begin{bmatrix} \text{topoi} = [\tau_{similar}] : \text{list}(Topos) \end{bmatrix} \\
\text{sh} : \begin{bmatrix}
\text{eud} = [\,\varepsilon_{metal\_reason}\,] : \text{list}(Enthymeme) \\
\text{topoi} = [\,] : \text{list}(Topos) \\
\text{l-m} : \begin{bmatrix}
\text{prev} : Rec \\
e : \begin{bmatrix}
x : T \\
y : T \\
z = \text{Petter} : Ind \\
T : Type \\
c_1 : \text{metal}(x) \\
c_2 : \text{hiphop}(y) \\
c_3 : \text{relevant}(T) \\
c_4 : \text{do}(z,y) \\
c_5 : \text{reason}(z, c_4, x)
\end{bmatrix}
\end{bmatrix}
\end{bmatrix}
\end{bmatrix}
$$

b. $e_1$ :
$$
\begin{bmatrix}
t = \tau_{similar} : Topos \\
c_1 : \text{in}(t,[\tau_{similar}]) \\
c_2 : \text{underspec.}(\varepsilon_{metal\_reason}, t))
\end{bmatrix}
$$

(4.28) $f_{integrate\_topos'}(s_1)(e_1) =$
$$
\lambda r : \begin{bmatrix}
\text{pr} : \begin{bmatrix} \text{topoi} : \text{list}(Topos) \end{bmatrix} \\
\text{sh} : \begin{bmatrix}
\text{eud} : \text{list}(Enthymeme) \\
\text{topoi} : \text{list}(Topos)
\end{bmatrix}
\end{bmatrix} \cdot \lambda e : \begin{bmatrix}
t : Topos \\
c_1 : \text{in}(t, r.\text{pr.topoi}) \\
c_2 : \text{underspec.}(\text{fst}(r.\text{sh.eud}), t))
\end{bmatrix} \cdot
$$
$$
\begin{bmatrix} \text{sh} : \begin{bmatrix} \text{topoi} = [\, e.t \mid r.\text{private.topoi}] : \text{list}(Topos) \end{bmatrix} \end{bmatrix} (r_1)(e_1) =
$$
$$
\begin{bmatrix} \text{sh} : \begin{bmatrix} \text{topoi} = [\tau_{similar}] : \text{list}(Topos) \end{bmatrix} \end{bmatrix}
$$

To obtain the type of the updated information state for $J$, we do an asymmetric merge of the type of $r_1$ and the result type, as seen in (4.29).

(4.29)

$$
\begin{bmatrix}
\text{pr} : \begin{bmatrix} \text{topoi} = [\tau_{similar}] : \text{list}(Topos) \end{bmatrix} \\
\text{sh} : \begin{bmatrix} \text{eud} = [\, \varepsilon_{metal\_reason}] : \text{list}(Enthymeme) \\ \text{topoi} = [\,] : \text{list}(Topos) \\ \text{l-m} : \begin{bmatrix} \text{prev} : Rec \\ e : \begin{bmatrix} x : T \\ y : T \\ z = Petter : Ind \\ T : Type \\ c_1 : \text{metal}(x) \\ c_2 : \text{hiphop}(y) \\ c_3 : \text{relevant}(T) \\ c_4 : \text{do}(z,y) \\ c_5 : \text{reason}(z, c_4, x) \end{bmatrix} \end{bmatrix} \end{bmatrix}
\end{bmatrix} \; \boxed{\wedge}
$$

$$
\begin{bmatrix} \text{sh} : \begin{bmatrix} \text{topoi} = [\tau_{similar}] : \text{list}(Topos) \end{bmatrix} \end{bmatrix} =
$$

$$
\begin{bmatrix}
\text{pr} : \begin{bmatrix} \text{topoi} = [\tau_{similar}] : \text{list}(Topos) \end{bmatrix} \\
\text{sh} : \begin{bmatrix} \text{eud} = [\, \varepsilon_{metal\_reason}] : \text{list}(Enthymeme) \\ \text{topoi} = [\tau_{similar}] : \text{list}(Topos) \\ \text{l-m} : \begin{bmatrix} \text{prev} : Rec \\ e : \begin{bmatrix} x : T \\ y : T \\ z = Petter : Ind \\ T : Type \\ c_1 : \text{metal}(x) \\ c_2 : \text{hiphop}(y) \\ c_3 : \text{relevant}(T) \\ c_4 : \text{do}(z,y) \\ c_5 : \text{reason}(z, c_4, x) \end{bmatrix} \end{bmatrix} \end{bmatrix}
\end{bmatrix}
$$

This update of $J$'s information state reflects that she is reasoning incrementally, and has a preconception about $P$'s reasoning based on what he has said this far. In situations where dialogue participants know each other very well and/or the context allows it, participants may well infer topoi based on underspecified enthymemes, which turn out to be exactly the ones intended by the speaker. Furthermore the possibility of asking follow-up questions and other types of feedback make it efficient to reason based on underspecified enthymemes in situations where the stakes are not too high.

To summarise this section so far, we may say that when trying to interpret an enthymeme, a dialogue participant first tries to access a topos that serves as underpinning for the enthymeme. Most obviously this means a topos which is a bit more general than the enthymeme. However, if no such topos is accessible to the dialogue participant, he may tentatively integrate another topos accessible on his private gameboard, if this topos is similar to—but actually more specific than—the enthymeme under discussion since the antecedent part involves more constraints.

### 4.2.3  Re-raising Topoi

When we engage in conversation we normally try to interpret underspecified or implicit content drawing on information already introduced on the shared DGB. This is the case with for example resolution of anaphora. Thus we would want an algorithm for applying update rules meant to pick out a topos to underpin the enthymeme currently under discussion, to first apply the rule $f_{reraise\_topos}$ which looks for a suitable topos which is already part of common ground, that is already present on the DGB, and not until that fails, apply the rules described in Sections 4.2.1 and 4.2.2 which look into the conversational participant's private depository of salient topoi.

The rule in (4.30) says that if the information state has a topos on 'shared.topoi' supporting the max-EUD (the most recently conveyed enthymeme), we are licensed to update that information state so that the topos in question is moved to the top of the list of topoi.

In (4.30), we use a function $\mu$. If $b$ is a list and $a \in b$, the function $\mu$ applied to $b$, $\mu(a, b)$, moves $a$ to the top of list $b$ regardless of what position $a$ has had previously. The use of ordered lists for topoi present on the shared DGB captures some aspects of salience. When a new topos is added it is always placed at the top of the list. This entails that the list of topoi is connected to the chronological order in which the topoi were added to the discourse model. However, this order may change if a topos which is already integrated on shared topoi is reraised in the conversation.

$$(4.30) \quad f_{reraise\_topos} =$$
$$\lambda r: \left[ shared : \begin{bmatrix} eud : list(Enthymeme) \\ topoi : list(Topos) \end{bmatrix} \right].$$
$$\lambda e: \begin{bmatrix} t : Topos \\ c_1 : in(t, r.shared.topoi) \\ c_2 : specification(fst(r.shared.eud), t) \end{bmatrix}.$$
$$\left[ shared : \left[ topoi = \mu(e.t, r.sh.topoi) : list(Topos) \right] \right]$$

### 4.2.4   Re-evaluating Topoi

In everyday conversational settings we tend to make inferences without having, in a logical sense, adequate evidence. For this reason dialogue participants sometimes need to reevaluate the principles on which they base their interpretations of enthymemes.

As we move on to the final part of Petter's utterance, (4.21b), we are faced with precisely this problem—the enthymeme which is now first on the list of enthymemes under discussion does not match the topos first on the list of shared topoi. The reason for this is that when integrating (4.21a), $J$ integrates the enthymeme $\varepsilon_{reason}$ in (4.31a), and accommodates a topos underpinning this enthymeme, $\tau_{similar}$. When encountering (4.21b), $J$ learns that in fact $P$ had a different enthymeme in mind, $\varepsilon_{reason'}$ in (4.31b). The intuition here is that the new enthymeme requires a new topos to be added to the DGB.

$$(4.31)\quad \text{a. } \varepsilon_{reason} = \lambda r: \begin{bmatrix} T = \text{music} : Type \\ x = \text{metal} : T \\ z = \text{Petter} : Ind \\ c_1 : \text{relevant(T)} \end{bmatrix} \cdot \begin{bmatrix} y = \text{hiphop} : r.T \\ c_2 : \text{do}(r.z, y) \end{bmatrix}$$

$$\text{b. } \varepsilon_{reason'} = \lambda r: \begin{bmatrix} T : Type \\ x = \text{metal} : T \\ c_1 : \text{relevant(T)} \\ z = \text{Petter} : Ind \\ c_{hate} : \text{hate}(z, x) \end{bmatrix} \cdot \begin{bmatrix} y = \text{hiphop} : r.T \\ c_2 : \text{do}(r.z, y) \end{bmatrix}$$

The only difference between the two enthymemes is that the antecedent type of $\varepsilon_{reason'}$ includes one constraint, $c_{hate}$, which is not present in $\varepsilon_{reason}$. $\varepsilon_{reason'}$ is thus a specification of $\varepsilon_{reason}$.

In 4.2.2 we discussed what it means for an enthymeme to be a specification of a topos and what it means for an enthymeme to be underspecified in relation to a topos. There are situations—such as the present one of $J$ trying to make sense of $P$'s utterance—where the enthymeme seems to be *incompatible* with the topos at the top of the list of 'sh.topos' (max-topos). Here the enthymeme $\varepsilon_{reason'}$ says that since $P$ hated metal, he started doing hip hop, and the topos $\tau_{similar}$ says that if someone likes something that person might also get involved in other, similar, activities. The antecedents of $\varepsilon_{reason'}$ and $\tau_{similar}$ include concepts that we would probably want to model as mutually exclusive, namely *like* and *hate*. The formula in (4.32) is our version of a meaning postulate, and reads "$T_1$ precludes $T_2$", that is there is no situation which is both of type $T_1$ and of type $T_2$.

(4.32)   If $\begin{bmatrix} x : Ind \\ c : hate(x) \end{bmatrix} = T_1$ and $\begin{bmatrix} x : Ind \\ c : like(x) \end{bmatrix} = T_2$ then $T_1 \perp T_2$

The only topos on the list of shared topoi at the point where $J$ has just integrated $\varepsilon_{reason'}$ is such that the max-EUD cannot be a specification of it, nor can the topos be a specification of the max-EUD, since $\varepsilon\_reason' \perp \tau_{similar}$. Thus the conditions for applying $f_{reraise\_topos}$ are not fulfilled. So, we move on to once again applying rule $f_{integrate\_topos}$. A topos that would work here would be one capturing the notion of "the lesser of two evils", $\tau_{Lte}$. The idea of this topos is that if, in a particular context or situation, you have two things to choose from and one is bad, you pick the other one.

(4.33)   $\tau_{Lte} = \lambda r: \begin{bmatrix} T : Type \\ x : T \\ y : T \\ z : Ind \\ c_1 : relevant(T) \\ c_2 : hate(z, y) \end{bmatrix} \cdot \begin{bmatrix} e : start\_doing(r.z, r.x) \end{bmatrix}$

We assume thus, that $J$'s information state when she has integrated $\varepsilon_{reason'}$ is of the type in (4.34).

(4.34)   $T_J \sqsubseteq \begin{bmatrix} private : \begin{bmatrix} topoi = [\tau_{Lte}] : list(Topos) \end{bmatrix} \\ shared : \begin{bmatrix} eud = [\varepsilon_{reason'}, \varepsilon_{reason}] : list(Enthymeme) \\ topoi = [\tau_{similar}] : list(Topos) \end{bmatrix} \end{bmatrix}$

Since the application of update rule $f_{reraise\_topos}$ fails in this situation, we move on to apply $f_{integrate\_topos}$ to the information state $s_J$ of type $T_J$.

(4.35)   $f_{integrate\_topos}(s_J) =$
$\begin{bmatrix} shared : \begin{bmatrix} eud = [\varepsilon_{reason'}, \varepsilon_{reason}] : list(Enthymeme) \\ topoi = [\tau_{Lte}, \tau_{similar}] : list(Topos) \end{bmatrix} \end{bmatrix}$

### 4.2.5   Accommodating Resource Topoi

In his classic paper *Scorekeeping in a language game*, Lewis (1979) argues that if you "say something that requires a missing presupposition, that presupposition will straight away spring into existence". Lewis refers to this phenomenon as *accommodation* (See also Karttunen, 1974 and Stalnaker, 1974).

When a speaker makes an utterance like that in (4.36), the claim—that the rollers must be carefully looked after since they are of much higher quality compared to the kind that is normally used—presupposes a topos warranting high quality as a reason for the rollers being well looked after. This topos could be something along the lines of "if something is valuable, it should be well looked after". The topos must, if we accept the enthymeme conveyed, be integrated on the shared DGB. We may refer to this integration as a kind of accommodation.

(4.36)  A: I'm going to take a, a roller ⟨pause⟩ these are very expensive, very classy rollers.

   A: ⟨cough⟩ Much higher quality than the bioprinting [sic] rollers that we may be used to using.

   A: And therefore they must be carefully looked after.

(BNC: F77 341–343)

However, in the case of presuppositions, it is clear from the triggering sentence exactly what is presupposed. In the case of an accommodated topos, it is clear only that *some* topos is drawn on to warrant the enthymeme in the discourse. Above, we have considered two ways of updating shared topoi on the DGB— $f_{integrate\_topos}$ (4.16) and $f_{integrate\_topos'}$ (4.26), which move a topos from an agent's private DGB and integrate it on the shared DGB—and $f_{reraise\_topos}$ which finds an appropriate topos on the shared DGB and moves it to the front of the list of shared topoi.

In addition to the types of accommodation mentioned, there are other possible types of topos accommodation. First, adding a topos to the shared DGB which is not part of the depository of private salient topoi (corresponding to the list on 'private.topoi') but must be retrieved from long term memory (we refer to this depository as the agent's rhetorical resources). Another type of accommodation is when a conversational participant does not have access to a topos which matches the enthymeme currently under discussion, and tentatively construes one based on the enthymeme under discussion.

In a situation such as (4.36), if a dialogue participant is not aware of the principle "costly/high quality things should be taken care of", he might integrate a topos such as "if a roller is expensive it should be taken care of" or, more generally, "if an artefact is expensive it should be taken care of". This topos may then be tentatively added to the resources of the individual, and eventually— if reinforced in further interaction—be considered a reliable topos.

The first of these scenarios, where a topos is available in the long term memory of the dialogue participant (shown in (4.37)), we refer to as $f_{integrate\_resource\_topos}$.

$(4.37)$   $f_{integrate\_resource\_topos} =$

$$\lambda r: \begin{bmatrix} \text{private} : [\text{topoi} : \text{list}(topos)] \\ \text{shared} : \begin{bmatrix} \text{eud} : \text{list}(Enthymeme) \\ \text{topoi} : \text{list}(Topos) \end{bmatrix} \end{bmatrix} \cdot$$

$$\lambda e: \begin{bmatrix} \text{t} : Topos \\ c_1 : \text{in\_rhet\_resources(t)} \\ c_2 : \text{specification(fst}(r.\text{shared.eud}), \text{t}) \end{bmatrix} \cdot$$

$$[\text{shared} : [\text{topoi} = [e.\text{t} \mid r.\text{shared.topoi}] : \text{list}(Topos)]]$$

We also need a rule to account for cases where the enthymeme is underspecified. We see such a rule in $(4.38)$.

$(4.38)$   $f_{integrate\_resource\_topos'} =$

$$\lambda r: \begin{bmatrix} \text{private} : [\text{topoi} : \text{list}(topos)] \\ \text{shared} : \begin{bmatrix} \text{eud} : \text{list}(Enthymeme) \\ \text{topoi} : \text{list}(Topos) \end{bmatrix} \end{bmatrix} \cdot$$

$$\lambda e: \begin{bmatrix} \text{t} : Topos \\ c_1 : \text{in\_rhet\_resources(t)} \\ c_2 : \text{underspecification(fst}(r.\text{shared.eud}), \text{t}) \end{bmatrix} \cdot$$

$$[\text{shared} : [\text{topoi} = [e.\text{t} \mid r.\text{shared.topoi}] : \text{list}(Topos)]]$$

In all of the cases above we would say that accommodation occurs, if we take accommodation to mean integration of a pragmatic inference on the shared DGB. However, in the scenario above, where a dialogue participant tentatively adds a topos to the gameboard based on the enthymeme under discussion, we not only accommodate a topos, we also add something to our resources that was not there before. This kind of topos accommodation will be discussed further in Chapters 5 and 6.

## 4.3   Summary

In this chapter we first looked at an example where the enthymematic structure is made explicit by a *why*-question. We considered how *why*-questions relate to enthymemes and how answers to questions can be evaluated based on how the enthymemes conveyed relate to accessible topoi.

We also considered an example where dialogue participants interpret the same enthymeme drawing on different topoi. To accommodate this type of dialogue event we extended our set of rules. We also had to make adjustments to the order in which rules are applied, i.e. the update algorithm.

One reason that dialogues can develop in the way described above is that speakers use enthymemes which are *underspecified* in relation to the topos drawn on. In our case the first enthymeme is underspecified in relation to the topos based on which *J* interprets it, as well as in relation to the topos that *P* seems to have in mind. It may well be argued that there is a preference for the first interpretation, and *P* is thus being deliberately misleading in first presenting an underspecified enthymeme. Note that we have defined underspecified enthymemes, but which topoi that may be conceived of as appropriate underpinning for any particular enthymeme is an empirical question. It is possible that an enthymeme which is underspecified according to our definition, would easily convey the intended enthymeme in a particular context, and vice versa.

We have focused on the issue of underspecified enthymemes and how they can still be used to accommodate particular topoi. However, in the discussion of evaluation of topoi in relation to the enthymeme under discussion, we made some simplifying assumptions. For example, we might want to introduce rules that remove enthymemes which include premises which are incompatible with more recently added enthymemes. Some of these issues will be addressed in the next two chapters.

# CHAPTER 5

# Participating in Enthymematic Dialogue

Thus far we have focused on how a theory of enthymemes and topoi contributes to semantic and pragmatic interpretation of dialogue. In this chapter we will focus more on how agents engaged in conversation produce dialogue contributions drawing on topoi which they themselves have access to, as well as other dialogue participants' capacity to identify enthymemes and underpinning topoi. First, we will consider the link between enthymemes and cognitive load. We will discuss the notion of redundancy in dialogue in the context of Walker's (1996) research on so called *information redundant utterances* (IRUS), and how we perceive these utterances as serving to add new information to a discourse situation by pointing to specific topoi.

We will discuss how enthymematic arguments are embedded in conversational games associated with speech act types such as assertion, suggestion, request, etc. We will also consider how we can model the invention of enthymematic arguments, as well as how an enthymematic relation may be accommodated based on accessible topoi.

## 5.1 Enthymemes and Cognitive Load

### 5.1.1 *Information Redundancy in Dialogue*

A significant feature of natural language—particularly dialogue—is economy. This has been noted by many scholars in the fields of pragmatics and discourse studies, and given rise to some of the well known and generally accepted theories previously discussed in this book. Walker (1996) mentions the second part of Grice's (1975) maxim of quantity, as an example of a generally assumed redundancy constraint, that is, the notion that communicative contributions should not be redundant with regard to informational content.

This maxim, "do not make your contribution more informative than required", has often been interpreted as "make your contribution as short as possible", resulting in all utterances whose content may be deduced from context or retrieved from memory being considered IRUS. Walker (1996) argues that IRUS are often not redundant at all (thus actually adhering to the maxim of quantity rather than violating it). Rather, IRUS serve to help lower the cognitive load of an interlocutor interpreting a dialogue contribution. For example, in (5.1), the

© ELLEN BREITHOLTZ, 2021 | DOI:10.1163/9789004436794_006

second part of the utterance is informationally redundant in the sense that the other dialogue participant is likely to be aware of who is president.

(5.1)  A: Clinton has to take a stand on abortion rights for poor women.
       A: HE'S THE PRESIDENT (Walker, 1996, p. 188)

The second part of the utterance above provides the non-redundant information that the fact that Clinton is president is the *reason* the speaker thinks that he has to take a stand on abortion rights for poor women. As we will demonstrate, many of the utterances that Walker refers to convey enthymemes and are underpinned by topoi.

According to Walker the principle of avoiding redundancy, which has often taken precedence in work on dialogue modelling and overshadowed other factors affecting communicative choice, is based on four assumptions about dialogue:

(5.2)  a. Unlimited working-memory: everything an agent knows is always available for reasoning;
       b. Logical omniscience: agents are capable of applying all inference rules, so any entailment will be added to the discourse model;
       c. Fewest utterances: utterance production is the only process that should be minimised;
       d. No autonomy: assertions and proposals by agent *A* are accepted by default by agent *B*.

Walker presents corpus data in which agents frequently violate the redundancy constraint, indicating that the fewest utterances assumption is not correct—sometimes other aspects of communication are more important than economy.

Walker's analysis leads her to formulate three main functions of IRUs:

(5.3)  a. To provide evidence supporting beliefs about mutual understanding and acceptance.
       b. To manipulate the locus of attention of the discourse participants by making a proposition salient.
       c. To augment the evidence supporting beliefs that certain inferences are licensed.

Walker also discusses experiments, which were designed according to the results of the corpus study. These experiments show that IRUs do indeed contribute to mitigating the effect of an agent's resource limits.

Let us now take a look at one of Walker's examples of an IRU.[1] The context of this excerpt is two colleagues walking to work. They are both familiar with the surroundings and the routes available.

(5.4)   a. *A*: Let's walk along Walnut Street
        b. *A*: It's shorter (Walker, 1996, p. 188)

It is known to *A* that *B* knows that Walnut Street is shorter, so by the redundancy constraint *A* should only have said (5.4a). Walker claims that (5.4b) is considered an IRU based on the assumption of unlimited working memory, i.e. that all knowledge and information an agent has access to is equally available at all times. Walker hypothesises that the mentioning of the well-known fact that Walnut Street is shorter is a way for *A* to ease *B*'s cognitive load. Another example is (5.5), which is an excerpt of a discussion about individual retirement accounts.

(5.5)   a. *A*: Oh no, individual retirement accounts are available as long as you
           are not a participant in an existing pension.
        b. *B*: Oh I see. Well [...] I do work for a company that has a pension.
        c. *A*: Ahh. Then you're not eligible for [the tax year of] eighty one.
           (Walker, 1996, p. 187)

Walker's analysis of this example is that (5.5c) is considered an IRU based on the assumption that agents are logically omniscient, since *B* would have to apply an inference rule to conclude (5.5c). The function of *A*'s stating (5.5c) is, according to Walker, to augment the evidence supporting beliefs that certain inferences are licensed.

### 5.1.2 *A Rhetorical Approach to IRUs*

A difficult question in this context is how to decide when to add an IRU and when not to. Some redundancy may help relieve the working memory of a dialogue system user or a participant in human-human conversation, while too much information will only increase the cognitive load. We will discuss how a rhetorical perspective may be of use in this balancing act, and suggest that enthymemes, underpinned by topoi, may provide a model for analysing these utterances.

---

1   This example has been discussed previously in the context of conventional and conversational implicature, Sections 2.2 and 2.3.

We would like to suggest a way of looking at IRUs which elucidates Walker's ideas about their function, and offers an alternative to the four assumptions of the redundancy constraint. The three functions of IRUs in Walker's study have in common that they aim to lead the listener to a certain conclusion, either by supporting a belief the listener already has, or by directing, or even redirecting, the attention of the listener. In other words, IRUs are rhetorical. Examples (5.4) and (5.5) are both illustrations of this. The fact that (5.4b) is considered redundant according to the redundancy constraint seems to reflect not only the unlimited working memory assumption, but also the assumption that dialogue participants do not have a will of their own in the sense that they by default accept assertions and proposals by other agents. In fact, it is the relative autonomy of *B* that makes it possible for him not to accept *A*'s proposition. By providing a reason for choosing Walnut Street, *A* performs a rhetorical act that potentially increases the likelihood that the suggestion will be accepted by *B*.

Example (5.5) also indicates that *A* wants to make sure that *B* draws a specific conclusion. It seems likely that *A*, if she did not find it of some importance that *B* draws the conclusion (5.5c), might not bother to make the inference explicit—*B* could still be expected to make the inference. However, for *B* to do that would not necessarily make him logically omniscient—the assumption Walker (1996) claims to be the reason for considering (5.5b) an IRU—just capable of making *some* inferences.

Interestingly, many of Walker's examples of IRUs and their respective antecedents constitute structures similar to that of an enthymeme. The mentioning of one carefully chosen premise directs the attention of the listener in the direction that the speaker wants, and makes the listener a bit more likely to accept the proposition presented in the conclusion. The enthymeme might of course serve to persuade or even mislead a listener, but the same mechanism can also make it easier for a conversational participant to accept an honest and constructive proposal made by another agent. This would be helpful when quick decisions need to be made, or when demanding parallel activities require attention.

Let us go back to the colleagues walking to work. Example (5.4) above could easily be analysed within a rhetorical framework. Mentioning (5.4b) could be a way for *A* to point to the argument about the shortest route, perhaps because they are running late. There could be other reasons to walk along Walnut Street, perhaps that it is more quiet. *A* might know that *B* usually prefers a busy street, but that she does not particularly like to walk, which would make the short-argument more persuasive. If they were not in a hurry, and *A* wanted them to walk along Walnut Street because it is nicer to walk along a quiet street than a busy one, *A* would probably say 'Let's walk along Walnut Street. It's quieter' thus validating her suggestion.

However, it is also possible that *A* would want to walk along Walnut Street for some reason that she does not want *B* to know about. So, by providing the premise "it's shorter", A makes it easier for B to interpret the suggestion to walk along Walnut Street in the intended way, that is, associated with particular inferences and not with others. The provided premise may or may not point to a genuine reason of A's for suggesting Walnut Street. However, it is also possible that A, by supplying the premise, is merely externalising her own way of thinking, not considering B's mental states. For a discussion on externalised inference, see Pickering and Garrod (2004), Mills and Gregoromichelaki (2010) and Gregoromichelaki et al. (2011).

So, giving the premise "it's shorter" points to an argument drawing on certain topoi, without which the utterance would be difficult to make sense of. The "hidden premise", i.e. the premise that *B* adds to the argument, would be something that makes sense in the context, having to do with for example time (as above) or effort (we don't want to walk longer than necessary). The additional premise is necessary in order to make the enthymeme fit with the relevant topos.

A rhetorical perspective that uses enthymematic arguments as an explanatory model for how information is given and withheld, would be based on a different set of assumptions about dialogue than those Walker formulates as the basis of the redundancy constraint. Thus we propose four rhetorically motivated principles as an alternative to the four principles of economy in dialogue in (5.2):

(5.6)   a. Limited working-memory: suggestions help agents to reach a certain decision
        b. Logical capacity: agents are capable of applying some inference rules, some entailments will be added to the discourse model;
        c. Utterance production: should be balanced so as to maximise persuasion
        d. Autonomy: assertions and proposals by agent *A* are not accepted by default by agent *B*, and different agents may or may not share goals and intentions.

As humans we need reasons to validate propositions we are presented with. We know this intuitively—it is difficult to complete a task if we are just presented with single pieces of information that do not seem to be connected. The same conclusion can be drawn based on different premises, and we often want to know which argument the speaker is referring to before we accept a proposition. There are situations where the standard way to instruct is by single utterances (or orders), such as in the military, or in other contexts where the roles are very well defined, and the *modus operandi* of the activity well rehearsed, such as in surgery.

We agree with Walker's conclusion that IRUs serve to ease cognitive load in different ways. We also suggest that the reason for this is that the enthymematic structure helps the recipient of the IRU to make up her mind, or correctly interpret an utterance. If the IRU provided links the assertion or suggestion made to a topos which the recipient finds acceptable she is more likely to agree with the proposition.

## 5.2    Enthymemes and Dialogue Context

In the previous chapter we discussed what we could call *assertion enthymemes*, like the one in (5.7).

(5.7)    Anon 3:    the monarchy are non political ⟨pause⟩ and therefore, when they choose to speak it's usually out of a genuine concern for that problem.                                                    (BNC: FLE 233)

In (5.7) the speaker claims that when (representatives of) the monarchy speak, it is out of genuine concern, supporting this claim with another claim, that they are non-political. Whether or not this is perceived as an accessible, relevant and acceptable argument by other conversational participants depends partly on to what extent they find that it is consistent with a relevant topos. This enthymeme seeks to establish a certain take on what the world is like.

However, reasoning in dialogue is often reasoning towards an action or decision. Enthymemes in arguments like (5.4) for example, consist of a conclusion or consequent part which conveys a speech act like request or exhortation. They belong to what Aristotle called *deliberative* rhetoric, which is commonly found in political discourse (Corbett and Connors, 1999).

The goal of deliberative discourse is to convince someone to carry out (or not carry out) a future action. In the context of politics this could be things like go to war, extend the public transport system of a city, or cut taxes. However, everyday conversations also often involve deliberative discourse. Conversational participants have to decide things like who to invite to a party, which car to buy, which restaurant to go to, or which film to see. In the context of deciding, interlocutors present arguments to each other. Also, many of the tasks for which we want to use dialogue systems are linked to advice giving, instructing etc. where the point of the system is to advise users based on assembled information and considerations of the context.

In the rest of this chapter we will focus on action-directed enthymemes embedded in a machinery of conversational games, taking as our point of departure the excerpt presented previously in (5.4). We will suggest how conversational games can be used to move a dialogue forward and how the kind of conversational game you choose to carry out a communicative project is related to the rhetorical force of the enthymeme conveyed.

Let us now consider (5.8).

(5.8)    A: Let's walk along Walnut Street.
         A: It's shorter.

In (5.8) speaker $A$ uses an enthymematic argument to communicate to another dialogue participant $B$ that they should choose Walnut Street rather than other possible routes, and that the reason for suggesting Walnut Street is that it is shorter than other options. We see this enthymeme in $\varepsilon_{shorter}$ in (5.9)—a function from a situation of a type where Walnut Street is shorter than some alternative, to a type of situation where $A$ and $B$ walk along Walnut Street. Note that we cannot know the exact nature of the enthymeme in terms of the number of features present, for example the number of routes available to $A$ and $B$.

$$
(5.9) \quad \varepsilon_{shorter} = \lambda r: \begin{bmatrix} x = \text{W.St.} : Ind \\ y = \text{other\_route} : Ind \\ z = \text{SELF} : Ind \\ w : \text{set}(Ind) \\ c_1 : \text{route}(x) \\ c_2 : \text{route}(y) \\ c_3 : \text{shorter\_than}(x,y) \\ c_4 : \text{in}(z, w) \end{bmatrix} \cdot \begin{bmatrix} e : \text{walk\_along}(r.w, r.x) \end{bmatrix}
$$

Using an enthymeme like the one in (5.9) is essentially a conversational strategy for carrying out a communicative project. In Chapter 3 we discussed the gameboard feature "project" and how we relate it to "communicative activity".

When an activity is carried out, it is made up of a number of projects, the goals of which are ideally fulfilled during the course of the interaction. For example, the activity type "medical consultation" typically includes a number of projects which need to be carried out, such as establishing the patient's symptoms, diagnosing the patient and explaining to the patient how his condition should be treated (Berbyuk Lindström, 2008). The activity "chatting with neighbour while gardening" is less formal, and it is not strongly associated with particular projects to be carried out in a specific order. However, if we were to examine data from this activity, we would be likely to identify communicative projects regarding things like current affairs, the weather, gardening, etc. This does not mean that the agents involved in the conversation have anticipated any of these projects, as would probably be the case in the medical consultation scenario.

Activity types also differ in terms of to what extent the roles are set or institutionalised. In the case of medical consultation, certain behaviour in the carrying out of a project is closely related to an activity role like "patient". In many activity types, however, activity roles do not play an important part for the order in which dialogue participants are expected to make their contributions. Neither do they always affect the type of contribution which we expect from a particular dialogue participant. However, even in an informal activity there are role related requirements for participating in the activity. For example, for participating in an informal conversation between friends, you have to know the other conversational participants, and the role "friend" comes with certain obligations like being honest, supportive and kind. However, assuming the role of "friend" is not associated with a particular pattern of conversation, as is the case when assuming the role of "doctor" or "patient" in a medical consultation conversation.

## 5.3    Conversational Games

As we mentioned briefly in Section 3.2.3, we consider the carrying out of a communicative project to be associated with a set of conversational games. The notion of *dialogue game* is well established in research on dialogue and is described for example in Carlson (1982) and Levin and Moore (1977). The descriptions of dialogue games in the literature do not generally distinguish between games that only lay down the rules for how to perform very general communicative functions, and rules stating which sub-projects need to be realised in order to carry out a communicative project.

Inspired by the *string theory of events* in work by Fernando (2006), Cooper and Ginzburg (2015), and Cooper (2016) describe a conversational game as a type of string of events where each event is (more or less) expected by the agents involved in the realisation of the string. If $T_1$ and $T_2$ are types of events, then, $T_1 ^\frown T_2$ is the type of strings of events $a ^\frown b$ such that $a : T_1$ and $b : T_2$.

On this view, it is not only conversational games that are perceived as string types—activity, project and conversational game may all be described as strings of events. On this view the distinction between a conversational game and a communicative project is not structural. Rather, the difference is related to the domain. An activity type is domain specific, that is it involves particular roles which are strongly associated with specific rights, obligations, etc. as well as associated settings and artefacts. A communicative project tends to be less domain specific—for example *agreeing on something* is a communicative project which may occur in various activity types. However, the carrying out of an activity of a particular kind often also requires specific communicative projects to be carried out.

Conversational games, on the other hand, are more general and reflect conversational practices which are or could be part of most communicative activities, such as asking or replying to questions, backtracking, giving feedback, etc. We define a conversational game as the minimal set of linguistic actions that need to be performed in order to realise a communicative project—similar to "speech act sequence" in van Dijk (1979). Examples of conversational games could be "request game", "suggestion game", "clarification game" and "assertion game".

## 5.4    The Suggestion Game

A relevant game type in relation to the dialogue in (5.8), is the suggestion game. In this section we will describe this game in terms of informal rules and conditions which state what should be allowed within the game:

- The suggestion game is played by at least two players, though more players are possible.
- The players have a shared project which they intend to carry out together.
- One of the dialogue participants makes a suggestion. For the sake of the game it does not matter which player has made the first move. We refer to whoever has done so as player 1.
- The suggestion by player 1 may optionally be followed by a motivation for the suggestion, again by player 1.
- Another player (who is then player 2) responds to the suggestion by accepting or rejecting the move. Note that this move does not necessarily have to be an actual response. Depending on the level of grounding we are willing to accept, abstaining from protesting might be enough to signal acceptance of a given suggestion.

We could describe the suggestion game as illustrated in Figure 1.

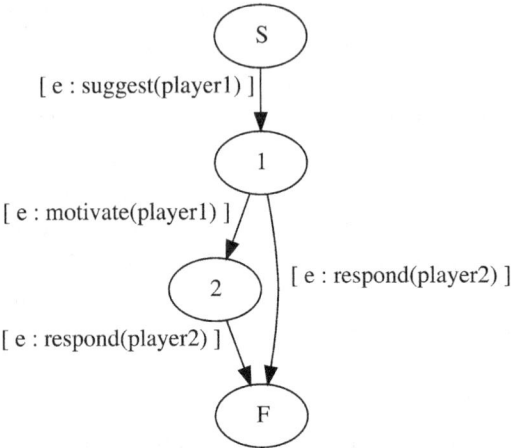

FIGURE 1     The Suggestion game

The rules above would suffice to account for an interaction where Player 1 makes a suggestion $\varphi$ to player 2, who responds by either accepting or rejecting it. However, a general set of rules that would account for the suggestion game would also have to allow for a less straightforward carrying out of the project "deciding which route to take". There could be questions, for example clarification questions or questions regarding other aspects of the context (time, place etc.) or the suggested route. Another possibility is that player 2 asks for a reason for choosing the suggested route. This would be perfectly acceptable dialogue behaviour, and players must be allowed, within the suggestion game, to move into games of other types like the clarification game or the motivation game.

We see the ability to move between games as a general rule for all conversational games. This reflects the expectations we have when engaging in dialogue—if you ask someone a question, you know that it is likely that you will get a reply. However, we can still account for dialogue behaviour which does not conform to one particular game, since we allow dialogue participants to introduce new games—and even new projects—and we also allow dialogue participants not to play the game.

So, we want rules which allow for the suggestion game to be played in a number of different ways, including detours into other games. But let us leave that aside for the moment, and just consider the possibilities realised in (5.8). If we want to represent this dialogue in terms of updates of information states, we need rules handling not only the explicit moves represented in Figure 1, but also *tacit* updates of the DGB. Tacit moves within a game represent inferences and other internal processes. We will now have a look at some of the updates of $A$'s and $B$'s DGB throughout (5.8).

## 5.5 Analysing a Suggestion Dialogue

### 5.5.1 *Initial Tacit Moves*

Since the notion of conversational game is linked to the acceptable moves in a conversation, rather than to the concrete results which conversational participants hope to get out of the interaction (as in the case of a communicative project) we introduce a new field—*games*—onto the gameboard.

In order to start a conversation, an agent searches her resources for a conversational strategy (a conversational game) to carry out the project. In case of the dialogue in (5.8), where one dialogue participant suggests to another which route they should take to work, a relevant game type is the suggestion game just described in Section 5.4. It is not until the first move is made and the conversational participants thus consider it shared information that this is the game which is being played, that the game appears on the shared game board.

At the beginning of the interaction the DGB of dialogue participant $A$ is empty apart from the field 'project', which we assume to be shared since the necessity of picking a route is obvious to both $A$ and $B$ in the context. As we remember from Chapter 4, a communicative project is a limited task or activity which is being carried out at least to some extent by means of communication. We represent a project as a type of event to be brought about by a number of agents. In (5.10) we see the type of a decision project, $T_{DecisionProject}$. $A_1$, ..., $A_n$ are dialogue participants and *Issue* the thing that is to be decided upon.

$$(5.10) \quad T_{DecisionProject} = \left[ e : \text{decide} \left( \{A_1, ..., A_n\}, Issue \right) \right]$$

For the purposes of this dialogue, only one communicative project needs to be carried out. However, by letting the type of *project* on the DGB be list(*RecType*), we are also able to model several projects to be carried out one after the other to fulfil some complex goal (linguistic or other). We would also be able to account for projects suddenly appearing in the information states of dialogue participants due to sudden events, such as "find shelter from the rain".

$$(5.11) \quad \begin{bmatrix} \text{private} : RecType \\ \text{shared} : \left[ \text{project} = \left[ \left[ e : \text{decide}(\{A, B\}, \text{route}) \right] \right] : \text{list}(RecType) \right] \end{bmatrix}$$

(5.11) shows the type of the speaker, $A$'s, information state at the beginning of the interaction in (5.8). For now we are interested only in the information state of dialogue participant $A$, not that of the listener, dialogue participant $B$. "Route" represents the issue of which route to take, in (5.8).

The first update of the dialogue gameboard is an update of 'private games', that is the repository of conversational games which are salient with respect to a dialogue participant in a given context. Before we move on to how we want to represent this update in TTR, let us have a look at the nature of projects and games in terms of types.

As illustrated in (5.10) we perceive a project as a record type representing the type of an event where a number of individuals (in this case $A$ and $B$), jointly perform some action (in this case making a decision) regarding some non-decided-upon issue. In this case, the issue which is being deliberated is which route to take to work.

We may think of the development of a conversation as a finite state automaton where the arrows leading from one state to another correspond to the linguistic moves of the conversation, as represented in Figure 1. Instead of focusing on the states between the moves, we could focus on the sequence of moves themselves when defining a conversational game. We would then get a string of move types. The type in (5.12) for example, is of strings of moves comprising the type of *suggestion game*, $T_{SuggestionGame}$—a suggestion by player 1 followed by an optional *motivation* by player 1, followed by a *response* (acceptance or rejection) by player 2. We represent move types as record types. A game of the type in (5.12) is made up of a suggestion, followed by an optional motivation by the dialogue participant who made the suggestion, followed by a response (either an *accept-* or a *reject* move) by the other player.[2]

(5.12)  $T_{SuggestionGame}=\left[e : suggest(player1)\right]^\frown\left[e : motivate(player1)\right]^{\leqslant 1\frown}$
$\left[e : respond(player2)\right]$

The notation $\left[e : motivate(player1)\right]^{\leqslant 1}$ means that the suggestion move is followed by at most one motivation move ($^{\leqslant 1}$). One could argue that a suggestion might be followed by more than one move motivating the suggestion, and it would of course be possible to alter $^{\leqslant 1}$ to $^{\leqslant 2}$ or $^{\leqslant 3}$ depending on how many motivation moves the model should allow. The string in (5.12) represents the type of a suggestion game on an abstract level—from this type we learn the

---

2   In Chapter 4, we represented move types as ptypes constructed from three-place predicates, such as suggest($x$, $y$, $ctnt$), where $x$ is the speaker, $y$ is the addressee and $ctnt$ is the content. In this chapter, we will sometimes use one-place predicates like suggest($x$), where $x$ is the speaker, to represent a slightly more abstract move type (where addressee and content are left unspecified). We will also use yet more abstract move types like *Suggest* which do not specify any arguments. One may think of these types as related in a subtype hierarchy, so that for example suggest($x$, $y$, $ctnt$) $\sqsubseteq$ suggest($x$) $\sqsubseteq$ *Suggest*.

sequence of move types involved and the relation between the *roles* that are necessary to play the game. However, in order for the game to work as a motor in the dialogue driving the updates, we need to assign the roles of the game to the individuals present in the context. For example, the player who initiates the game by making a suggestion has to be distinct from the player who acknowledges that suggestion.

### 5.5.2    *Rules for Updating Private Games*

There are at least two different scenarios which would lead to an update of private games. First, there is the type of situation where the presence of a project on the DGB causes an agent to search his long term memory for a strategy by which to carry out that project, and load it onto the DGB. The second is when there is already a game on private games that would suffice to carry out the project. Assume for example that $A$ has been thinking since he got out of bed in the morning that he wants to pass Walnut Street on his way to work. He has been meaning to suggest it for a while (or maybe hoping that $B$ will suggest it), thus the suggestion game is activated on his private DGB. When $A$ and $B$ reach a junction the issue of which route to take becomes necessary to address, and the project appears on the shared DGB. In this case the only update necessary on $A$'s DGB is to place $T_{SuggestionGame}$ first in the list of games, while $B$ has to retrieve the game from long term memory and load it onto private games. As mentioned in the previous chapter, the idea is that the update rules are combined with a control algorithm selecting which rule to apply in a given context. In Figure (2) we see a visualisation of the algorithm controlling the update of private games.

### 5.5.2.1    Update Private Games

We want the first rule $f_{ud\_pr\_games}$ to apply in a context where an agent has a project on her gameboard, but the game first on the list of private games is not relevant to carry out the project. The agent is then licensed to either reraise a game already on private games (but not first on the list) or to load a relevant game from resources onto private games. Now, one question that arises here is what it means to be a relevant game in relation to a particular project. One way of describing this would be in terms of licences in an agent's resources. If an agent has in her resources a link between a type of project $T_P$ and a type of game $T_G$, she has a licence to carry out a communicative project of type $T_P$ by means of $T_G$, and may load it onto 'private.games' on her DGB.

Which types of games are relevant to carry out particular types of projects is an empirical question. We think of the update rules licensing the carrying out of a project by means of a particular type of game as reflecting the pragmatic norms of a community. One way of modelling how an agent selects a

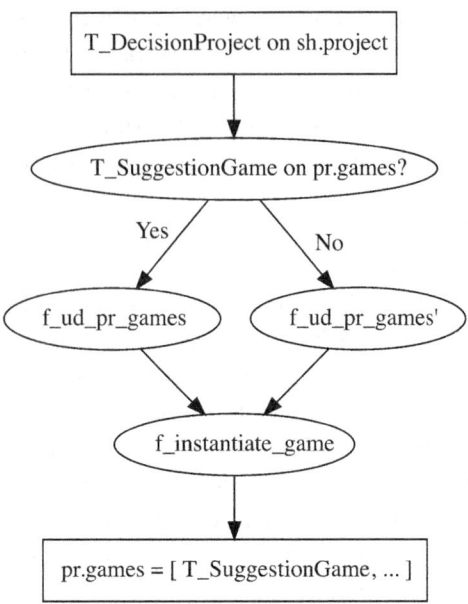

FIGURE 2    Update of private games

strategy—for example choosing between an indirect and a direct speech act—
would be to extend the model with a probabilistic component (see for example
Eshghi and Lemon (2014)). However, in the limited model we are focusing on
here, we assume that we have access to only one type of game which is relevant
to the project at hand. Moreover, it seems to us that a limited set of project types
and game types would suffice to account for a large number of dialogue situations. Thus, for each project type we would introduce a set of postulates defining which games could be relevant to carry out a project of that type. We use
the notation "relevant_to($T_1, T_2$)" to represent relevance of $T_1$ in relation to $T_2$.

When a communicative project appears on an agent's DGB and the agent initiates carrying out the project there are, as mentioned above, two possibilities.
Either there is a game present in the private games field of the DGB by means of
which the project can be carried out, or there is not. In the first case we want to
make sure that the appropriate game is moved up to the first slot on the list of
private games. In the second case, we want to pick an appropriate game from
the agent's long term memory, and place it first on the list of private games. The
update of 'private.games' thus consists of three rules: $f_{ud\_pr\_games}$ for reraising a
game, $f_{ud\_pr\_games'}$ for uploading a game from resources, and—to complete the
update—$f_{inst\_game}$. In an instantiated game the roles (player1, player2, etc.) are
assigned to dialogue participants from the point of view of the participant on
whose gameboard the instantiated game appears. This means in the case of the

suggestion game, that when $A$ starts carrying out a decision making project by initiating a game of type $T_{SuggestionGame}$, she has also taken on the role of 'player 1' in that game. In every move type of the instantiated game on her DGB the move to be carried out by player 1 will be assigned to SELF, the ones by player 2 to OTHER.

Even though instantiated games involve assignments of roles to dialogue participants, we still want to be able to treat them as types. For this reason, the type of games is a *join type*. A join type is a disjunction such that, for any two types $T_1$ and $T_2$ you can form the join $T_1 \vee T_2$. a : $T_1 \vee T_2$ just in case either a : $T_1$ or a : $T_2$ (Cooper and Ginzburg, 2012). This means that the type of games, $T_{Game}$, in our theory is a join of the types non-instantiated game, $T_{NonInstGame}$ and instantiated game, $T_{InstGame}$ as defined in (5.13):

(5.13)  $a : T_{Game}$ iff $a : T_{NonInstGame}$ or $a : T_{InstGame}$

By defining the type of game as a join, we make sure that we can handle situations where, for example, something sudden and unexpected happens, and dialogue participant needs to postpone the initiation of a game already on the DGB. We will look at the instantiation process in more detail further on in this section.

(5.14)  $f_{ud\_pr\_games} =$
$$\lambda r: \begin{bmatrix} \text{pr} : \begin{bmatrix} \text{games} : \text{list}(T_{Game}) \end{bmatrix} \\ \text{sh} : \begin{bmatrix} \text{project} = [\ T_{DecisionProject}] : \text{list}(RecType) \end{bmatrix} \end{bmatrix} \cdot \lambda e: \begin{bmatrix} \text{g} : T_{SuggestionGame} \\ c_1 : \text{in}(g, r.\text{pr.games}) \end{bmatrix} \cdot$$
$$\begin{bmatrix} \text{pr} : \begin{bmatrix} \text{games} = [\mu(e.g, r.\text{pr.games})\ ] : \text{list}(T_{Game}) \end{bmatrix} \end{bmatrix}$$

In (5.14), $f_{ud\_pr\_games}$ takes a situation of the type where there is a decision project on 'shared.project' and, if there is a game of type $T_{SuggestionGame}$ on private games in that record, the function returns a type of situation where that game type is first on 'private.games'. (See (4.2.3) on the function of $\mu$.)

We think of the update rule $f_{ud\_pr\_games}$, as seen in (5.15) as a function from an information state where an agent has a decision project on her gameboard but no game of type $T_{SuggestionGame}$ on the list of games on 'private.games',[3] to an information state where the agent has a decision project on 'shared.project' and a suggestion game first on 'private.games'. In this case the game $T_{SuggestionGame}$ has to be retrieved from parts of the agent's resources which are external to the DGB.

---

3  There may be other games on the list of private games, just not the game *suggestion game*.

(5.15)  $f_{ud\_pr\_games'} =$

$$\lambda r: \begin{bmatrix} \mathrm{pr} : \begin{bmatrix} \mathrm{games} : \mathrm{list}(T_{Game}) \end{bmatrix} \\ \mathrm{sh} : \begin{bmatrix} \mathrm{project} = \begin{bmatrix} T_{DecisionProject} \end{bmatrix} : \mathrm{list}(RecType) \end{bmatrix} \end{bmatrix} \cdot \lambda e: \begin{bmatrix} \mathrm{g} : T_{SuggestionGame} \\ \mathrm{c_1} : \neg\mathrm{in}(g, r.\mathrm{pr.games}) \end{bmatrix}$$

$$\begin{bmatrix} \mathrm{pr} : \begin{bmatrix} \mathrm{games} = [e.\mathrm{g} \mid r.\mathrm{pr.games}] : \mathrm{list}(T_{Game}) \end{bmatrix} \end{bmatrix}$$

The functions in (5.14) and (5.15) are similar to the update functions discussed by Cooper (2016, pp. 24–26). In order to obtain the required update of such a function we need to apply it to the *current information state*—that is the information state at the start of the update—of the agent whose information state we seek to capture. Let us consider a scenario where agent $A$ has previously considered suggesting Walnut Street, but was distracted by an event which the agent has just observed. This caused another conversational game, $T_{G_x}$, to appear on the DGB. His initial information state is thus of the type in (5.16), which we refer to as $T_{current}$.

(5.16)  a.  $T_{current} = \begin{bmatrix} \mathrm{pr} : \begin{bmatrix} \mathrm{games} = [T_{G_x}, T_{SuggestionGame}] : \mathrm{list}(T_{Game}) \end{bmatrix} \\ \mathrm{sh} : \begin{bmatrix} \mathrm{project} = \begin{bmatrix} T_{DecisionProject} \end{bmatrix} : \mathrm{list}(RecType) \end{bmatrix} \end{bmatrix}$

  b.  $s_{current} : T_{current}$

Before we apply the function we need to make sure that the type of the current information state is a subtype of the domain type of $f_{ud\_pr\_games}$. We should point out here that the type of the current information state might very well have other fields such as a shared game, a latest utterance, shared beliefs, etc., and still be a subtype of the domain type of $f_{ud\_pr\_games}$.

In (5.17) we see the application of $f_{ud\_pr\_games}$ to $s_{current}$, followed by an asymmetric merge (see Section 4.1.1.1) of the result of that function application and the type $T_{current}$ of $s_{current}$ (as well as $e_1$ witnessing the condition that $T_{SuggestionGame}$ is in $s_{current}.\mathrm{pr.games}$).

(5.17)  a.  $f_{ud\_pr\_games}(s_{current})(e_1)=$
$\begin{bmatrix} \mathrm{pr} : \begin{bmatrix} \mathrm{games} = [T_{SuggestionGame}, T_{G_x}] : \mathrm{list}(T_{Game}) \end{bmatrix} \end{bmatrix}$
  b.  $T_{current}$ $\boxed{\wedge}$ $\begin{bmatrix} \mathrm{pr} : \begin{bmatrix} \mathrm{games} = [T_{SuggestionGame}, T_{G_x}] : \mathrm{list}(T_{Game}) \end{bmatrix} \end{bmatrix}=$
$\begin{bmatrix} \mathrm{pr} : \begin{bmatrix} \mathrm{games} = [T_{SuggestionGame}, T_{G_x}] : \mathrm{list}(T_{Game}) \end{bmatrix} \\ \mathrm{sh} : \begin{bmatrix} \mathrm{project} = [[e : \mathrm{decide}(\{A_1, A_2\}, Issue)]] : \mathrm{list}(RecType) \end{bmatrix} \end{bmatrix}$

### 5.5.2.2    Instantiation of Game

After an update putting a game which is a subtype of $T_{SuggestionGame}$ first on the list of private games (either by $f_{ud\_pr\_games}$ or $f_{ud\_pr\_games'}$), we need to instantiate the game, that is associate the roles of the game with the players in this particular situation. To do this we apply the function $f_{inst\_T_{SuggestionGame}}$ to a record assigning the values 'SELF' and 'OTHER' to the roles of the suggestion game.

$$(5.18) \quad f_{inst\_T_{SuggestionGame}} =$$
$$\lambda r: \begin{bmatrix} player_1 : Ind \\ player_2 : Ind \end{bmatrix} \cdot \begin{bmatrix} e : suggest(r.player_1) \end{bmatrix} ^\frown \begin{bmatrix} e : motivate(r.player_1) \end{bmatrix}^{\leqslant 1} ^\frown$$
$$\begin{bmatrix} e : respond(r.player_2) \end{bmatrix}$$

For dialogue participant $A$ in our current example this assignment would be that in (5.19).

$$(5.19) \quad r = \begin{bmatrix} player_1 = SELF \\ player_2 = OTHER \end{bmatrix}$$

In (5.20) we see the application of $f_{inst\_T_{SuggestionGame}}$ to $r$.

$$(5.20) \quad f_{inst\_T_{SuggestionGame}}(r) =$$
$$\begin{bmatrix} e : suggest( \begin{bmatrix} player_1 = SELF \\ player_2 = OTHER \end{bmatrix}.player_1 ) \end{bmatrix} ^\frown$$
$$\begin{bmatrix} e : motivate( \begin{bmatrix} player_1 = SELF \\ player_2 = OTHER \end{bmatrix}.player_1 ) \end{bmatrix}^{\leqslant 1} ^\frown$$
$$\begin{bmatrix} e : respond( \begin{bmatrix} player_1 = SELF \\ player_2 = OTHER \end{bmatrix}.player_2 ) \end{bmatrix} =$$
$$\begin{bmatrix} e : suggest(SELF) \end{bmatrix} ^\frown \begin{bmatrix} e : motivate(SELF) \end{bmatrix}^{\leqslant 1} ^\frown$$
$$\begin{bmatrix} e : respond(OTHER) \end{bmatrix}$$

The instantiated suggestion game would in this situation thus be $T_{SuggestionGameInst}$, as seen in (5.21):

$$(5.21) \quad T_{SuggestionGameInst} = \begin{bmatrix} e : suggest(SELF) \end{bmatrix} ^\frown \begin{bmatrix} e : motivate(SELF) \end{bmatrix}^{\leqslant 1} ^\frown$$
$$\begin{bmatrix} e : respond(OTHER) \end{bmatrix}$$

### 5.5.3 Updating the Agenda

An important aspect of the notion of conversational game is that players (conversational participants), by identifying an utterance as being part of a particular game, get an idea of which moves are likely to follow and what part they should expect to play over the next few turns of the dialogue. In this sense conversational games may be seen as engines driving dialogues forward. Once a game is loaded onto the gameboard and roles are assigned to individuals in the context, an agent involved in a conversation can at any stage of the game look at her gameboard and know what options are available if she wants to keep playing the game. Before the update of the agenda, agent $A$—if playing the suggestion game—has on her private games the instantiated game $T_{SuggestionGameInst}$ which we see in (5.22).

Now, we want an update rule that would load the first available move of the game which is to be carried out by SELF, onto the agenda. We have a set of rules pertaining to the suggestion game that governs the dynamics of the agenda, which is inherent in the suggestion game in (5.21). This set of rules is similar to that used to update the agenda in Cooper (2016). However, in Cooper's approach, there are rules pushing moves onto the agenda which are to be made by agents other than 'SELF'. Since we have a conversational game specifying what we expect of others and ourselves in the employment of that particular game, we have chosen to use the agenda only for moves that are to be made by the agent whose agenda they are on. The agenda is part of the 'private'-field of an agent's gameboard, and is represented as a record type (move type). Each move type has a label 'e' paired with one of a set of speech act types like *Suggest*, *Ask*, *Assert*, etc. There are a number of constraints on such move types having to do with the roles of the agents involved in dialogue, $c_{actor}$. There could also be more constraints. Further, there is a label 'ctnt' for content, which—after the first update of the agenda—will not yet be associated with a specified content.

The first rule to be employed of the rules of the suggestion game is a "starting rule" in (5.22), stating that if a player has an empty agenda and a suggestion game on his private gameboard, he may, within the suggestion game, push a suggestion onto the agenda. We refer to this rule as $f_{update\_agenda\_suggestion}$.

$$(5.22) \quad f_{update\_agenda\_suggestion} = \\ \lambda r: \left[ pr: \begin{bmatrix} \text{agenda} = [\ ] : \text{list}(RecType) \\ \text{games} = [T_{SuggestionGameInst}] : \text{list}(T_{Game}) \end{bmatrix} \right]. \\ \left[ pr: \left[ \text{agenda} = [\begin{bmatrix} \text{e} : \text{suggest}(\text{SELF}) \\ \text{ctnt} : RecType \end{bmatrix}] : \text{list}(RecType) \right] \right]$$

The content of the move type that ends up on the agenda is unspecified. $f_{update\_agenda\_suggestion}$ is applied to a record of the type in (5.23):

$$(5.23) \quad \begin{bmatrix} pr: \begin{bmatrix} \text{agenda} = [\ ] : \text{list}(RecType) \\ \text{games} = [T_{SuggestionGameInst}] : \text{list}(T_{Game}) \end{bmatrix} \\ \text{sh} : [\text{project} = [[\text{e} : \text{decide}(\{A, B\}, \text{route})]] : \text{list}(RecType)] \end{bmatrix}$$

We apply the function in (5.22) to the current information state of the type in (5.23), and asymmetrically merge the current state type with the result of function application. In (5.24) we see the type of *A*'s information state after the rule has been applied.

$$
(5.24) \quad
\begin{bmatrix}
\text{pr} : 
\begin{bmatrix}
\text{agenda} = [\ \begin{bmatrix} e : \text{suggest}(\text{SELF}) \\ \text{ctnt} : RecType \end{bmatrix}\ ] : \text{list}(RecType) \\
\text{games} = [\,T_{SuggestionGameInst}] : \text{list}(T_{Game})\,)
\end{bmatrix} \\
\text{sh} : \begin{bmatrix} \text{project} = [[\,e : \text{decide}(\{A, B\}, \text{route})]] : \text{list}(RecType) \end{bmatrix}
\end{bmatrix}
$$

The next update rule provided by the conversational game (although this rule is actually general and applicable to any conversational game) is a rule saying that if we have an item on the agenda which is to be performed by SELF and whose content is specified, that is, the label 'ctnt' has one specific value ([ctnt=*T:RecType*]), then the agent is allowed to make that move and push the next move onto the agenda (we will get back to this rule soon). However, at the moment the item on the agenda is not specified in terms of content—the label is just typed *RecType* (ctnt:*RecType*). In order to add a content specific move to the agenda, the agent needs to search her resources for relevant facts and ways of reasoning about the situation and the project at hand.

### 5.5.4    *Drawing on Topoi to Specify Move Content*

So far in this chapter we have considered mechanisms of things like speech act sequences and turn taking. We will now move on to consider how a dialogue participant may reason given the topoi which are available to him or her in relation to a particular goal.

For example, let us assume that an agent is involved in a conversational game according to which he is expected to make a suggestion regarding some future action. One way for the agent to decide which suggestion to make, is to reason based on the relevant topoi available to him.

There is evidence that the strong assumptions of intentionality associated with, for example, Gricean pragmatics and Relevance Theory, sometimes do not hold (Gregoromichelaki et al., 2011). Thus, conversational participants do not necessarily reason about how their moves will be interpreted. Rather, reasons for making specific claims, suggestions and other moves in conversation are not always arrived at through conscious reasoning. In such cases a motivation or reason for the content of a claim or suggestion may be added post hoc, if the agent is asked to motivate his actions.

However, there are contexts where claims or suggestions are arrived at after planning involving conscious reasoning. This is important not least in the context of modelling a dialogue system. A dialogue system which has identified that it is supposed to make the first move in a suggestion game requires a structured way of choosing how this move should be specified. That is, which content it should have, based on the available possibilities. The suggestion made should be based on reasoning that may also be accounted for. Thus, at this point in the dialogue in (5.4), we assume that the agent is about to make a suggestion based on its role in the current interaction. However, we assume that the precise content of this suggestion is not yet specified.

### 5.5.4.1    Integrate Private Resource Topos and Belief

In order to be able to specify the content of the agenda, the agent must access relevant information. The update we are looking for is an update of private topoi and beliefs. This update rule should add information to the agent's private beliefs and topoi which is relevant to the project at hand. The relevance of the project is slightly different here than for adding a private game to the gameboard. In the latter case the relation between the project "decide(which route to choose)" and the suggestion game clearly has more to do with the fact that a decision is to be made than with what the decision concerns. In contrast, in the case of topoi and relevant beliefs it seems more likely that the choice of topos is more domain specific. The simplest way of doing this is to have a rule saying that if you have an information state that includes a particular project $P$ and an unspecified item on the agenda, then you can load a particular set of topoi and beliefs onto the gameboard.

Before we move on to present a more detailed account of this update rule, let us consider $\tau_{shorter}$—representing a topos saying that if one route is shorter than another, take that route. As in previous chapters we represent topoi and enthymemes as functions from records to record types. The topos which is loaded onto the 'private' field of $A$'s gameboard should capture the notion that if we have a choice between a shorter route and a longer route, we take the shorter one.

This rule of thumb is not absolute—a shorter route might take much longer because of roadworks, or be associated with other unappealing features and therefore not preferable. The agents involved in the situation might also for some reason prefer a longer walk. In many cases however, the rule of thumb that we should choose shorter rather than longer routes applies. Informally, we can say that the domain type includes two routes of which one is shorter than the other and one agent (or set of agents) who has to make a choice between two routes of which one is shorter. The result type is the type of situation where the agents walk along the shorter route. In (5.25) we see a suggestion of what such a topos might look like.

(5.25)   $\tau_{shorter} =$

$$\lambda r: \begin{bmatrix} x : Ind \\ y : Ind \\ z : Ind \\ c_{agent} : agent(z) \\ c_{route} : route(x) \\ c_{route_1} : route(y) \\ c_{shorter\_than} : shorter\_than(x, y) \\ c_{choose\_between} : is\_choosing\_between(z, x, y) \end{bmatrix} \cdot \begin{bmatrix} e : take(r.z, r.x) \end{bmatrix}$$

We think of beliefs in an agent's long term resources as assumptions about the world including, but not limited to, facts. We model beliefs as record types. The relevant belief in this case would be that Walnut Street is shorter than the other possible route—let us call it Maple Street. We refer to this belief, represented by the record type in (5.26), as $T_{bWSt\_s}$.

(5.26)   $T_{bWSt\_s}:$ $\begin{bmatrix} x = \text{Walnut Street} : Ind \\ y = \text{Maple Street} : Ind \\ c_{shorter\_than} : shorter\_than(x, y) \end{bmatrix}$

Let us now look at the update rule for integrating topoi and beliefs on the private DGB. We want the rule to apply when an agent has a move type on the agenda which is not specified for content. The rule should capture what is a context relevant way of reasoning. At this point the content of the item on the agenda is not fully specified. Thus there is information about the function of the move that is to be made (to make a suggestion) while we do not know anything about the content. The label 'ctnt' in the move type on the agenda is therefore associated with the type *ERec*, whose only witness (the only thing that is of that type) is the empty record. For a definition of the empty record, see Cooper (2016, p. 47).

In (5.27) we see the update function $f_{integrate\_pr\_resource\_topos}$.

$(5.27)$  $f_{integrate\_pr\_resource\_topos} =$

$$\lambda r: \begin{bmatrix} pr: \begin{bmatrix} agenda = [\begin{bmatrix} e: Type \\ ctnt: ERec \end{bmatrix}]: list(RecType) \\ topoi: list(Topos) \\ beliefs: RecType \end{bmatrix} \\ sh: [project = [\ T_{DecisionProject}]: list(RecType)] \end{bmatrix} .$$

$$\lambda e: \begin{bmatrix} t: Topos \\ c_1: in(t, resources) \\ c_2: relevant\_to(t, fst(r.sh.project)) \\ belief: RecType \\ c_3: in(belief, resources) \\ c_4: relevant\_to(belief, fst(r.sh.project)) \end{bmatrix} .$$

$$\begin{bmatrix} pr: \begin{bmatrix} topoi = [e.t \mid r.pr.topoi]: list(RecType) \\ beliefs = \begin{bmatrix} current: e.belief \\ prev: r.pr.beliefs \end{bmatrix}: RecType \end{bmatrix} \end{bmatrix}$$

The rule above in $(5.27)$ says that if you have a move type on the agenda whose content is of type *ERec*, and there is a topos in your resources such that it is relevant to the project at hand (the first item on the list of projects, or max-project following max-QUD in Ginzburg's terminology) and a belief such that it is relevant to the project at hand, then you are allowed to integrate that topos and that belief on your private DGB. We have ignored the possibility that the integration of beliefs and topos might not be simultaneous and that just one of them could be enough to underpin the specification of content of the next move. For example, there might be cases where a topos alone is sufficient to sanction a specification of the agenda. This would be the case for example if one agent makes a suggestion and the other agent accepts, believing that people usually have a good reason for making a suggestion. This could possibly lead to the other agent accepting without having taken any additional information into account.

Though we are aiming at modelling the kind of updates that would allow an agent to participate in a particular type of dialogue by accounting for the kind of dialogue behaviour present in such a situation, we do not claim that our model necessarily mirrors the cognitive procecesses that actually take place. It seems likely that the topoi involved and other beliefs interact rather than one of them preceding the other. Thus we choose to represent both of these updates in one rule. However, it would be possible to turn them into two separate rules if one would wish to represent a dependency between beliefs and topoi where the integration of one precedes the integration of the other.

### 5.5.4.2    Integrate Private Topos

In the previous chapter, Section (4.2.1), we considered the integration of shared topoi on the DGB. We suggested a pair of rules where one looks for relevant topoi already on shared topoi (but not at the top of the list), and moves them to the top of the list. If there is no such topos already on shared topoi, another function looks in private topoi for a relevant topos and—if there is such a topos—loads it onto shared topoi. In the situation we are currently considering, we might want to add a similar rule. This rule would search private topoi for a relevant topos and—if such a topos is present—place it first on the list of private topoi, using the function $\mu$ as described in Section 4.2.3.

$$(5.28)\quad f_{integrate\_pr\_topos} =$$

$$\lambda r:\left[\text{pr}:\begin{bmatrix}\text{agenda} = [\begin{bmatrix}e : \textit{Type}\\ \text{ctnt} = \textit{ERec} : \textit{RecType}\end{bmatrix}] : \text{list}(\textit{RecType})\\ \text{topoi} : \text{list}(\textit{Topos})\end{bmatrix}\\ \text{sh} : [\text{project} = [[e : \text{decide}(\{A, B\}, \text{route})]] : \text{list}(\textit{RecType})]\right].$$

$$\lambda e:\begin{bmatrix}t : \textit{Topos}\\ c_1 : \text{in}(t, r.\text{pr.topoi})\\ c_2 : \text{relevant\_to}(t, \text{fst}(r.\text{sh.project}))\end{bmatrix}.$$

$$[\text{pr} : [\text{topoi} = \mu(e.t, r.\text{pr.topoi}) : \text{list}(\textit{RecType})]]$$

### 5.5.4.3    Specify Content of Suggestion on Agenda

We have one more silent move left to account for before we reach the point where a linguistic move is actually made, and that is an update of the agenda where information in the dialogue participant's private depository of salient topoi and beliefs is used to add content to the move type first on the agenda. Unlike the update rules for private games and private topoi and beliefs, the rule for specifying the agenda is not about loading information from an agent's resources onto her gameboard, but about assembling information already on the gameboard, turning it into a content-specific type and pushing that type onto the agenda.

We do not present any theory of how the information on the gameboard is turned into actual utterances. We will just say that the information on topoi and beliefs affect the content of the utterance. For example, in a case where a route is to be suggested, a topos regarding routes, such as $\tau_{shorter}$ combined with beliefs about the available routes can be combined to contribute content to the suggestion move. The most recently added items on topoi and beliefs are relevant to the move the agent is about to make.

The update function would thus be a function from a record of a type where there is a project, a game, a topos and a set of beliefs—but no specified content on the agenda—to a type of information state where there is a move type on the agenda where the label 'ctnt' is associated with a specific content. This rule is represented below in (5.29):

$(5.29)\quad f_{specify\_suggestion\_content} =$

$$\lambda r: \begin{bmatrix} pr: \begin{bmatrix} agenda = [\begin{bmatrix} e:Suggest \\ ctnt = ERec:RecType \end{bmatrix}]:list(RecType) \\ topoi:list(Topos) \\ beliefs:list(RecType) \end{bmatrix} \\ sh:[project:list(RecType)] \end{bmatrix} .$$

$$\lambda e: \begin{bmatrix} t:Topos \\ c_1:in(t,\, r.pr.topoi) \\ c_2:relevant\_to(t,\, fst(r.sh.project)) \\ belief:RecType \\ c_3:in(belief,\, r.pr.beliefs) \\ c_4:relevant\_to(belief,\, fst(r.sh.project)) \\ ctnt:RecType \\ c_5:derived\_from(ctnt,\, \{t, belief\}) \end{bmatrix} .$$

$$\left[ pr: \left[ agenda = [\begin{bmatrix} e:Suggest \\ ctnt = e.ctnt:RecType \end{bmatrix}]:list(RecType) \right] \right]$$

### 5.5.4.4   Identify Suggestion Game

Based on the latest utterance made, dialogue participant $B$ is able to identify in which conversational game she is being invited to play. Also, dialogue participant $A$ must now consider the game that was up until now private, as explicitly shared. This update rule is specific to the speech act type *Suggest*. If the latest utterance is a suggestion, then we are allowed to load the suggestion game onto the DGB. We see the rule $f_{identify\_suggestion\_game}$ in (5.30):

$(5.30)\quad f_{identify\_suggestion\_game} =$

$$\lambda r: \begin{bmatrix} sh: \begin{bmatrix} l\text{-}m: \begin{bmatrix} prev:RecType \\ e:Suggest \end{bmatrix} \\ games:list(T_{Game}) \end{bmatrix} \end{bmatrix} .$$

$$[sh:[games = [T_{SuggestionGame} \mid r.sh.games]:list(T_{Game})]]$$

When the suggestion game is pushed onto $B$'s shared game, it also has to be instantiated. This is done as in (5.18), but with the assignments adjusted so that the player who has the assignment OTHER on $A$'s DGB has the assignment SELF, and vice versa.

$$(5.31) \quad \begin{bmatrix} \text{player1} = \text{OTHER} \\ \text{player2} = \text{SELF} \end{bmatrix}$$

We have now considered some ways in which the notion of conversational game can be employed to account for updates necessary for actively participating in a conversation. In the following section we will suggest how games can also be useful in the process of accommodating enthymematic relations, that is, assigning a rhetorical relation between two dialogue moves where one is an antecedent and the other a consequent of a enthymematic argument.

### 5.5.5   Accommodation of Enthymemes

The participants in (5.8) are faced with a situation which is common in dialogue—that the rhetorical relation is not made explicit by means of a word like "therefore", "since" or "because". The relation between "Let's take Walnut Street" and "It's shorter" must thus be inferred by dialogue participant B. We refer to this as accommodating the enthymeme, parallel to the accommodation of topoi discussed in Chapter 4.

However, in the case of enthymeme accommodation it is the enthymematic *relation* that is accommodated rather than any semantic content. The question is: On what does dialogue participant B base the accommodation of the enthymeme? In fact, it is probably the case that many factors contribute to the accommodation of the EUD. In the Walnut Street example, (5.8), we have a lexically encoded imperative or exhortation that clearly indicates that we are dealing with a suggestion. Thus, the conversational game which we can expect to be on the shared DGB for all dialogue participants, at this point involves the possibility of a move of type *assertion* to follow, motivating the content of the suggestion move. Therefore, even though (5.8) does not include a term explicitly signaling that an enthymeme is under discussion, knowledge of basic conversational practice would give this away. However, it seems to also depend on the identification of some topos which supports this interpretation. Intuitively, the rule in (5.32) applies to a situation of a type where an assertion has been made preceded by a suggestion.

(5.32)  $f_{accommmodate\_enthymeme} =$

$$\lambda r: \begin{bmatrix} \text{pr} : \begin{bmatrix} \text{topoi} : \text{list}(Topos) \end{bmatrix} \\ \text{sh} : \begin{bmatrix} \text{l-m} : \begin{bmatrix} \text{prev} : \begin{bmatrix} \text{ctnt} : RecType \\ \text{e} : Suggest \end{bmatrix} \\ \text{ctnt} : RecType \\ \text{e} : Assert \end{bmatrix} \end{bmatrix} \end{bmatrix} \cdot$$

$$\lambda e: \begin{bmatrix} \text{t} : Topos \\ c_1 : \text{in}(\text{t}, r.\text{pr.topoi}) \\ c_2 : \text{spec}(\text{t}, \lambda r' : r.\text{sh.l-m.ctnt} \cdot r.\text{sh.l-m.prev.ctnt}) \end{bmatrix} \cdot$$

$$\begin{bmatrix} \text{sh} : \begin{bmatrix} \text{eud} = [\lambda r' : r.\text{l-m.ctnt} \cdot r.\text{sh.l-m.prev.ctnt}] : \text{list}(Enthymeme) \end{bmatrix} \end{bmatrix}$$

## 5.6    Summary

In this chapter we have discussed the issue of how enthymemes may contribute to lower the cognitive load of dialogue participants. Rather than stating, suggesting or requesting something without providing a reason, a dialogue participant can add an utterance giving a reason for the state of affairs described in the previous utterance. Such supporting utterances have been shown to often not convey any new factual information, that is, they are informationally redundant. However, Walker (1996) shows that they still—despite adding linguistic material—make the processing of the entire utterance quicker than if they had been withheld.

We have argued that IRUs can be linked to enthymemes, and that they facilitate the accommodation of a salient topos that could underpin the enthymeme. This could be particularly important in contexts where one agent tries to persuade another not of what is the state of the world, but of changing the world in some way, that is, of doing something. Basing a suggestion on a topos enables an agent to justify it directly by supplying the premise of an enthymematic argument where the suggestion is the consequent.

We suggest some update rules in which conversational games related to speech act type may govern which kind of moves can be expected in a conversation instantiating a particular game type. We focused on the silent updates necessary for a dialogue participant to participate in a dialogue and make moves whose speech act type and order depends on which conversational game the agent is participating in, and whose content depends among other things on the topoi the agent has access to.

### 5.6.1  Enthymemes and Artificial Intelligence

If IRUs and enthymemes are indeed linked in the way we have argued above, this sheds some light on why enthymemes are such an important part of rhetorical discourse—they simply make it easier to accept the beliefs the speaker wants the audience to encompass or the actions she wants the audience to perform.

Taking rhetoric into account in artificial intelligence (AI) has proven successful in some cases, for example, Miller (2003) reports that rhetorical ethos is central for creating an agent capable of passing the Turing test, that is, not being recognised as a machine by a human user for a certain period of time. Andrews et al. (2006) show that social cues and emotion (pathos) contribute to more human like (and thus more user friendly) dialogue systems.

As the work by Walker (1996) suggests, IRUs can facilitate the processing of the linguistic contributions of an artificial agent by a human. Integrating these insights with a formal theory of enthymematic reasoning provides us with a theory telling us which IRUs are actually helpful in a particular context—the ones supported by salient topoi. This may be particularly useful in contexts where the user of for example a spoken dialogue system is under heavy cognitive load. One such example is in-vehicle dialogue systems.

In a data collection carried out within the DICO project[4] (Villing, 2009) to test how in-vehicle conversation adapts to shifting cognitive load, Breitholtz and Villing (2008) report many examples of enthymematic arguments, most of which also involve IRUs. The data consist of dyadic in-vehicle interactions where one subject—the passenger—is given a map and a list of destinations and is asked to provide the other subject—the driver—with driving instructions. Both subjects have access to the same situational context, such as street view, traffic intensity, etc. Despite this the passenger often justifies instructions by supplying information about the state of the traffic and street ahead.

For example, in (5.33) it is clear to the driver as well as the passenger that the street they are driving on is ending. By supplying the premise (5.33b) the passenger points to an enthymeme based on a number of premises, most of which have been stated earlier (for example that Rose Street crosses the street they are driving down), and a topos that has to be inferred (if you are looking for a crossing street, and you haven't yet passed it, and there is only one crossing street left, this has to be the street you are looking for).

---

4 DICO is a project that aims to demonstrate how state-of-the-art spoken language technology can enable access to communication, entertainment and information services as well as to environment control in vehicles. A priority in the project is cognitive load management for safe in-vehicle dialogue.

(5.33)   a.  *A*: Rosengatan ja det måste vara nästa
             *Rose Street yes it must be next*
         b.  *A*: för vi kommer inte så mycket längre
             *cause we don't get much further.*

We suggest that the reason they do this is because the enthymematic structure helps the recipient of the IRU to make up her mind or correctly interpret
an utterance—if the IRU provided links the assertion or suggestion made to a
topos she finds acceptable she is more likely to agree with the proposition. This
indicates that many artificial agents, e.g. in domains of instruction and advice
giving, would communicate more efficiently if they were extended to include
enthymematic competence.

These findings demonstrate the need to motivate for rhetorical purposes
rather than to provide new information about one's reasons. In the context
of speech interfaces for e.g. GPS systems in cars the need to justify instructions becomes even more urgent, among other reasons because human users
of artificial intelligence tend to need the reassurance of explanation. This is
especially true in complex tasks such as giving driving instructions based on
a combination of geographical knowledge, current traffic and—possibly—the
preferences of the driver.

# CHAPTER 6

# Rhetorical Reasoning in Dialogue

Thus far we have introduced enthymemes and topoi in a gameboard analysis of dialogue, and suggested ways in which to represent the role of rhetorical reasoning in interpretation and production of dialogue. In this chapter we will consider a few different problems and situations requiring reasoning. The focus is not so much on the updates of the dialogue, but on the topoi and associated enthymemes which can be identified in, or derived from, the discourse.

When we interpret an enthymeme we draw on principles of reasoning—topoi—that we have acquired through interaction with others and the world around us. However, many enthymemes are so specific that they require much abstraction to be recognised as belonging to, or being underpinned by, a particular topos. Moreover, sometimes enthymemes in discourse require that we manipulate and/or combine several topoi to reach one that directly warrants the enthymeme. There are also situations where an enthymeme evokes two or more topoi which are incompatible, or which, when applied in a given context, lead to incompatible conclusions.

In this chapter we will consider some of these issues. First, we will look at two textbook examples of non-monotonic reasoning, and suggest how these can be framed in a game board model of rhetorical reasoning cast in TTR. Secondly, we will move on to a slightly longer dialogue excerpt, where topoi play a role for coherence and meaning interpretation. Finally, we will consider how we may model the acquisition of topoi based on enthymemes in dialogue. None of these analyses are fully fleshed out, but rather suggestions of strands of research where the notion of rhetorical reasoning might be helpful.

## 6.1    A Rhetorical Perspective on Non-monotonicity

An important feature of classical logic is that if a formula is derivable from a theory (a set of sentences[1]), then it must also be derivable from an expansion of that theory. Let us say for example that $\Gamma$ is a set of formulae, $A$ is a formula and $A$ is a logical consequence of $\Gamma$ ($\Gamma \vdash A$). Then $\Gamma, B \vdash A$ is true as well.

---

1   By which we mean formulae with no free occurrences of variables.

Natural reasoning, on the other hand, is *situated*. This means that contextual factors—such as the point of view of individual agents with certain beliefs—influence the reasoning. In such situated reasoning we sometimes draw conclusions which we later have to retract in the light of new information. One reason for this is that we often consider problems about which we have limited information. To handle cases like these, various types of non-monotonic logic were proposed in the early eighties by for example McDermott and Doyle (1980); Reiter (1980) and McCarthy (1980). Approaches to non-monotonic logic often suggest that we represent human reasoning in terms of *defaults*, as proposed by Reiter (1980), with later followers such as Horty (2012).

The principle of default logic is that there are rules which are usually true, but which may in some cases be overridden by other, more specific rules. However, in some cases—such as the "Nixon-diamond problem" (Reiter and Criscuolo, 1981)—we cannot represent all accessible information as one consistent set of rules, even if we allow for specific rules to override less specific ones. This type of reasoning is not uncommon in conversation and other types of natural discourse—see for example McCarthy (1980); Schulz and Van Rooij (2006)—and poses a challenge to formal approaches to dialogue and discourse.

In this section we give an account of two problems often discussed in the literature on non-monotonic reasoning. Both of these reflect that we have access to topoi which, when applied in a particular context, might be inconsistent or lead to incompatible conclusions. Our account treats the rules of non-monotonic logic as topoi accessible to an agent. The first problem we will consider concerns a situation where we receive new information which, by being more specific, cancels out the topos previously drawn on and replaces it with another. The second problem is more complicated since it has to do with topoi where one is not a specification of the other, but where two topoi applied in the same context lead to different conclusions.

### 6.1.1    *The Tweety Triangle*

The "Tweety triangle" puzzle exemplifies a dialogue situation where we draw on a topos which has to be discarded further on in the dialogue, in the light of new information. In this case the accommodated topos warrants the enthymeme conveyed in the dialogue, but when new information is added, the new enthymeme under discussion is no longer warranted by the topos originally evoked. In short, the puzzle comes down to this: when we say that Tweety is a bird, and therefore Tweety flies, we draw on a principle saying that if something is a bird, then it flies. In first order logic this is expressed as (6.1).

(6.1)    $\forall x\,(\text{bird}(x) \rightarrow \text{fly}(x))$

We know, however, that there are some types of birds which do not fly, like penguins and ostriches. So we also have access to rules like

(6.2)    a. $\forall x\,(\text{penguin}(x) \rightarrow \neg\text{fly}(x))$
         b. $\forall x\,(\text{penguin}(x) \rightarrow \text{bird}(x))$

This means that the rule in (6.1) has to be modified:

(6.3)    $\forall x\,((\text{bird}(x) \wedge \neg\text{penguin}(x)) \rightarrow \text{fly}(x))$

In most natural discourse, we allow for exceptions like this, but we do not necessarily have rules for every single exception. It would be possible to include more exceptions for other types of non-flying birds. However, this could be difficult since there might be species of non-flying birds which we do not know of (but we know they *might* exist). Also, there might be individual birds which, for various reasons, do not fly. So, what we really want is a rule that expresses "under normal circumstances, birds fly" or "if we are not dealing with an exception, then birds fly". This is usually done through *default rules* as in (6.4), which should be interpreted as "if $x$ is a bird and there is nothing to contradict that $x$ flies, then $x$ flies".

(6.4)    $\dfrac{\text{bird}(x).\ \text{fly}(x)}{\text{fly}(x)}$

Let us now think of the Tweety-problem as situated in a dialogue context. We assume that $A$ and $B$ are involved in a conversation, and for some reason they discuss whether Tweety the bird flies or not, and the following exchange takes place:

(6.5)    a. $A$: Tweety flies—he is a bird!
         b. $B$: No, he doesn't—he's a penguin!

In the scenario above the utterances of $A$ and $B$ convey two enthymemes—Tweety flies since he is a bird, and Tweety does not fly since he is a penguin.

$A$'s enthymeme is underpinned by a topos saying that if we have a situation where something is a bird, we can assume that we also have a situation where that something flies, $\tau_1$. $B$'s objection, on the other hand, evokes a topos saying that if something is a penguin, this something does not fly, $\tau_2$. Given that

Tweety is a penguin, the topos about penguins could be considered more reliable, and $A$ would have to reconsider her judgement. According to Horty (2012), the reason why the rule about penguins overrides the one about birds, is that the rule saying that penguins do not fly is more specific than the one saying that birds do. It is more specific since penguin is a type of bird, but bird is not a type of penguin. We think of this kind of subtyping as a topos saying that if something is a penguin it is a bird, $\tau_3$. In (6.6) we see the enthymemes involved in this exchange and in (6.7) the topoi evoked.

(6.6)    a. $\varepsilon_1 = \lambda r:\begin{bmatrix} x = \text{Tweety} : Ind \\ c_{\text{bird}} : \text{bird}(x) \end{bmatrix} \cdot \begin{bmatrix} c_{\text{fly}} : \text{fly}(r.x) \end{bmatrix}$

   b. $\varepsilon_2 = \lambda r:\begin{bmatrix} x = \text{Tweety} : Ind \\ c_{\text{penguin}} : \text{penguin}(x) \end{bmatrix} \cdot \begin{bmatrix} c_{\text{do\_not\_fly}} : \text{do\_not\_fly}(r.x) \end{bmatrix}$

(6.7)    a. $\tau_1 = \lambda r:\begin{bmatrix} x : Ind \\ c_{\text{bird}} : \text{bird}(x) \end{bmatrix} \cdot \begin{bmatrix} c_{\text{fly}} : \text{fly}(r.x) \end{bmatrix}$

   b. $\tau_2 = \lambda r:\begin{bmatrix} x : Ind \\ c_{\text{penguin}} : \text{penguin}(x) \end{bmatrix} \cdot \begin{bmatrix} c_{\text{do\_not\_fly}} : \text{do\_not\_fly}(r.x) \end{bmatrix}$

   c. $\tau_3 = \lambda r:\begin{bmatrix} x : Ind \\ c_{\text{penguin}} : \text{penguin}(x) \end{bmatrix} \cdot \begin{bmatrix} c_{\text{bird}} : \text{bird}(r.x) \end{bmatrix}$

Let us assume that, at the outset of the exchange in (6.7), the project which $A$ has in mind is to reach an agreement with $B$ on whether Tweety flies or not. On the topic of Tweety $A$ has access to a set of relevant resources. Among these is the topos $\tau_1$, which is loaded onto private topoi on $A$'s DGB, and a belief about Tweety, represented here by a record type like the one in (6.8).[2]

(6.8)    $T_{Tweety\_flies} = \begin{bmatrix} x = \text{Tweety} : Ind \\ c_{\text{bird}} : \text{bird}(x) \\ c_{\text{fly}} : \text{fly}(x) \end{bmatrix}$

In (6.9) we see the type of $A$'s initial information state, with the topos $\tau_1$, and the belief $T_{Tweety\_flies}$ on $A$'s private DGB. The proposition that $\tau_1$ is present on the private DGB should be interpreted as $\tau_1$ having been brought to the fore in $A$'s mind, but not (yet) taken by $A$ to be shared in the conversation.

2  Record types representing contextually relevant individuals which are accessed during a dialogue are reminiscent of file cards representing referents of definite noun phrases in Heim (1983), and mental files in Recanati (2012).

$$(6.9) \quad \text{IS}_{A_1} : \begin{bmatrix} \text{private} : \begin{bmatrix} \text{agenda} = [\ ] : \text{list}(\text{RecType}) \\ \text{topoi} = [\ \tau_1] : \text{list}(\text{Topos}) \\ \text{beliefs} = \text{T}_{\text{Tweety\_flies}} : \text{RecType} \end{bmatrix} \\ \text{shared} : \text{RecType} \end{bmatrix}$$

After $A$ has uttered (6.5a), the enthymeme $\varepsilon_1$—that Tweety flies since he is a bird—is under discussion. As a result of this, $\tau_1$ is evoked and integrated into the shared DGB, as seen in 6.10.

$$(6.10) \quad \text{IS}_{A_3} : \begin{bmatrix} \text{shared} : \begin{bmatrix} \text{eud} = [\varepsilon_1] : \text{list}(\text{Enthymeme}) \\ \text{topoi} = [\tau_1] : \text{list}(\text{Topos}) \end{bmatrix} \end{bmatrix}$$

We could imagine a few different scenarios here, the first being that $B$ does not recognise $\tau_1$. Unlikely as this may seem, if it were to occur, $B$ could make a clarification request along the lines of "what do you mean he's a bird?", questioning the relevance of the premise. $A$ could then reply by pointing to $\tau_1$, if something is a bird, it flies. $B$ could agree or disagree with this, and if $B$ objects, $A$ would have to provide some support for the claim. If $B$ agrees, she could evaluate the argument and possibly object, but in this case not object to the topos that birds generally fly, but to the conclusion that the individual Tweety flies, as seen in $\varepsilon_1$. The second scenario is that $B$ does have access to the topos that birds fly, $\tau_1$, and that she thereby is able to accommodate $\varepsilon_1$. So the topos $\tau_1$ is integrated on $B$'s shared DGB, along with $\varepsilon_1$. Thus, $B$ agrees that this enthymeme is indeed under discussion. $B$ then further evaluates the enthymeme by searching her resources for the type "Tweety". We assume that $B$ believes that Tweety is a penguin, as represented in $B$'s type for Tweety, $T_{TweetyB}$, in (6.11):

$$(6.11) \quad T_{Tweety_B} = \begin{bmatrix} x = \text{Tweety} : \text{Ind} \\ c_{\text{bird}} : \text{bird}(x) \\ c_{\text{penguin}} : \text{penguin}(x) \end{bmatrix}$$

Note that the type in (6.11) might have many other constraints, such as "black and white", "eats fish", etc. However, we restrict ourselves now to those aspects of $B$'s Tweety-type which are relevant for this dialogue. Now, $B$ continues the evaluation by searching her resources for topoi which may be relevant to the enthymeme on the one hand and on the other hand to the type of Tweety. She finds two such topoi, namely $\tau_2$ "if something is a penguin, it does not fly", and $\tau_3$, "if something is a penguin, it is a bird". As stated above, this rule tells us that "penguin" is a subtype of "bird".

In (6.12) we see $B$'s information state at this point:

$$(6.12) \quad \begin{bmatrix} \text{private} : \begin{bmatrix} \text{agenda} : \text{list}(RecType) \\ \text{topoi} = [\tau_2, \tau_3] : \text{list}(Topos) \\ \text{beliefs} = \tau_{Tweety_B} : RecType \end{bmatrix} \\ \text{shared} : \begin{bmatrix} \text{eud} = [\varepsilon_1] : \text{list}(Enthymeme) \\ \text{topoi} = [\tau_1] : \text{list}(Topos) \\ \text{com} = \begin{bmatrix} x = \text{Tweety} : Ind \\ c_{\text{bird}} : \text{bird}(x) \end{bmatrix} : RecType \end{bmatrix} \end{bmatrix}$$

Now $B$ may compare $\tau_1$, which was evoked and accommodated in the light of $A$'s enthymematic argument $\varepsilon_1$, with the topoi she herself has loaded onto her private DGB, $\tau_2$ and $\tau_3$. On the one hand we have $\tau_1$, "if something is a bird, it flies", on the other $\tau_2$, "if something is a penguin, it does not fly" and $\tau_2$, "if something is a penguin, it is a bird".

Now $B$ has access to two topoi which are relevant for evaluating Tweety's ability to fly. One according to which he can fly because he is a bird, and one according to which he cannot fly because he is a penguin. Since the topos $\tau_3$ says that "penguin" and "bird" are in a subtype-supertype relation, $\tau_2$ is more specific than $\tau_1$, $\tau_2$ constitutes a stronger argument as long as it is applicable to Tweety.

At this point in the dialogue, $B$ has evaluated the enthymeme under discussion and does not agree. An item is integrated on on $B$'s agenda to refute $A$'s argument (the assertion "Tweety can't fly") followed by the assertion "He's a penguin!". (6.13) is the type of $B$'s information state after this utterance. The topos $B$ would expect $A$ to accommodate is at least $\tau_2$, (see 6.7b), since this topos is required to underpin the enthymeme.

$$(6.13) \quad \begin{bmatrix} \text{pr} : \begin{bmatrix} \text{agenda} = [] : \text{list}(RecType) \\ \text{topoi} : [\lambda r: \begin{bmatrix} x : Ind \\ c_{\text{bird}} : \text{bird}(x) \\ c_{\text{penguin}} : \text{penguin}(x) \end{bmatrix} . \\ \quad [c_{\text{do\_not\_fly}} : \text{do\_not\_fly}(r.x)]] : \text{list}(Topos) \end{bmatrix} \\ \text{sh} : \begin{bmatrix} \text{eud} : [\lambda r: \begin{bmatrix} x = \text{Tweety} : Ind \\ c_{\text{bird}} : \text{bird}(x) \\ c_{\text{penguin}} : \text{penguin}(x) \end{bmatrix} . \\ \quad [c_{\text{do\_not\_fly}} : \text{do\_not\_fly}(r.x)]] : \text{list}(Enthymeme) \\ \text{l-m} : \begin{bmatrix} e : \text{assert}(B, A, \text{ctnt}) \\ \text{ctnt} = [e : \text{bird}(\text{Tweety})] : RecType \end{bmatrix} \\ \text{topoi} : [\lambda r: \begin{bmatrix} x : Ind \\ c_{\text{penguin}} : \text{penguin}(x) \end{bmatrix} . \\ \quad [c_{\text{do\_not\_fly}} : \text{do\_not\_fly}(r.x)]] : \text{list}(Topos) \end{bmatrix} \end{bmatrix}$$

Let's assume that $A$ accommodates this topos. $A$ then has to evaluate the latest enthymeme under discussion in relation to the enthymeme he himself produced, and the activated topoi. If $A$ has access to the same type for Tweety as $B$ has, or at least a type which shares the constraint that Tweety is a penguin, and a topos which says that penguin is a subtype of bird, $A$ will be able to evaluate $B$'s argument and his own argument in the light of $B$'s argument, and come to the conclusion that $B$'s argument is stronger since it is more specific (cf. Horty, 2012). However, if $C$ would enter the discussion and say that Tweety actually flies, since he has a pair of artificial wings, both $A$ and $B$ would have to reevaluate their position. The type of "Penguin-bird who has artificial wings" is more specific than "Bird" or "Penguin-bird", and therefore a topos stating that someone who has artificial wings flies would be stronger, in case the constraint "has artificial wings" is in the Tweety-type.

### 6.1.2    *The Nixon Diamond*

Another problem often discussed in the context of non-monotonic reasoning is the so-called "Nixon Diamond", often visualised as in Figure (3) (Reiter and Criscuolo, 1981; Strasser and Antonelli, 2019). In this puzzle, the following situation is described:

(6.14)    a. Nixon is a Quaker
          b. Nixon is a Republican
          c. Quakers are pacifists
          d. Republicans are not pacifists

If we were to formulate rules based on the information in (6.14), these rules would make up an inconsistent theory. If we apply (6.14a) and (6.14c), we arrive at the conclusion that Nixon is a pacifist. However, if we apply (6.14b) and (6.14d), we arrive at the opposite conclusion, as illustrated in Figure 3.

Traditionally, problems like these are treated either *sceptically* or *credulously* (Strasser and Antonelli, 2019). On the sceptical approach only inferences that are consistent with all the facts and inference rules of a theory are accepted. In the Nixon case that means that neither the conclusion that Nixon is a pacifist, nor the one that he is a non-pacifist, are accepted. The credulous reasoner, on the other hand, accepts as many inferences as possible, as long as they are not inconsistent with other accepted inferences. In the Nixon case this means accepting either the inference that Nixon is a pacifist or the inference that he is a non-pacifist.

However, neither of these approaches tells us how agents interactively reason to draw one conclusion or the other, possibly based on different takes on a situation or type of situation, or because their goals differ. The arguments made may be aimed at e.g. retrospectively justifying a speaker's position rather than reaching a conclusion based on an accepted set of topoi, or at reaching a specific outcome supported by some topoi but not others. We therefore suggest that we look at problems related to human non-monotonic reasoning from a rhetorical perspective in a dialogue setting.

The Nixon diamond-puzzle is slightly different from the puzzle discussed in Section 6.1.1. In the case of the Tweety puzzle there is a subtype relationship between "penguin" and "bird", which means that "penguin" entails "bird". Therefore, in the case of Tweety, we can follow the principle that a more specific rule, $\tau_2$ "penguins do not fly", (6.7b), takes precedence over a less specific rule like $\tau_1$, "birds fly", (6.7a). In the case of the Nixon diamond there is no entailment relation between "Quaker" and "Republican". Instead, the puzzle arises from two types entailing incompatible types (pacifist and non-pacifist respectively), while both being applicable to one individual.

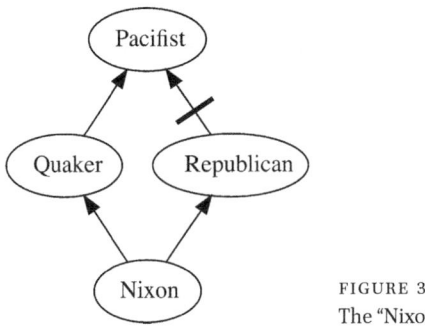

FIGURE 3
The "Nixon Diamond"

To illustrate what a rhetorical approach to non monotonic reasoning would look like, let us imagine again a conversation between two people discussing whether Nixon is (or was) a pacifist or a non-pacifist. Two of the arguments presented by the dialogue participants are the following:

(6.15)   a. *A*: Nixon is not a pacifist—he's a Republican!
          b. *B*: He's a pacifist—he's a Quaker!

Initially in this conversation, *A* assigns Richard Nixon a type which may be restricted in a number of ways, but has at least the restrictions *non_pacifist* and *Republican*. We see this type in (6.16). $T_{Nixon_A}$ is a subtype of the less specific type $T_{Nixon_{non\_pac}}$.

$$(6.16) \quad T_{Nixon_A} = \begin{bmatrix} x = \text{Nixon} : Ind \\ c_{\text{non\_pacifist}} : \text{non\_pacifist(x)} \\ c_{\text{republican}} : \text{republican(x)} \end{bmatrix}$$

$$(6.17) \quad T_{Nixon_{non\_pac}} = \begin{bmatrix} x = \text{Nixon} : Ind \\ c_{\text{non\_pacifist}} : \text{non\_pacifist(x)} \end{bmatrix}$$

*A* also has access to a topos saying that if someone is a Republican, that person is a non-pacifist. We refer to this topos, "Republicans are non-pacifists" in (6.18), as $\tau_1$.

$$(6.18) \quad \tau_1 = \lambda r: \begin{bmatrix} x : Ind \\ c_{\text{republican}} : \text{republican(x)} \end{bmatrix} \cdot \begin{bmatrix} c_{\text{non\_pacifist}} : \text{non\_pacifist(r.x)} \end{bmatrix}$$

In (6.19) we see *A*'s information state just before she produces the utterance (6.15a). On the agenda is a claim that Nixon is not a pacifist, and on private topoi the topos $\tau_1$, saying that Republicans are non-pacifists.

$$(6.19) \quad \begin{bmatrix} pr : \begin{bmatrix} \text{agenda} = [\begin{bmatrix} e : \text{claim(SELF)} \\ \text{ctnt} : T_{Nixon_{non\_pac}} \end{bmatrix}] : \text{list}(RecType) \\ \text{topoi} = [\tau_1] : \text{list}(Topos) \\ \text{beliefs} = T_{Nixon_A} : RecType \end{bmatrix} \end{bmatrix}$$

We assume that *A* has a conversational game similar to the suggestion game discussed in Chapter 5, Figure 1, loaded onto her DGB. This game—let us call it the *claim game*—allows for a player to make a claim followed by a move to support this claim, corresponding to the motivation move of the suggestion game. After this move the other player may either agree, disagree, or refute the argument by means of a new round of the claim game.

In order to completely account for the dialogue in (6.15) we would have to make further adjustments to the update rules presented in Chapters 4 and 5. However, as in our account of the Tweety puzzle, we have omitted some steps of our analysis in order to focus on the dynamics of enthymemes, topoi and beliefs.

After having stated that Nixon is not a pacifist, (6.15a), *A*'s shared information state is updated. *A* now considers it a shared comittment that Nixon is a non-pacifist. In (6.20) we see the type of *A*'s shared information state at this point:

$$(6.20) \quad \begin{bmatrix} \text{sh}: \begin{bmatrix} \text{eud} = [\,] : \text{list}(\textit{Enthymeme}) \\ \text{topoi} = [\,] : \textit{Topos} \\ \text{l-m}: \begin{bmatrix} \text{prev}: \textit{RecType} \\ \text{e}: \text{claim}(\textsc{self}) \\ \text{ctnt}: T_{\textit{Nixon}_{\textit{non\_pac}}} \end{bmatrix} \\ \text{com} = T_{\textit{Nixon}_{\textit{non\_pac}}} : \textit{RecType} \end{bmatrix} \end{bmatrix}$$

When $A$ has uttered his argument in favour of Nixon not being a pacifist—that Nixon is a Republican—'sh.com' and 'l-m' are updated on $A$'s DGB, and the enthymeme $\varepsilon_1$—"Nixon is a Republican, therefore he is not a pacifist"—is added. $A$ now expects $\varepsilon_1$ to be shared in the conversation (6.21). We see the type of $A$'s information state after these updates in (6.22):

$$(6.21) \quad \varepsilon_1 = \lambda r: \begin{bmatrix} \text{x} = \text{Nixon}: \textit{Ind} \\ c_{\text{republican}}: \text{republican}(\text{x}) \end{bmatrix} \cdot \begin{bmatrix} c_{\text{non\_pacifist}}: \text{non\_pacifist}(r.\text{x}) \end{bmatrix}$$

$$(6.22) \quad \begin{bmatrix} \text{sh}: \begin{bmatrix} \text{eud} = [\varepsilon_1] : \text{list}(\textit{Enthymeme}) \\ \text{topoi} = [\,] : \text{list}(\textit{Topos}) \\ \text{l-m}: \begin{bmatrix} \text{prev}: \begin{bmatrix} \text{prev}: \textit{RecType} \\ \text{e}: \begin{bmatrix} \text{e}: \text{claim}(\textsc{self}) \\ \text{ctnt}: T_{\textit{Nixon}_{\textit{non\_pac}}} \end{bmatrix} \end{bmatrix} \\ \text{e}: \begin{bmatrix} \text{e}: \text{motivate}(\textsc{self}) \\ \text{ctnt}: \begin{bmatrix} \text{x} = \text{Nixon}: \textit{Ind} \\ c_{\text{republican}}: \text{republican}(\text{x}) \end{bmatrix} \end{bmatrix} \end{bmatrix} \\ \text{com} = T_{\textit{Nixon}_{\textit{non\_pac}}}: \textit{RecType} \end{bmatrix} \end{bmatrix}$$

Now, since $A$ knows that she is presenting an enthymeme, and that there exists a link between the antecedent and consequent of (6.15a), $A$ assumes that the topos $\tau_1$ underpinning $\varepsilon_1$, is now shared. Thus, $\tau_1$—if someone is a Republican, that person is a non-pacifist—is integrated on her shared DGB as seen in (6.23).

$$(6.23) \quad \begin{bmatrix} \text{sh}: \begin{bmatrix} \text{eud} = [\varepsilon_1] : \text{list}(\textit{Enthymeme}) \\ \text{topoi} = [\tau_1] : \text{list}(\textit{Topos}) \end{bmatrix} \end{bmatrix}$$

Let us now focus on the information state of dialogue participant $B$. When $A$ has uttered (6.15b) the topos $\tau_1$ and a belief about Nixon that is relevant to the conversation (that is, one that involves at least the constraint that Nixon is a Republican) are integrated on $B$'s private DGB. Based on this the enthymeme $\varepsilon_1$ is also accommodated.

At the point in the dialogue where $A$ has just uttered (6.15b), we thus assume that $B$'s shared information state is of the type in (6.24).

$$(6.24) \quad \begin{bmatrix} \text{sh}: \begin{bmatrix} \text{eud} = [\varepsilon_1] : \text{list}(\textit{Enthymeme}) \\ \text{topoi} = [] : \text{list}(\textit{Topos}) \\ \text{l-m}: \begin{bmatrix} \text{prev}: \textit{RecType} \\ \text{e}: \begin{bmatrix} \text{e}: \text{claim}(\text{OTHER}) \\ \text{ctnt}: T_{\textit{Nixon}_{non\_pac}} \end{bmatrix} \end{bmatrix} \end{bmatrix} \end{bmatrix}$$

By the rule $f_{integrate\_topos}$ (see Section 4.1.3), the topos $\tau_1$ is integrated on $B$'s shared DGB.

In order to evaluate $\varepsilon_1$ $B$ accesses his knowledge of Nixon, represented as the type in (6.25). This type has, among others, the constraint *Quaker*. Since the belief that Nixon is also a Republican is already shared, this is also a constraint on (6.25).

$$(6.25) \quad T_{Nixon_B} = \begin{bmatrix} \text{x} = \text{Nixon}: \textit{Ind} \\ \text{c}_{\text{Quaker}}: \text{Quaker}(\text{x}) \\ \text{c}_{\text{Republican}}: \text{Republican}(\text{x}) \end{bmatrix}$$

For some reason, either because $B$ wants to argue that Nixon is a pacifist, or because *Quaker* is simply a more salient quality of Nixon for him than *Republican*, the topos which is pushed onto $B$'s private topoi is $\tau_2$, as seen in (6.26).

$$(6.26) \quad \tau_2 = \lambda r \begin{bmatrix} \text{x}: \textit{Ind} \\ \text{c}_{\text{quaker}}: \text{Quaker}(\text{x}) \end{bmatrix} \cdot \begin{bmatrix} \text{c}_{\text{pacifist}}: \text{pacifist}(r.\text{x}) \end{bmatrix}$$

Dialogue participant $B$ now must take two topoi into account. According to one of these, which he considers shared, if you are a Republican you are not a pacifist. According to the other, which is private, if you are a Quaker you are a pacifist. On the other hand $B$ has to consider the type of an individual who is both a Quaker and a Republican. On $B$'s private topoi we find a topos saying that Quakers are pacifists ($\tau_2$), and on shared topoi a topos saying that Republicans are not pacifists ($\tau_1$). The topos $\tau_2$ underpins a move being added to $B$'s agenda which is part of an enthymematic argument refuting the claim made by $A$, that Nixon is a pacifist.

$B$ assumes that (6.15b) conveys an enthymeme saying that Nixon is not a pacifist, since he is a Republican, $\varepsilon_2$ below. This enthymeme also evokes the topos $\tau_2$, which $B$ now expects to be shared in the conversation.

$$(6.27) \quad \varepsilon_2 = \lambda r: \begin{bmatrix} x = \text{Nixon} : Ind \\ c_{\text{republican}} : \text{quaker}(x) \end{bmatrix} \cdot \begin{bmatrix} c_{\text{pacifist}} : \text{pacifist}(r.x) \end{bmatrix}$$

In (6.28) we see $B$'s information state after uttering (6.15d).

$$(6.28) \quad \begin{bmatrix} \text{private} : \begin{bmatrix} \text{agenda} = [\,] : \text{list}(RecType) \\ \text{topoi} = [\,] : \text{list}(Topos) \end{bmatrix} \\ \text{shared} : \begin{bmatrix} \text{eud} = [\varepsilon_2, \varepsilon_1] : \text{list}(Enthymeme) \\ \text{l-m} : \begin{bmatrix} e : \text{sssert}(\text{SELF}) \\ \text{ctnt} : \begin{bmatrix} e = \text{nixon} : Ind \\ c_{\text{Quaker}} : \text{Quaker}(x) \end{bmatrix} \end{bmatrix} \\ \text{topoi} = [\tau_2, \tau_1] : \text{list}(Topos) \end{bmatrix} \end{bmatrix}$$

Now $B$'s take on the state of the dialogue is that there are two enthymemes under discussion—Nixon is a Quaker and therefore a pacifist, and Nixon is a Republican and therefore a non-pacifist. On $B$'s view it is also the case that topoi underpinning both arguments have been evoked in the dialogue. Since "pacifist" and "non-pacifist" can never be in a subtype—supertype relation to each other, $A$ and $B$ must interactively evaluate the arguments based on how general they take the rules expressed in the topoi to be and whether they think that one of the rules is more committing than the other. One could for example say that if someone is a Quaker, that person has to be a pacifist, otherwise he would no longer be a Quaker, while being a Republican could mean nothing more than having voted for a Republican candidate—not necessarily embracing all political views typically taken by Republicans. It is obviously also possible to reason in favour of the conclusion that Nixon is a non-pacifist in a similar way.

We believe that this kind of argumentation could be modelled along the lines of the analysis of our example dialogue so far, but we leave the details of this analysis for future work. For a monolithic logical system the presence of inconsistent conclusions and the impact of individual preferences on the acceptability of topoi, as well as the ambiguity of terms used, present a problem. However, this is not a problem in dialogue, since dialogue participants can at any point back track, make clarification requests, specify and negotiate arguments and motivations, meaning, etc. Thus, in order to capture reasoning in interaction, we need to allow for different conclusions being drawn by different participants, and also for participants reaching different conclusions depending on context and point of view.

## 6.2     Drawing on Topoi in Conversation

In the previous sections in this chapter we have considered examples which were made up to illustrate some problems introduced by the non-monotonicity often found in common sense reasoning. However, in spontaneous dialogue, reasoning is often messier than that. For example, reasoning may be intertwined with lexical disambiguation and anaphora resolution and—especially if the conversational participants have a close personal relationship—it is hard for an external analyst to tell which topoi are accessible to the participants in a particular interaction.

In order to account for the reasoning in such interactions, more manipulations of enthymemes and topoi involved may thus be necessary compared to what is needed to account for clear cut examples from the literature.

In this section we will return to an exchange previously discussed in Chapter 1, about whether dogs should be allowed upstairs or not. We argue that one component in this reasoning process is the set of topoi that are evoked throughout the conversation, and we will suggest how the dialogue participants can arrive at the reasoning behaviour displayed in this excerpt through manipulations of the surface enthymemes and the topoi that underpin them.

In doing so, we are not claiming that we can determine the exact resources which any particular dialogue participant would have at their disposal when taking part in this dialogue. Rather we set ourselves the task of describing which topoi and enthymemes could be accessed by an agent in order for the dialogue to play out the way it does. There is a great, if not unlimited, number of possible topoi through which the same result could be achieved. What is important is to show that our theory enables us to formulate at least one of these. Let us first have a look at the dialogue again:

(6.29)  CHERRILYN:    Most dogs aren't allowed up ⟨pause⟩ upstairs.
                     He's allowed to go wherever he wants ⟨pause⟩ do what-
                     ever he likes.
       FIONA:        Too right!
                     So they should!
                     Shouldn't they?
       CHERRILYN:    Yeah I mean ⟨pause⟩ dog hairs rise anyway so
       FIONA:        What do you mean, rise?
       CHERRILYN:    The hair ⟨pause⟩ it rises upstairs.
                     I mean I, you know friends said it was, oh God I
                     wouldn't allow mine upstairs because of all the
                     ⟨pause⟩ dog hairs!
                     Oh well ⟨pause⟩ they go up there anyway.

FIONA:              So, but I don't know what it is, right, it's only a few
                    bloody hairs!                    (BNC file KBL:4196–4206)

The dialogue in (6.29) is essentially about whether dogs should be allowed
everywhere in the house, or—more specifically—upstairs. Important for the
analysis of this conversation is the notion of communicative project (3.2.3.2).
The overall project seems to be to establish and expand common ground
regarding where dogs should be allowed and why, and the argumentation
orients either in favour of or against dogs being allowed upstairs. However,
it is possible to distinguish sub-projects, like the clarification sequence after
Cherrilyn's utterance *Yeah I mean, dog hairs rise anyway so*. We will look at
the enthymemes conveyed and topoi available to the dialogue partners at
certain points in time throughout the dialogue, starting with Cherrilyn just
after she has uttered *He is allowed to go wherever he wants, do whatever he
likes*.

Fiona's response to Cherrilyn's claim that her dog is allowed to go everywhere, the utterance *Too right! So they should! Shouldn't they?* ends with a tag
question. Tag questions may have at least two functions—to signal uncertainty
in the speaker, or to bring the interlocutor into the conversation (Andersen,
1998). In this context the function of the question could be either or both of
these. Cherrilyn has already communicated her view when she said that her
dog is allowed to go wherever he wants (including upstairs) and do whatever
he likes, but she does so implicitly. In her response *Too right, so they should,
shouldn't they?* Fiona shows agreement with the proposition that dogs should
be allowed upstairs.

Now, Cherrilyn could produce any out of many different utterances in response to Fiona's agreement, but she chooses *Yeah, I mean, dog hairs rise anyway*. There is obviously no way of telling precisely why and based on which
assumptions Cherrilyn says this. However, she seems to be taking a stand for
dogs being allowed to go upstairs, since she claims that her own dog is allowed
to "go wherever he likes".

The continuation of this dialogue implies that Cherrilyn intends her utterance in (6.29), *Yeah, I mean, dog hairs rise anyway*, as support for her earlier
claim.

In (6.30) we see the enthymematic argument conveyed by Cherrilyn's utterances, where the proposition that dog hairs rise is given as a reason for Cherrilyn's dog being allowed upstairs. We refer to this enthymeme—"dog hairs rise,
therefore my dog is allowed upstairs" as $\varepsilon_1$, represented in TTR as a function
from a situation type where dog hairs rise, to a situation where Cherrilyn's dog
is allowed upstairs.

$$(6.30) \quad \varepsilon_1 = \lambda r: \begin{bmatrix} y : Ind \\ c_{doghairs} : \text{doghairs}(y) \\ c_{rise} : \text{rise}(y) \end{bmatrix} \cdot \begin{bmatrix} x = \text{cherrilyn's\_dog} : Ind \\ c_{dog} : \text{dog}(x) \\ \text{e-loc} : Loc \\ c_{upstairs} : \text{upstairs}(\text{e-loc}) \\ c_{be\_allowed} : \text{be\_allowed}(x, \text{e-loc}) \end{bmatrix}$$

We assume that Cherrilyn's information state is updated with the enthymeme $\varepsilon_1$, which she now considers to be under discussion. If Cherrilyn expects the interaction to be successful, that is, if she expects Fiona to correctly interpret her utterance in relation to the previous discourse, Cherrilyn must assume that a topos or set of topoi underpinning the enthymeme is also accommodated by Fiona. Thus, Cherrilyn's gameboard will be updated with the relevant topos or set of topoi via either update rule $f_{integrate\_topos}$ (Section 4.2.2 and Appendix 1, section 2) and $f_{integrate\_resource\_topos}$ (Section 4.2.5 and Appendix 1, section 2), depending on the salience of the integrated topos[3] with regard to the interlocutor, in this case Fiona.

Contextual clues and intonation might contribute to Fiona's ability to accommodate an enthymematic relation between the utterance *Yeah, dog hairs rise anyway* and the previously established and agreed upon notion that dogs should be allowed upstairs. However, there is still need for a topos warranting the reasoning in $\varepsilon_1$.

The most straightforward way of obtaining the topos that underpins $\varepsilon_1$ is by removing the manifest fields of the enthymeme.[4] In this case that means that the underpinning topos would be "dog hairs rise, therefore dogs are allowed upstairs". However, Fiona signals a lack of understanding by asking "what do you mean rise". This indicates that the topos is not acceptable to her.

So, we assume that Fiona interprets Cherrilyn's utterances as expressing an enthymematic argument, meaning that $\varepsilon_1$ is integrated on Fiona's shared gameboard at this point in time. Fiona then tries to find a topos warranting $\varepsilon_1$. Failing to do so, she makes a clarification request which indicates that none of the meanings of *rise* which she is aware of helps her reach a relevant interpretation of the utterance. Fiona's clarification request is an explicit signal that she has not been able to accommodate a topos or set of topoi warranting $\varepsilon_1$.

---

3   For a discussion of this see Section 4.2.5.
4   See Section 4.2.1 and Section 4.2.2 for a discussion about different ways in which enthymemes and topoi can be related.

In her response to the clarification request Cherrilyn does not only elaborate which interpretation of *rise* she had in mind, she also adds a sequence to explain the reasoning behind her utterance *dog hairs rise anyway*. The sequence *friends said it was, oh God I wouldn't allow mine upstairs because of all the dog hairs* actually evokes a topos—$\tau_{dogs\_shed}$—the relevance of which Cherrilyn rejects by saying *dog hairs rise anyway*.

So, let us look more closely at the underpinning topoi and the reasoning that would be necessary for arriving at $\varepsilon_1$ drawing on these topoi.

### 6.2.1    The Topoi of Dog Hairs

One topos that everybody involved seems to agree on is that if a dog with hairs is at a certain place at a certain time, there will be hairs of that dog at that place at a later point in time. We call this topos $\tau_{hairy\_dogs\_shed}$, as represented in (6.31).

$$(6.31) \quad \tau_{\text{hairy\_dogs\_shed}} = \lambda r: \begin{bmatrix} x : Ind \\ c_{\text{dog}} : \text{dog}(x) \\ y : \text{set}(Ind) \\ c_{\text{hairs}} : \text{hairs}(y) \\ c_{\text{of}} : \text{of}(y, x) \\ e\text{-loc} : Loc \\ e\text{-time} : Time \\ c_{\text{be}} : \text{be}(x, e\text{-loc}, e\text{-time}) \end{bmatrix} \cdot \begin{bmatrix} z : \text{set}(Ind) \\ c_{\text{hairs}_1} : \text{hairs}(z) \\ c_{\text{of}_1} : \text{of}(z, r.x) \\ e\text{-time}_1 : Time \\ c_< : r.e\text{-time} < e\text{-time}_1 \\ c_{\text{be}_1} : \text{be}(z, r.e\text{-loc}, e\text{-time}) \end{bmatrix}$$

We may generalise the topos in (6.31) by removing the field labelled with 'y' in the domain type and all the fields which depend on the y-field, $c_{\text{hairs}}$ and $c_{\text{of}}$. There is nothing in the return type that depends on these fields, and therefore a generalisation is possible. The topos we obtain after the generalisation says that if there is a dog upstairs at some point in time there will be hairs there at a later point in time (no matter if the dog is hairy or not). We call this topos $\tau_{\text{dogs\_shed}}$.

$$(6.32) \quad \tau_{\text{dogs\_shed}} = \lambda r: \begin{bmatrix} x : Ind \\ c_{\text{dog}} : \text{dog}(x) \\ y : \text{set}(Ind) \\ e\text{-loc} : Loc \\ e\text{-time} : Time \\ c_{\text{be}} : \text{be}(x, e\text{-loc}, e\text{-time}) \end{bmatrix} \cdot \begin{bmatrix} z : \text{set}(Ind) \\ c_{\text{hairs}_1} : \text{hairs}(z) \\ c_{\text{of}_1} : \text{of}(z, r.x) \\ e\text{-time}_1 : Time \\ c_< : r.e\text{-time} < e\text{-time}_1 \\ c_{\text{be}_1} : \text{be}(z, r.e\text{-loc}, e\text{-time}) \end{bmatrix}$$

In this case we are interested in dogs shedding in a specific location—upstairs. The $\tau_{dogs\_shed}$ could be made more specific, by adding fields to the domain type (see Appendix 2). We then obtain a topos specifying that $\tau_{dogs\_shed}$ applies to situations where the location is upstairs, that is if a dog is upstairs at some point in time, there will be doghairs upstairs at a later point in time. Since *upstairs* is a subtype of *location*, (6.33), which we refer to as $\tau_{dogs\_up\_shed\_up}$, is a specification of $\tau_{dogs\_shed}$ in (6.32).

$$(6.33) \quad \tau_{dogs\_up\_shed\_up} = \lambda r: \begin{bmatrix} x : Ind \\ c_{dog} : dog(x) \\ y : set(Ind) \\ e\text{-loc} : Loc \\ c_{upstairs} : upstairs(e\text{-loc}) \\ e\text{-time} : Time \\ c_{be} : be(x, e\text{-loc}, e\text{-time}) \end{bmatrix} \cdot \begin{bmatrix} z : set(Ind) \\ c_{hairs_1} : hairs(z) \\ c_{of_1} : of(z, r.x) \\ e\text{-time}_1 : Time \\ c_< : r.e\text{-time}<e\text{-time}_1 \\ c_{be_1} : be(z, r.e\text{-loc}, e\text{-time}_1) \end{bmatrix}$$

Cherrilyn and Fiona would also, presumably, have access to a topos stating that doghairs upstairs are undesirable. We refer to this topos as $\tau_{hairs\_up\_undes}$.

$$(6.34) \quad \tau_{hairs\_up\_undes} = \lambda r: \begin{bmatrix} x : Ind \\ c_{dog} : dog(x) \\ e\text{-loc} : Loc \\ c_{upstairs} : upstairs(e\text{-loc}) \\ z : set(Ind) \\ c_{hairs_1} : hairs(z) \\ c_{of_1} : of(z, x) \\ e\text{-time}_1 : Time \\ c_{be_1} : be(z, e\text{-loc}, e\text{-time}_1) \end{bmatrix} \cdot \begin{bmatrix} c_{undesirable} : undesirable(r) \end{bmatrix}$$

Now, in order to arrive at a topos saying that dogs upstairs are undesirable, $\tau_{dogs\_up\_undes}$, we need to combine the topoi $\tau_{dogs\_up\_hairs\_up}$ and $\tau_{hairs\_up\_undes}$. We do this through *composition*.

### 6.2.2    Composition of Topoi and Enthymemes

To discuss composition of two topoi or enthymemes, we first need to talk about how to derive *fixed-point types* for functions in TTR (for an in-depth discussion, see Cooper, 2005a). In this context a fixed point type represents a holistic, or static, perspective on the two situation types involved in a topos. For example, if we have a topos saying that "if the weather is warm, people spend time at the beach", we may from this topos construe a type of situation which is warranted by the topos, namely one where the weather is warm and people spend time at the beach. In more formal terms, the fixed point type of a function $f$, $\mathscr{F}(f)$, is obtained by extending the type of the domain of $f$ with the dependent type that characterises its range (Cooper, 2005a); see Appendix 2, section 3 for a formal definition.

To obtain a fixed-point type for $\tau_{dogs\_up\_hairs\_up}$ we need to merge the domain type and the result type adjusting the references to $r$ in the dependencies, as shown in (6.35). We will refer to this type as $\mathscr{F}(\tau_{dogs\_up\_hairs\_up})$, and we could say it represents a situation where there is a dog upstairs at some point in time and dog hairs upstairs at a later point in time.

$$(6.35) \quad \mathscr{F}(\tau_{dogs\_up\_hairs\_up}) = \begin{bmatrix} \text{x} : Ind \\ c_{dog} : dog(x) \\ \text{e-loc} : Loc \\ c_{upstairs} : upstairs(\text{e-loc}) \\ \text{e-time} : Time \\ c_{be} : be(x, \text{e-loc}, \text{e-time}) \\ \text{z} : set(Ind) \\ c_{hairs_1} : hairs(z) \\ c_{of_1} : of(z, x) \\ \text{e-time}_1 : Time \\ c_< : \text{e-time} < \text{e-time}_1 \\ c_{be_1} : be(z, \text{e-loc}, \text{e-time}_1) \end{bmatrix}$$

(6.36)   The composition $\tau_1 \circ \tau_2$ of two topoi $\tau_1$ and $\tau_2$ such that
$\tau_1 = \lambda r\colon T_1 \cdot T_2(r)$, $\tau_2 = \lambda r\colon T_3 \cdot T_4(r)$, and $\mathscr{F}(\tau_1) \sqsubseteq T_3$, is $\lambda r\colon \mathscr{F}(\tau_1) \cdot T_4(r)$

According to the definition in (6.36) the fixed-point type of a topos must be a subtype of the domain-type (antecedent) of the topos with which it is to be composed. Since $\mathscr{F}(\tau_{dogs\_up\_hairs\_up})$ is a subtype of the domain type of $\tau_{hairs\_up\_undes}$, they may be composed. The composition of these topoi—$\tau_{dogs\_up\_}$ $_{hairs\_up}$ $\circ$ $\tau_{hairs\_up\_undes}$—is $\tau_{dogs\_and\_hairs\_up\_undes}$ in (6.37).

$(6.37)$ $\lambda r : \mathcal{F}\left(\tau_{dogs\_up\_hairs\_up}\right) \cdot \left[c_{undesirable} : undesirable(r)\right] =$

$$\lambda r: \begin{bmatrix} x : Ind \\ c_{dog} : dog(x) \\ e\text{-}loc : Loc \\ c_{upstairs} : upstairs(e\text{-}loc) \\ e\text{-}time : Time \\ c_{be} : be(x, e\text{-}loc, e\text{-}time) \\ z : set(Ind) \\ c_{hairs_1} : hairs(z) \\ c_{of_1} : of(z, x) \\ e\text{-}time_1 : Time \\ c_< : e\text{-}time < e\text{-}time_1 \\ c_{be_1} : be(z, e\text{-}loc, e\text{-}time_1) \end{bmatrix} \cdot \left[c_{undesirable} : undesirable(r)\right]$$

Through generalisation, we finally arrive at a topos stating that if a dog is upstairs, that is an undesirable situation:

$(6.38)$  $\tau_{dogs\_up\_undes} = \lambda r:$ $\begin{bmatrix} x : Ind \\ c_{dog} : dog(x) \\ e\text{-}loc : Loc \\ c_{upstairs} : upstairs(e\text{-}loc) \\ e\text{-}time : Time \\ c_{be} : be(x, e\text{-}loc, e\text{-}time) \end{bmatrix} \cdot \left[c_{undesirable} : undesirable(r)\right]$

The topos in (6.38) seems to be recognized by Cherrilyn and Fiona, in the sense that they are both aware that this is a generally accepted way of reasoning. Also, it serves as underpinning for a second enthymeme in this dialogue—an enthymeme evoked by Cherrilyn's report of her friends' comment *I wouldn't allow mine upstairs because of all the dog hairs!*, which would also be underpinned by a topos like $\tau_{undes\_disal}$ in (6.39).

$(6.39)$  $\tau_{undes\_disal} = \lambda r:$ $\begin{bmatrix} s : Rec \\ c_{undesirable} : undesirable(s) \end{bmatrix} \cdot disallow(r.s))$

In order to reason as they do, Cherrilyn's friends have to accept not only the topos $\tau_{dogs\_up\_hairs\_up}$, but also a topos saying the opposite—if there are no dogs upstairs, there will be no dog hairs upstairs. In other words, Cherrilyn's friends interpret the implication between dogs up and hairs up as a biconditional. This type of reasoning may be logically faulty, but it has been shown implication is often interpreted this way (Stenning and van Lambalgen, 2008), and this interpretion may be more useful in many real life situations. For example, if we do a job we get paid, and if we do not do the job we do not get paid—it is not the case that we may get paid even if we do not do the job.

However, when Cherrilyn points out that her friend's reasoning—and that of all other dogs-upstairs-disallowers—is not valid, it could be argued that she in fact forces the conversation, or the conversation participants, to accommodate a more logically accurate way of reasoning, or a higher degree of exactness of reasoning.

So, by pointing to the fact that hairs rise, drawing on the topos $\tau_{hairs\_down\_hairs\_up}$ in (6.40), Cherrilyn has demonstrated that it is not possible to avoid hairs upstairs by keeping dogs downstairs. Also, we would need a topos saying that if two possible actions lead to the same result, you should choose the action which is preferable in some respect, for example because it takes less effort or because it gives some additional desirable result.

(6.40)   a. if there are doghairs downstairs at some point in time there will be doghairs upstairs at a later point in time

b. $\lambda r$:
$$
\begin{bmatrix}
x : Ind \\
c_{dog} : dog(x) \\
y : set(Ind) \\
c_{hairs_1} : hairs(y) \\
c_{of_1} : of(y, x) \\
e\text{-}loc : Loc \\
c_{downstairs} : downstairs(e\text{-}loc) \\
e\text{-}time : Time \\
c_{be} : be(y, e\text{-}loc, e\text{-}time)
\end{bmatrix}
\cdot
\begin{bmatrix}
z : set(Ind) \\
c_{hairs_1} : hairs(z) \\
c_{of_1} : of(z, r.x) \\
e\text{-}loc_1 : Loc \\
c_{upstairs} : upstairs(e\text{-}loc) \\
e\text{-}time_1 : Time \\
c_< : r.e\text{-}time < e\text{-}time_1 \\
c_{be_1} : be(z, e\text{-}loc_1, e\text{-}time_1)
\end{bmatrix}
$$

So there is a question of balancing the undesirable consequences of dogs upstairs with the desirable consequences. Cherrilyn's point is that it does not matter which of these takes precedence, since both options—allowing dogs upstairs or not allowing dogs upstairs—result in the same type of situation: hairs upstairs.

Fiona, on the other hand, questions the topos that dogs should not be allowed upstairs from another angle: She claims that dog hairs upstairs is not a serious problem, which renders the discussion of whether hairs get upstairs or not less relevant. The topos which she is challenging is $\tau_{hairs\_up\_undes}$.

Our analysis of this example illustrates how the topoi underpinning an argument must be recognisable to interlocutors in order for the communication to be successful. To obtain a topos that would warrant the conclusion that dogs should be allowed upstairs based on the premise that dog hairs rise, many manipulations on topoi are required.

In her first utterance "dog hairs rise anyway", Cherrilyn fails to relevantly connect the enthymeme to the topoi to which she has access, so she clarifies not only by elaborating on the appropriate interpretation of *rise*, but also by pointing to an enthymeme partly based on competing topoi. This dialogue is thus an example of a spontaneous conversation of the kind we mentioned in connection to the Nixon puzzle, where the set of topoi drawn on by individual dialogue participants is not necessarily consistent, and where dialogue participants sometimes utilise topoi which they do not agree with. This is not surprising *per se*—as humans we are capable of reasoning about actual and hypothetical situations considering matters from different points of view depending on the context. However, modelling this kind of reasoning requires a theory that allows inconsistent rules and rules which can be manipulated with regard to context.

## 6.3 Acquiring Topoi in Interaction

In Chapter 1 we mentioned that topoi can be seen as cultural indicators. This means that the topoi which members of a group live by can be seen as a characterisation of the socio-cultural environment of that group. Similarly, an individual's personal set of topoi can be seen as defining the experiences of that individual. However, such sets are by no means closed—we acquire new topoi throughout life, some are explicitly pointed out to us, some we learn through inference. Consider, for example, the exchange in (6.41) taken from a corpus of argumentative three-party dialogues (Lavelle et al., 2012).

(6.41)   *A*: I wanna wanna know what she plays but
          [you know what I mean]
          *B*: [apparently she's the next Mozart]
          *A*: the next Mozart so piano                          (GP13 47–50)

*A*'s final utterance in (6.41) conveys the enthymeme in (6.42)—She is the next Mozart, hence, she plays the piano.

(6.42)   she is the next Mozart
         ‾‾‾‾‾‾‾‾‾‾‾‾‾‾‾‾‾‾‾‾‾‾‾
           she plays the piano

Let us assume a situation where *B* does not know which instrument Mozart played. When encountering the enthymeme in (6.42), *B* may accommodate a topos saying that if someone is a Mozart, they play the piano. Not only can this topos tentatively be made common ground in the dialogue, it can also be incorporated into $B$'s long-term resources. Previously, we have thought of the rhetorical resources of a dialogue participant as something external to the DGB. However, in order to model, within our current theory, an update where topoi are added to the long term resources of an agent, we will introduce 'resources' as a third field on the DGB. In $f_{acquire\_topos}$ below, the type associated with the label 'resources' is 'list($Topos$)', since the only resources we will consider here are topoi.

The function handling the update of resources by means of topos accommodation says that if there is no topos accessible in your rhetorical resources such that it can be used to warrant the enthymeme currently under discussion, you may add a topos which is identical to the enthymeme under discussion to the topoi that are shared in the conversation, and also incorporate it in your rhetorical resources. In order to formulate such a rule, we must first define negation for record types. Following Cooper and Ginzburg (2015) we define negation as in (6.43):[5]

(6.43)   For any type $T$, an object $a$ is of type $\neg T$, $a: \neg T$, iff there is some $T'$ such that $a: T'$ and $T'$ precludes $T$ $(T' \perp T)$

The update rule $f_{acquire\_topos}$ says that if there is no topos in the rhetorical resources of an agent of which the enthymeme currently under discussion is a specification, then the agent is licensed to add a topos identical to that enthymeme not only to the topoi which are shared in the conversation, but also to their rhetorical resources. In future interactions, this topos might be adjusted or generalised further, or rejected if the agent learns that it is unacceptable to many of her interlocutors.

(6.44)   $f_{acquire\_topos} =$

$$\lambda r: \begin{bmatrix} \text{resources} : \text{list}(\textit{Topos}) \\ \text{shared} : \begin{bmatrix} \text{eud} : \text{list}(\textit{Enthymeme}) \\ \text{topos} : \text{list}(\textit{Topos}) \end{bmatrix} \end{bmatrix} \cdot \lambda e: \neg \begin{bmatrix} \text{t} : \textit{Topos} \\ c_1 : \text{in}(\text{t}, r.\text{resources}) \\ c_2 : \text{spec}(\text{t}, \text{fst}(r.\text{shared.eud})) \end{bmatrix} \cdot$$

$$\begin{bmatrix} \text{resources} = [\text{fst}(r.\text{shared.eud}) \mid r.\text{resources}] : \text{list}(\textit{Topos}) \\ \text{shared} : [\text{topoi} = [\text{fst}(r.\text{shared.eud}) \mid r.\text{shared.topos}\ ] : \text{list}(\textit{Topos})] \end{bmatrix}$$

Situations where we encounter enthymemes for which we cannot find a suitable underpinning topos can be expected to be more frequent when individ-

---

5   See also Section 4.2.4 and Appendix 2, Section 1.1 on preclusion.

uals find themselves in novel types of situations. This is the case for adults experiencing unfamiliar socio-cultural contexts as well as for children who are struggling to get a grip on functional and acceptable reasoning. It has been suggested that enthymematic reasoning plays a role for lexical disambiguation (Pustejovsky, 1998), and we suggest that it also may play a role for acquisition of new concepts by means of accommodation of new topoi. However, due to a tendency to overextension, discussed for example by Barrett (1978) and Clark (2015), the meaning children associate with an expression sometimes deviates from the conventional meaning of that expression in the language community.

An example of this can be found in the following interaction of a mother reading a bedtime story to a four-year-old child from Breitholtz (2015):

(6.45)  MOTHER:  When Snow White was still a baby her mother died. After some time her father, the king, remarried. His new wife was beautiful but vain and wicked.

        CHILD:  Yes mum—a widow!

To anyone familiar with the conventional meaning of the word *widow*, it seems obvious that the child has got it wrong. However, how did she get it wrong? And can the mechanisms of how she got it wrong explain how most of us eventually get it right?

The mother's utterance in (6.45) says explicitly that Snow White's stepmother is vain and wicked. Thus we may assume that the type of Snow White's step mother that is common ground in the dialogue this far is the one in (6.46).[6]

$$(6.46) \quad T_{step\_mother} : \begin{bmatrix} x = \text{Snow White's stepmother} : Ind \\ c_{vain} : \text{vain}(x) \\ c_{wicked} : \text{wicked}(x) \end{bmatrix}$$

The child's utterance together with that of the mother convey a co-constructed enthymeme saying that Snow White's stepmother is vain and wicked, therefore, she is a widow. We refer to this enthymeme as $\varepsilon_1$, as seen in (6.47). Intuitively, $\varepsilon_1$ represents the idea that if you have a situation of the type where someone is vain and wicked, you can predict the type of situation where that person is a widow.

---

6  This could also be a subtype of 6.46 including other constraints like "woman". However, we leave aside such considerations here for clarity.

$$(6.47) \quad \varepsilon_1 = \lambda r: \begin{bmatrix} x = \text{Snow White's stepmother}: Ind \\ c_{\text{vain}}: \text{vain}(x) \\ c_{\text{wicked}}: \text{wicked}(x) \end{bmatrix} \cdot \left[ c_{\text{widow}}: \text{widow}(r.x) \right]$$

For the child to make this argument, we must assume that she has access to a topos warranting $\varepsilon_1$, for example $\tau_1$ below. The question is—how was this topos established?

$$(6.48) \quad \tau_1 = \lambda r: \begin{bmatrix} x: Ind \\ c_{\text{vain}}: \text{vain}(x) \\ c_{\text{wicked}}: \text{wicked}(x) \end{bmatrix} \cdot \left[ c_{\text{widow}}: \text{widow}(r.x) \right]$$

It seems reasonable to say that if the child believes that someone being vain and wicked is a reason for concluding that that person is a widow, the child perceives *vain and wicked* as essential components of the meaning of the word *widow*. But how was this idea established? No one is likely to have told the child that *widow* means *vain and wicked*, or that widows are vain and wicked. We argue that this is a result of children's tendency to overextension mentioned above, and the general ability of accommodation (previously discussed in section 4.2.5).

One possible source of input leading the child to construe a topos that would warrant $\varepsilon_1$ is other fairy tales such as *Cinderella*:

(6.49)  "After a few years Cinderella's father took a new wife, a widow with two daughters of her own"

From this passage, we learn that Cinderella's stepmother is a widow. As the story evolves, we receive evidence that she is also vain and wicked. From the story of *Cinderella* a topos regarding widows may be tentatively construed, namely the one in (6.50):

$$(6.50) \quad \tau_2 = \lambda r: \begin{bmatrix} x: Ind \\ c_{\text{widow}}: \text{widow}(x) \end{bmatrix} \cdot \begin{bmatrix} c_{\text{vain}}: \text{vain}(r.x) \\ c_{\text{wicked}}: \text{wicked}(r.x) \end{bmatrix}$$

This topos says that if we have a situation of the type where someone is a widow, we also have a type of situation where that person is vain and wicked.

There are many ways in which human reasoning does not adhere to the rules of classical logic—some of these we have discussed in this book. The transition from $\tau_2$ to $\tau_1$ in this example is an instance of one of the most obvious deviations of human reasoning with respect to classical logic—biconditional strengthening, that is, interpreting conditionals as biconditionals (Wason, 1968; Sztencel, 2018).

We could think of this as a principle of human reasoning and introduce a rule in our model saying that if we have a topos $\lambda r : T_1 \cdot T_2$, we are licensed to add to our resources a topos $\lambda r : T_2 \cdot T_1$. We could also think of the reasoning process as more associative, and related to the kind of associations that arise in neural activity where co-activation of two neural patterns eventually leads to external stimulation of one engendering the second pattern even in the absence of a stimulus, often referred to as Hebbian reinforcement (Hebb, 1949). From this point of view, a child may perceive a number of features co-occurring in one particular situation, and based on this may construe various types of dependencies between these features, and the ones that co-occur more often will eventually be more strongly connected. Thus, when encountering a type of situation where someone (Snow White's stepmother) is vain and wicked, the child draws on a type of situation in (6.51), a fixed-point type[7] of $\tau_2$.

$$(6.51) \quad \begin{bmatrix} x : Ind \\ c_{widow} : \text{widow}(x) \\ c_{wicked} : \text{wicked}(x) \\ c_{vain} : \text{vain}(x) \end{bmatrix}$$

Other topoi that would be possible to derive from (6.51) include ones saying that vain widows are wicked and that widows are wicked and vain. In fact, from all topoi we may, in principle, derive any topos that has the same fixed point type.

This way of thinking about the building up of rhetorical resources and concepts may seem very open ended. However, we do not argue that the topoi we have access to are necessarily biconditional or that any topos derived from a particular situation type is acceptable in reasoning, but in order to model the acquisition of new topoi our theory must allow for less restricted ways of making inferences.

To achieve a dynamic theory of language learning and reasoning, where we can account for things like the overextension common in children, while at the same time mostly avoid unacceptable predictions, we believe it necessary to include a statistical or probabilistic component. Exactly how this would be set up we leave aside for the time being, but it seems intuitively clear that the child, as she encounters the word "widow" in other situations, will revise the

---

7 See Section 6.2.2.

dependencies of the relevant topoi in her resources, and "vain" and "wicked" will gradually move from the centre of the meaning of *widow* to the periphery to become at most a connotation.

## 6.4    Summary

In this chapter we have seen examples illustrating how we use reasoning to establish the meaning of words as well as to disambiguate word meaning. Our approach allows us to represent misunderstanding and misinterpretation of meaning, since it is based on the conceptualisation of entities and individuals rather than on a God's eye view of meaning. Thus our account fits well with an approach to meaning where speakers constantly adjust meanings on the basis of experience, which can be found in work by for example Pustejovsky (1998), Cooper (2012), Gregoromichelaki et al. (2012), Ludlow (2014), Kempson et al. (2016) and Larsson and Myrendal (2017).

One of the advantages of using topoi rather than default rules as underpinning for the kind of non-monotonic reasoning we find in enthymemes, is that the set of topoi of one agent does not necessarily constitute a monolithic logical system. Thus the topoi in an individual's resources do not need to be consistent or lead to consistent conclusions even within one model or domain (Breitholtz, 2014a).

The ability to follow various strains of reasoning—also inconsistent ones—seems to be a prerequisite for the complex type of interactive language understanding and problem solving that humans master so well. However, in order to fully take advantage of the possibility to model this ability, we need to be able to account for the reasoning of agents with access to a wider range of topoi than those we have considered here.

A natural progression of the account presented here would be to extend our model to include a probabilistic component. This would enable us to make predictions regarding the enthymematic inferences of an agent with access to several topoi applicable in a particular situation. It would also allow for modelling the learning of new topoi through interaction with other agents.

Interesting work has been done by Cooper et al. (2014) on probabilistic semantics in TTR, and Clark and Lappin (2010) convincingly show how language learning is related to probability theory. Both of these approaches fit well with the approach that we suggest, and they offer a way to introduce a probabilistic component into the account of learning presented here.

# CHAPTER 7

# Conclusions and Future Work

## 7.1    Conclusions

In this book we have investigated the role of enthymemes and topoi in dialogue. These concepts, which are known from Aristotle's work, refer to rhetorical arguments and the warrants of such arguments respectively. A defining feature of an enthymeme is that the conclusion does not necessarily follow from its premises (unlike in a logical argument), and therefore the topoi that underpin enthymemes must be *acceptable* to the audience or interlocutor at which the argument is aimed. Hence, the reasoning based on topoi is sometimes referred to as "common sense" reasoning.

However, enthymematic reasoning goes beyond that. In fact any type of reasoning can be accounted for using enthymemes and topoi, ranging from situations where we do not find a topos acceptable (and which are thus not part of "common sense") but *recognisable*, to instances of strictly logical reasoning where the inference rules have been made explicit (Brandom, 1998).

In Chapter 1 we introduced the concepts of enthymeme and topos and considered how they may present themselves in dialogue, and how enthymematic reasoning is relevant to many of the challenges in interactional linguistics. In Chapter 2 we were interested in how enthymemes and topoi relate to different types of inferences and how they contribute to cohesion and meaning. In Chapter 3 we introduced a dialogue semantic account of how enthymematic reasoning causes updates of dialogue participants' information states, cast in TTR, a type theory with records. In Chapter 4 we looked at how some features of dialogical reasoning such as *why*-questions can be analysed in terms of enthymemes and topoi, and in Chapter 5 we moved on to consider how enthymematic reasoning relates to models of dialogue, context and cognition. In Chapter 6 we looked at how our theory accounts for non-monotonicity, ambiguous meaning in conversation and the acquisition of new topoi. In this final chapter we will sum up the main conclusions drawn in the previous chapters and suggest some directions for future work.

## 7.1.1    *Pragmatic Inference*

Few theories in linguistics or philosophy of language deny that some kind of background knowledge or set of beliefs about the world is necessary in order for a language user to draw pragmatic inferences. However, the organisation of this knowledge and the mechanisms for including it in dialogue models are still far from accounted for in pragmatics.

The anti-inferentialist theory of meaning in context (Recanati, 2004) does pay more attention to the role of world knowledge than theories like Gricean pragmatics and Relevance Theory. But it mainly acknowledges the role of world knowledge in the context of primary pragmatic processes such as disambiguation and enrichment, and less as underpinning pragmatic inferences like conversational implicatures.

In overtly rhetorical discourse such as political speeches the role of background knowledge or assumptions is particularly evident. In this context enthymemes are sometimes very conspicuous since they draw on potentially controversial topoi. This is not least true in the current, increasingly polarised, political climate.

In dialogue, particularly informal conversation, on the other hand, enthymematic arguments tend to be less noticeable, as many of the things that underpin our arguments in everyday conversation are associated with commonly acknowledged topoi. For example, when interpreting pieces of dialogue like "Let's walk along Walnut Street—it's shorter" we might not even reflect on the rhetorical structure, since the enthymeme conveyed is based on commonplace and uncontroversial topoi such as the assumptions that if you are going somewhere you want to get there as quickly as possible, if a route is short it is fast, etc.

In the literature on pragmatic inferences it is often suggested that the principles for making such inferences are universal and independent of context. We have shown that while we may draw on general principles to infer more than the truth-conditional content of an utterance, we cannot rely only on a small and closed set of high-level principles like Gricean maxims or relevance assumptions.

### 7.1.2   *Defining Genres*

In Chapter 5 we discussed some parameters that can be used to distinguish between genres of language use or conversational types. We mentioned *activity*, *communicative project* and *conversational game* as examples of such parameters. We may think of communicative projects as linked to the subgoals of the activity, and of conversational games as related to activities as well as to projects, in the sense that the speech act sequence (or sequence of adjacency pairs) typically employed to carry out a communicative project depends on the nature of the project itself, but also on the kind of activity in association with which the conversation occurs.

Let us imagine, for example, that a group of friends are going camping and they are dividing up the various tasks which are necessary to set up camp. In this scenario, the activity is "setting up camp". The communicative project of making decisions about tasks would probably be carried out by means of a different conversational game, or sequence of conversational games, than in a similar situation in the military where hierarchies are very well defined and there is no expectation that decisions should be made jointly.

We suggested that topoi should be added to the set of parameters defining conversational types. In this context, the notion of topoi is to some extent related to activity type, since certain topoi are strongly associated with particular activity types. For example, in a patient-doctor conversation we can expect topoi related to health, body, etc., to be more frequent than topoi regarding the economy or money. However, topoi also contribute to how the activity plays out, since the socio-cultural context in which the activity is embedded may affect *which* topoi of health are introduced in the interaction.

### 7.1.3    *Enthymemes in Conversational AI*

Related to the question of defining genres of conversation is the question of how to model context. When modelling artificial agents, world knowledge may be organised for example as schemas or frames. These can be seen as groups or clusters of connected concepts for things, people and events, usually related to a particular domain or activity such as dining in a restaurant. While we do not want to rule out the use of frames and schemas for modelling context, we suggest that modelling some world knowledge as topoi could be advantageous. Many topoi would be included in several schemas and it might sometimes be hard for an agent to identify a given situation as belonging to a particular schema or frame, whereas it may be easier to recognise an enthymematic argument as evoking a particular topos. With a set of topoi at its disposal rather than only a set of domain specific schemas, an artificial agent has a higher degree of flexibility and is free to draw on any topos in any domain, specify it, generalise it and combine it with other topoi just as people do. It seems to us that this approach is valuable if we want to build creative agents who can adjust to new situations.

In the context of dialogue systems we pointed out a connection between enthymemes and informationally redundant utterances (IRUS). IRUS have been shown to contribute to decreasing the cognitive load of dialogue participants. We argued that IRUS and their antecedents evoke enthymemes drawing on situation relevant topoi. The fact that suggestions, proposals or claims are presented with a supporting premise decreases cognitive load, since the addressee has to do less work to find the appropriate topos or topoi.

### 7.1.4  *Accommodation*

In the context of pragmatic inferences we extended the notion of accommodation to cover enthymemes and topoi. We discussed several different cases of topos accommodation, that is, when a topos is added to the discourse model because it is perceived as a necessary warrant of an enthymeme under discussion. In the modelling of a dialogue, accommodation of a topos results in integrating the topos on the shared DGB.[1] We distinguished different cases of topos accommodation based on the resources available to the language user and the salience of the topos in a given context.

The first case is when a dialogue participant anticipates the accommodation of a topos, that is, the topos is already salient and part of the discourse model for a dialogue participant. The accommodation in this case consists of the integration of already acknowledged and relevant topoi into the shared discourse model. In our model, this corresponds to the topoi being moved from the private to the shared DGB. This kind of topos accommodation was described in Section 4.2.1.

Secondly, we have the case where a topos is evoked that is available in the long term memory of a dialogue participant. In this case, the topos is recognisable to the dialogue participant, but it is not salient in the sense that it is already present in his or her mind in the discourse context. An example where this kind of accommodation occurs is the excerpt about "rollers" in (4.36).

Note that we do not make strong claims regarding the precise architecture of the private game board and other resources accessible to a dialogue participant. We could think of the rhetorical resources of an agent as part of that agent's private game board, or external to it. The point is that we sometimes need to differentiate between easily accessible topoi (ones that are salient and relevant for a particular speaker engaged in dialogue in a particular context) and less accessible topoi.

Another case of accommodation is when a dialogue participant cannot identify a topos that would warrant the enthymeme currently under discussion, but is still able to reconstruct and tentatively accommodate a topos that warrants the enthymeme. This means that we can accommodate topoi we did not previously recognise. We suggest that this kind of accommodation contributes to acquisition of new topoi, in that an agent may add new, tentatively

---

1  Since topoi are usually not made explicit, they are not straightforwardly integrated in the way that explicit dialogue moves are. For example, an answer to a question raised in the previous turn is automatically integrated as the latest move made in the dialogue. Topoi, on the other hand, are typically integrated through accommodation.

accommodated topoi to his resources, where they might over time become more prominent as the language user encounters more instances of these topoi in interaction with other language users. An example of this kind of accommodation can be found in Section 6.3.

In addition to the different types of topos accommodation, we also introduced a rule for accommodation of enthymemes based on topoi. The type of situation we are interested in here is when an agent infers an enthymematic structure between two utterances or parts of an utterance based on topoi that are easily associated with the discourse. This kind of accommodation contributes to cohesion in dialogue by warranting an enthymematic relation between two discourse units. An example of this kind of accommodation is the "Walnut Street" example in (5.4).

### 7.1.5    *Formalisation*

We have suggested a way of formalising enthymematic reasoning in TTR, drawing on previous work by Cooper and Ginzburg, thus extending the kinds of linguistic phenomena previously accounted for in the literature on TTR to also include enthymemes and topoi. Developing the formal analysis has contributed to many of the conclusions discussed above. One insight in particular regards the nature of enthymemes and topoi and the relation between them. Topoi tend not to be *instantiated*, viz. they usually apply to more than one individual of a certain type, while enthymemes are specific arguments used in particular dialogues and situations. In our formalisation we treat enthymemes and topoi as the same type of formal object—a function from a situation of a particular type to another type of situation.

It is possible that instantiated principles of reasoning become part of our rhetorical resources, if they concern individuals and events that are central enough to motivate this. That topoi and enthymemes are modelled as the same type of formal object means that we have a way of moving seamlessly between enthymemes and related topoi. This is necessary to account for how we expand our resources by integrating topoi based on enthymematic inferences from discourse. Such mechanisms may also explain how we can obtain new topoi by combining, generalising and restricting topoi which are already established in our resources. In our account of these operations we draw on the subtype-supertype relation that exists between parts of enthymemes and the topoi that underpin them.

### 7.1.6    *Non-monotonic Reasoning*

In Chapter 6 we suggest using topoi as resources for non-monotonic reasoning. Using a collection of topoi integrated in one DGB we can account not only for situations where topoi are hierarchical, but also for situations where several topoi apply, but taken together are inconsistent or lead to conclusions that are inconsistent. The reason for this is that a system of topoi is not a monolithic logical system. Allowing for mutually inconsistent topoi enables, for example, modelling of internal deliberation or a discussion where arguments are used which are potentially acceptable by themselves, but lead to an inconsistent system, such as the "Nixon Diamond" example discussed in Section 6.1.2.

## 7.2      Future Work

### 7.2.1      *Experimental and Corpus Studies*
The work presented in this book is mostly neither experimental nor quantitative, and a natural progression would be to test some of the hypotheses and models experimentally. For example, the connection between enthymemes and *Why*-questions could be systematically tested to see how people respond to such questions at different points in dialogue, and how this is related to the incremental update of their rhetorical resources.

It could also be fruitful to use experimental techniques to investigate the enthymemes people use in a dialogue, and to see what factors influence which argument people choose when more than one topos is available. It seems possible that how people respond to *Why*-questions is influenced by both the current turn, and the enthymematic arguments they have shared previously in the dialogue, with later turns leading to more explicit descriptions of topoi as participants incrementally refine and recognise their own arguments through the process of dialogue.

The hypotheses that enthymemes are somehow related to cognitive load could also be tested, for example in an in-vehicle environment (see for example Villing, 2009). Drivers would be given instructions in the form of valid enthymematic arguments (that is, enthymemes underpinned by a relevant topos), in the form of enthymematic arguments that do not have obvious connections to relevant topoi, or in the form of instructions without a supporting premise, leaving the question of the underpinning topos open. The subject's cognitive load would be measured continuously. An experiment like this would not only test the connection between cognitive load and acceptable enthymemes, but potentially also provide some information about which topoi are considered relevant in particular situations.

Quantitative corpus studies of enthymemes are problematic since enthymemes are not easy to find automatically, and manual searches that would produce enough data for quantitative studies are not feasible. One option that might be worth pursuing in this context is enthymeme mining (Razu-vayevskaya and Teufel, 2017; Maraev et al., 2020).

Implementing our model in a conversational AI system would be a way of testing the predictions made by our theory as well as the effects of using enthymemes on interctions between humans and artificial agents.

### 7.2.2 *Enthymematic Reasoning and Probabilistic Inference*

A consequence of the gradual nature of topoi is that the acceptability of an enthymeme is based on the non-binary acceptability in a particular context of the warranting topos. When we model a dialogue based on already existing data, we know which enthymemes are conveyed in the discourse and we may construe topoi which would result in the observed dialogue behaviour. How-ever, if we were to model artificial agents capable of interpreting, producing and reacting to new dialogue contributions, other issues arise.

One such issue is how an agent is to choose between available topoi based on the degree of acceptability of these topoi in the context. In recent work in this direction Maguire (2019) encodes enthymemes and topoi as Bayesian networks implemented in TTR. Combining techniques from Maguire (2019) and other probabilistic approaches to dialogue modelling, such as Cooper et al. (2014), with insights from the experimental studies sketched above would provide data for testing such a model.

### 7.2.3 *Theoretical Development*

The formal account presented in this book provides a way of formally account-ing for phenomena discussed in the literature on reasoning going back to antiq-uity, even in cases when the theories of reasoning presented cannot be cast in a traditional logical framework. Being able to formally account for some aspects of theories like Aristotelian dialectic, which has been shown to be fun-damentally pragmatic in nature (Mora-Márquez, 2017), would elucidate our understanding of some of these theories.

A precise theory of enthymemes and topoi also enables us to relate (non-formal) accounts of rhetoric and argumentation to formal and computational models in linguistics and language technology. One area where this is relevant is within "third wave" sociolinguistics (Eckert, 2012), where topoi could be used to characterise personae, particularly in argumentative contexts, using simi-lar techniques to those used by Burnett (2019) (see for example Breitholtz and Cooper, 2018; Noble et al., 2020).

A micro-rhetorical perspective on discourse and dialogue combines differ-ent strands of linguistic research which each contribute important perspec-tives on linguistic interaction. Including enthymemes and topoi in an analysis of dialogue has the potential of capturing notions of individual- and socio-cultural identity, as well as point of view. One example of a field of study where it is necessary to take socio-cultural aspects into account is humour and laughter, see for example Ginzburg et al. (2015) and Breitholtz and Maraev (2019).

## 7.3     Summary

In this book we have shown that by including enthymematic reasoning based on topoi in an account of dialogue, we can capture in a precise way how background assumptions and knowledge is integrated into the common ground of a dialogue. We have also sketched a way of formally accounting for phenomena at the semantics-pragmatics interface which opens up a wide range of opportunities for applied, experimental and theoretical future work.

# Update Rules

## 1 Enthymemes

### 1.1 Integrate Why?-Question Following Assertion, $f_{why\_assert}$ (p. 60)

$$\lambda r:\begin{bmatrix} sh:\begin{bmatrix} l\text{-}m:\begin{bmatrix} e:\begin{bmatrix} prev:Rec \\ e:assert(x,y,ctnt) \\ x=A:Ind \\ y=B:Ind \\ ctnt:RecType \end{bmatrix} \end{bmatrix} \\ qud:list(Question) \end{bmatrix} \end{bmatrix} \cdot$$

$$\begin{bmatrix} sh:\begin{bmatrix} l\text{-}m:\begin{bmatrix} e:\begin{bmatrix} prev:r.shared.l\text{-}m \\ e:ask(x,y,ctnt) \\ x=B:Ind \\ y=A:Ind \\ ctnt=fst(sh.qud):Question \end{bmatrix} \end{bmatrix} \\ qud=[(\lambda t:Type\cdot\lambda r':t\cdot r.sh.l\text{-}m.e.ctnt)\,|\,r.sh.qud]:list(Question) \end{bmatrix} \end{bmatrix}$$

### 1.2 Integrate Enthymeme Following Why?, $f_{integrate\_enthymeme\_why}$ (p. 64)

$$\lambda r:\begin{bmatrix} sh:\begin{bmatrix} l\text{-}m:\begin{bmatrix} prev:\begin{bmatrix} prev:\begin{bmatrix} e:\begin{bmatrix} prev:Rec \\ e:assert(x,y,ctnt) \\ x=A:Ind \\ y=B:Ind \\ ctnt:RecType \end{bmatrix} \\ e:\begin{bmatrix} e:ask(y,x,ctnt) \\ x=A:Ind \\ y=B:Ind \\ ctnt=fst(sh.qud):Question \end{bmatrix} \end{bmatrix} \\ e:\begin{bmatrix} e:assert(x,y,ctnt) \\ x=A:Ind \\ y=B:Ind \\ ctnt:RecType \end{bmatrix} \end{bmatrix} \\ qud=[\lambda t:Type\cdot\lambda r':t\cdot l\text{-}m.prev.prev.e.ctnt]:list(Question) \end{bmatrix} \\ \big[sh:[eud=[r.sh.qud(r.sh.l\text{-}m.e.ctnt)]:list(Enthymeme)]\big] \end{bmatrix} \cdot$$

## 1.3 Accommodate Enthymeme, $f_{accommmodate\_enthymeme}$ (p. 106)

$$\lambda r: \begin{bmatrix} pr : \begin{bmatrix} topoi : list(Topos) \end{bmatrix} \\ sh : \begin{bmatrix} l\text{-}m : \begin{bmatrix} prev : \begin{bmatrix} ctnt : RecType \\ e : Suggest \end{bmatrix} \\ ctnt : RecType \\ e : Assert \end{bmatrix} \end{bmatrix} \end{bmatrix} \cdot$$
$$\lambda e: \begin{bmatrix} t : Topos \\ c_1 : in(t, r.pr.topoi) \\ c_2 : spec(t, \lambda r' : r.sh.l\text{-}m.ctnt \cdot r.sh.l\text{-}m.prev.ctnt) \end{bmatrix} \cdot$$
$$\begin{bmatrix} sh : \begin{bmatrix} eud = [\lambda r' : r.l\text{-}m.ctnt \cdot r.sh.l\text{-}m.prev.ctnt] : list(Enthymeme) \end{bmatrix} \end{bmatrix}$$

## 2 Topoi

### 2.1 Integrate Topos, $f_{integrate\_topos}$ (p. 67)

$$\lambda r: \begin{bmatrix} private : \begin{bmatrix} topoi : list(Topos) \end{bmatrix} \\ shared : \begin{bmatrix} eud : list(Enthymeme) \\ topoi : list(Topos) \end{bmatrix} \end{bmatrix} \cdot \lambda e: \begin{bmatrix} t : Topos \\ c_1 : in(t, r.private.topoi) \\ c_2 : specification(fst(r.shared.eud), t) \end{bmatrix} \cdot$$
$$\begin{bmatrix} shared : \begin{bmatrix} topoi = [e.t \mid r.shared.topoi] : list(Topos) \end{bmatrix} \end{bmatrix}$$

### 2.2 Integrate Topos', $f_{integrate\_topos'}$ (p. 72)

$$\lambda r: \begin{bmatrix} private : \begin{bmatrix} topoi : list(topos) \end{bmatrix} \\ shared : \begin{bmatrix} eud : list(Enthymeme) \\ topoi : list(Topos) \end{bmatrix} \end{bmatrix} \cdot \lambda e: \begin{bmatrix} t : Topos \\ c_1 : in(t, r.private.topoi) \\ c_2 : underspec.(fst(r.shared.eud), t)) \end{bmatrix} \cdot$$
$$\begin{bmatrix} shared : \begin{bmatrix} topoi = [e.t \mid r.private.topoi] : list(Topos) \end{bmatrix} \end{bmatrix}$$

### 2.3 Reraise Topos, $f_{reraise\_topos}$ (p. 75)

$$\lambda r: \begin{bmatrix} shared : \begin{bmatrix} eud : list(Enthymeme) \\ topoi : list(Topos) \end{bmatrix} \end{bmatrix} \cdot \lambda e: \begin{bmatrix} t : Topos \\ c_1 : in(t, r.shared.topoi) \\ c_2 : specification(fst(r.shared.eud), t) \end{bmatrix} \cdot$$
$$\begin{bmatrix} shared : \begin{bmatrix} topoi = [\mu(e.t, r.sh.topoi)] : list(Topos) \end{bmatrix} \end{bmatrix}$$

### 2.4 *Integrate Resource Topos,* $f_{integrate\_resource\_topos}$ *(p.79)*

$$\lambda r: \begin{bmatrix} \text{private} : [\text{topoi} : \text{list}(topos)] \\ \text{shared} : \begin{bmatrix} \text{eud} : \text{list}(Enthymeme) \\ \text{topoi} : \text{list}(Topos) \end{bmatrix} \end{bmatrix} \cdot \lambda e: \begin{bmatrix} t : Topos \\ c_1 : \text{in\_rhet\_resources}(t) \\ c_2 : \text{specification}(\text{fst}(r.\text{shared.eud}), t)) \end{bmatrix} \cdot$$
$$\big[\text{shared} : [\text{topoi} = [e.t \mid r.\text{shared.topoi}] : \text{list}(Topos)]\big]$$

### 2.5 *Integrate Resource Topos',* $f_{integrate\_resource\_topos'}$ *(p.79)*

$$\lambda r: \begin{bmatrix} \text{private} : [\text{topoi} : \text{list}(topos)] \\ \text{shared} : \begin{bmatrix} \text{eud} : \text{list}(Enthymeme) \\ \text{topoi} : \text{list}(Topos) \end{bmatrix} \end{bmatrix} \cdot \lambda e: \begin{bmatrix} t : Topos \\ c_1 : \text{in\_rhet\_resources}(t) \\ c_2 : \text{specification}(t, \text{fst}(r.\text{shared.eud}))) \end{bmatrix} \cdot$$
$$\big[\text{shared} : [\text{topoi} = [e.t \mid r.\text{shared.topoi}] : \text{list}(Topos)]\big]$$

### 2.6 *Integrate Private Resource Topos and Belief,* $f_{integrate\_pr\_resource\_topos}$ *(p.102)*

$$\lambda r: \begin{bmatrix} \text{pr} : \begin{bmatrix} \text{agenda} = [\ \begin{bmatrix} e : Type \\ \text{ctnt} : ERec \end{bmatrix}] : \text{list}(RecType) \\ \text{topoi} : \text{list}(Topos) \\ \text{beliefs} : RecType \end{bmatrix} \\ \text{sh} : [\text{project} = [\ T_{DecisionProject}] : \text{list}(RecType)] \end{bmatrix} \cdot$$

$$\lambda e: \begin{bmatrix} t : Topos \\ c_1 : \text{in}(t, \text{resources}) \\ c_2 : \text{relevant\_to}(t, \text{fst}(r.\text{sh.project})) \\ \text{belief} : RecType \\ c_3 : \text{in}(\text{belief}, \text{resources}) \\ c_4 : \text{relevant\_to}(\text{belief}, \text{fst}(r.\text{sh.project})) \end{bmatrix} \cdot$$

$$\begin{bmatrix} \text{pr} : \begin{bmatrix} \text{topoi} = [e.t \mid r.\text{pr.topoi}] : \text{list}(RecType) \\ \text{beliefs} = \begin{bmatrix} \text{current} : e.\text{belief} \\ \text{prev} : r.\text{pr.beliefs} \end{bmatrix} : RecType \end{bmatrix} \end{bmatrix}$$

### 2.7 *Integrate Private Topos,* $f_{integrate\_pr\_topos}$ *(p.103)*

$$\lambda r: \begin{bmatrix} \text{pr} : \begin{bmatrix} \text{agenda} = [\ \begin{bmatrix} e : Type \\ \text{ctnt} = ERec : RecType \end{bmatrix}] : \text{list}(RecType) \\ \text{topoi} : \text{list}(Topos) \end{bmatrix} \\ \text{sh} : [\text{project} = [[e : \text{decide}(\{A, B\}, \text{route})]] : \text{list}(RecType)] \end{bmatrix} \cdot$$

$$\lambda e: \begin{bmatrix} t: Topos \\ c_1: in(t, r.pr.topoi) \\ c_2: relevant\_to(t, fst(r.sh.project)) \end{bmatrix} \cdot$$
$$\left[ pr: \left[ topoi = \mu(e.t, r.pr.topoi) : list(RecType) \right] \right]$$

## 2.8    *Acquire Topos,* $f_{acquire\_topos}$ *(p.130)*

$$\lambda r: \begin{bmatrix} resources: list(Topos) \\ shared: \begin{bmatrix} eud: list(Enthymeme) \\ topos: list(Topos) \end{bmatrix} \end{bmatrix} \cdot \lambda e: \neg \begin{bmatrix} t: Topos \\ c_1: in(t, r.resources) \\ c_2: spec(t, fst(r.shared.eud)) \end{bmatrix} \cdot$$
$$\begin{bmatrix} resources = [fst(r.shared.eud) \mid r.resources] : list(Topos) \\ shared: \left[ topoi = [fst(r.shared.eud) \mid r.shared.topos] : list(Topos) \right] \end{bmatrix}$$

## 3    Agenda

## 3.1    *Update Agenda with Suggestion,* $f_{update\_agenda\_suggestion}$ *(p. 98)*

$$\lambda r: \left[ pr: \begin{bmatrix} agenda = [\ ] : list(RecType) \\ games = [T_{SuggestionGameInst}] : list(T_{Game}) \end{bmatrix} \right] \cdot$$
$$\left[ pr: \left[ agenda = [\begin{bmatrix} e: suggest(SELF) \\ cnt: RecType \end{bmatrix}] : list(RecType) \right] \right]$$

## 3.2    *Specify Content of Suggestion on Agenda,* $f_{specify\_suggestion\_content}$ *(p. 104)*

$$\lambda r: \begin{bmatrix} pr: \begin{bmatrix} ag = [\begin{bmatrix} e: Suggest \\ cnt = ERec: RecType \end{bmatrix}] : list(RecType) \\ topoi: list(Topos) \\ beliefs: list(RecType) \end{bmatrix} \\ sh: \left[ project: list(RecType) \right] \end{bmatrix} \cdot$$
$$\lambda e: \begin{bmatrix} t: Topos \\ c_1: in(t, r.pr.topoi) \\ c_2: relevant\_to(t, fst(r.sh.project)) \\ belief: RecType \\ c_3: in(belief, r.pr.beliefs) \\ c_4: relevant\_to(belief, fst(r.sh.project)) \\ cnt: RecType \\ c_5: derived\_from(cnt, \{t, belief\}) \end{bmatrix} \cdot$$
$$\left[ pr: \left[ ag = [\begin{bmatrix} e: Suggest \\ cnt = e.cnt: RecType \end{bmatrix}] : list(RecType) \right] \right]$$

## 4 Games

### 4.1 *Update Private Games,* $f_{\text{ud\_pr\_games}}$ *(p. 95)*

$$\lambda r: \begin{bmatrix} \text{pr} : \begin{bmatrix} \text{games} : \text{list}(T_{Game}) \end{bmatrix} \\ \text{sh} : \begin{bmatrix} \text{project} = [\ T_{DecisionProject}] : \text{list}(RecType) \end{bmatrix} \end{bmatrix} \cdot \lambda e: \begin{bmatrix} g : T_{SuggestionGame} \\ c_1 : \text{in}(g, r.\text{pr.games}) \end{bmatrix} \cdot$$
$$\begin{bmatrix} \text{pr} : \begin{bmatrix} \text{games} = [\mu(e.g, r.\text{pr.games})\ ] : \text{list}(T_{Game}) \end{bmatrix} \end{bmatrix}$$

### 4.2 *Update Private Games',* $f_{\text{ud\_pr\_games'}}$ *(p. 96)*

$$\lambda r: \begin{bmatrix} \text{pr} : \begin{bmatrix} \text{games} : \text{list}(T_{Game}) \end{bmatrix} \\ \text{sh} : \begin{bmatrix} \text{project} = [T_{DecisionProject}] : \text{list}(RecType) \end{bmatrix} \end{bmatrix} \cdot \lambda e: \begin{bmatrix} g : T_{SuggestionGame} \\ c_1 : \neg\text{in}(g, r.\text{pr.games}) \end{bmatrix} \cdot$$
$$\begin{bmatrix} \text{pr} : \begin{bmatrix} \text{games} = [e.g \mid r.\text{pr.games}] : \text{list}(T_{Game}) \end{bmatrix} \end{bmatrix}$$

### 4.3 *Instantiation of Game,* $f_{\text{inst\_}T_{SuggestionGame}}$ *(p. 97)*

$$\lambda r: \begin{bmatrix} \text{player1} : Ind \\ \text{player2} : Ind \end{bmatrix} \cdot$$
$$\begin{bmatrix} e : \text{suggest}(r.\text{player1}) \end{bmatrix} \frown \begin{bmatrix} e : \text{motivate}(r.\text{player1}) \end{bmatrix}^{\leqslant 1} \frown \begin{bmatrix} e : \text{respond}(r.\text{player2}) \end{bmatrix}$$

### 4.4 *Identify Suggestion Game,* $f_{\text{identify\_suggestion\_game}}$ *(p. 104)*

$$\lambda r: \begin{bmatrix} \text{sh} : \begin{bmatrix} \text{l-m} : \begin{bmatrix} \text{prev} : RecType \\ e : Suggest \end{bmatrix} \\ \text{games} : \text{list}(T_{Game}) \end{bmatrix} \end{bmatrix} \cdot$$
$$\begin{bmatrix} \text{sh} : \begin{bmatrix} \text{games} = [\ T_{SuggestionGame} \mid r.\text{sh.games}] : \text{list}(T_{Game}) \end{bmatrix} \end{bmatrix}$$

# Definitions

## 1 Types and Relations between Types

### 1.1 *Preclusion (p. 76)*

A type $T_1$ precludes a type $T_2$ iff is there can be no $s$ such that $s : T_1$ and $s : T_2$.

### 1.2 *Negation (p. 130)*

For any type $T$, an object $a$ is of type $\neg T$, $a: \neg T$, iff there is some $T'$ such that $a: T'$ and $T'$ precludes $T$ ($T' \perp T$)

## 2 Specification of Topoi and Enthymemes

### 2.1 *Specification (p. 67)*

Assuming topos $\tau = \lambda r{:}T_1 \cdot T_2$ and enthymeme $\varepsilon = \lambda r{:}T_3 \cdot T_4$, $\varepsilon$ is a specification of $\tau$, i.e., specification($\varepsilon,\tau$) is witnessed, iff $T_3 \sqsubseteq T_1$ and for any $r$, $\varepsilon(r) \sqsubseteq \tau(r)$.

### 2.2 *Underspecification (p. 72)*

Assuming topos $\tau = \lambda r{:}T_1 \cdot T_2$ and enthymeme $\varepsilon = \lambda r{:}T_3 \cdot T_4$, $\varepsilon$ is an underspecification of $\tau$, i.e., underspecification($\varepsilon,\tau$) is witnessed, iff $T_1 \sqsubset T_3$ and for any $r$, $\varepsilon(r) \sqsubseteq \tau(r)$.

## 3 Operations on Enthymemes and Topoi

### 3.1 *Fixed-Point Types of Enthymemes and Topoi (pp. 125–126)*

If, for some type $T_1$, $f : (T_1 \to Type)$ then $\mathscr{F}(f)$ is a *fixed point type* for $f$, that is $a : \mathscr{F}(f)$ implies $a : f(a)$.

For a function (topos or enthymeme) $\lambda r{:}T_1 \cdot T_2(r)$, $\mathscr{F}(\lambda r{:}T_1 \cdot T_2(r)) = T_1 \wedge T'$ where $T'$ is like $T_2(r)$ except that any path $r.\pi$ is replaced by $\pi$.

### 3.2 *Composition (p. 126)*

The composition $\tau_1 \circ \tau_2$ of two topoi $\tau_1$ and $\tau_2$ such that $\tau_1 = \lambda r{:}T_1 \cdot T_2(r)$, $\tau_2 = \lambda r{:}T_3 \cdot T_4(r)$, and $\mathscr{F}(\tau_1) \sqsubseteq T_3$, is $\lambda r{:}\mathscr{F}(\tau_1) \cdot T_4(r)$

# References

Allwood, J. (2000). An activity based approach to pragmatics. In Bunt, H. and Black, W., editors, *Abduction, belief, and context in dialogue: studies in computational pragmatics*, pages 47–78. John Benjamins, Amsterdam.

Altmann, G. and Kamide, Y. (1999). Incremental interpretation at verbs: Restricting the domain of subsequent reference. *Cognition*, 73(3):247–264.

Andersen, G. (1998). Are tag questions questions? Evidence from spoken data. In *19th International Computer Archive of Modern and Medieval English (ICAME) Conference*, Belfast.

Andrews, P., Manandhar, S., and De Boni, M. (2006). Persuasive argumentation in human computer dialogue. In *AAAI Spring Symposium: Argumentation for Consumers of Healthcare*, pages 8–13.

Anscombre, J.-C. (1995). La théorie des topoi: Sémantique ou rhétorique? *Hermés*, 15.

Aristotle (1989). *Prior Analytics* (translated by Robin Smith). Hackett Publishing Company, Inc, Indianapolis, IN. (Original work published ca. 350 B.C.E.).

Aristotle (2007). *On Rhetoric, a theory of civic discourse* (translated by George A. Kennedy). Oxford University Press, Oxford. (Original work published ca. 340 B.C.E.).

Asher, N. and Lascarides, A. (2003). *Logics of Conversation*. Cambridge University Press, Cambridge.

Bakhtin, M. (1986). The problem of speech genres. In Emerson, C. and Holquist, M., editors, *Speech Genres and Other Late Essays*. University of Texas Press, Austin, TX.

Barrett, M.D. (1978). Lexical development and overextension in child language. *Journal of Child Language*, 5(2):205–219.

Barwise, J. and Perry, J. (1983). *Situations and Attitudes*. MIT Press, Cambridge, MA.

Berbyuk Lindström, N. (2008). Intercultural communication in health care. Non-Swedish physicians in Sweden. *Gothenburg Monographs in Linguistics*, 36.

Brandom, R. (1998). *Making it Explicit: Reasoning, Representing, and Discursive Commitment*. Harvard University Press, Cambridge, MA.

Breitholtz, E. (2014). *Enthymemes in Dialogue: A micro-rhetorical approach*. PhD thesis, University of Gothenburg.

Breitholtz, E. (2015). Are widows always wicked? Learning concepts through enthymematic reasoning. In *Type Theory and Lexical Semantics: ESSLLI 2015*, pages 49–55.

Breitholtz, E. and Cooper, R. (2011). Enthymemes as rhetorical resources. In *Proceedings of the 15th Workshop on the Semantics and Pragmatics of Dialogue—Full Papers*, pages 149–157. SEMDIAL.

Breitholtz, E. and Cooper, R. (2018). Towards a conversational game theory. In *Proceedings of Workshop on Sociolinguistic, Psycholinguistic and Formal Perspectives on Meaning*.

Breitholtz, E. and Maraev, V. (2019). How to put an elephant in the title: Modelling humorous incongruity with topoi. In *Proceedings of the 23rd Workshop on the Semantics and Pragmatics of Dialogue—Full Papers*, pages 118–126, London, United Kingdom. SEMDIAL.

Breitholtz, E. and Villing, J. (2008). Can Aristotelian enthymemes decrease the cognitive load of a dialogue system user? In *Proceedings of the 12th Workshop on the Semantics and Pragmatics of Dialogue—Full Papers*, pages 94–100. SEMDIAL.

Burnett, H. (2019). Signalling games, sociolinguistic variation and the construction of style. In *Linguistics and Philosophy*, 42.5 pages 419–450.

Carlson, L.H. (1982). *Dialogue games: An approach to discourse analysis*. PhD thesis, Massachusetts Institute of Technology.

Carston, R. (2006). Relevance Theory and the saying/implicating distinction. In *The Handbook of Pragmatics*, pages 633–656. Blackwell, Oxford.

Carston, R. and Hall, A. (2012). Implicature and explicature. In Schmid, H.-J., editor, *Cognitive Pragmatics*, Handbooks of Pragmatics, pages 47–84. De Gruyter Mouton, Berlin.

Chatzikyriakidis, S. (2014). Adverbs in a modern type theory. In *International Conference on Logical Aspects of Computational Linguistics*, pages 44–56.

Clark, A. and Lappin, S. (2010). *Linguistic Nativism and the Poverty of the Stimulus*. John Wiley & Sons, New York, NY.

Clark, E.V. (2015). Semantics and language acquisition. In Lappin, S. and Fox, C., editors, *The Handbook of Contemporary Semantic Theory*, pages 714–733. Wiley-Blackwell, Oxford.

Clark, H.H. (1996). *Using Language*. Cambridge University Press, Cambridge.

Clark, H.H., Brennan, S.E., et al. (1991). Grounding in communication. In *Perspectives on Socially Shared Cognition*, pages 127–149. American Psychological Association, Washington DC.

Clark, H.H. and Fox Tree, J.E. (2002). Using *uh* and *um* in spontaneous speaking. *Cognition*, 84(1):73–111.

Cooper, R. (2005a). Austinian truth, attitudes and type theory. *Research on Language and Computation*, 3:333–362.

Cooper, R. (2005b). Records and record types in semantic theory. *Journal of Logic and Computation*, 15(2):99–112.

Cooper, R. (2012). Type theory and semantics in flux. In Kempson, R., Asher, N., and Fernando, T., editors, *Philosophy of linguistics*, volume 14 of *Handbook of the philosophy of science*, pages 271–323. North Holland (Elsevier), Amsterdam.

Cooper, R. (2016). Type theory and language: From perception to linguistic communication. Draft manuscript accessed from https://sites.google.com/site/typetheorywith records/drafts/ttl161130.pdf.

Cooper, R. (2020). From perception to communication: An analysis of meaning and action using a theory of types with records (ttr). Draft manuscript accessed 2020-06-29 from https://github.com/robincooper/ttl/blob/master/ttl.pdf.

Cooper, R., Dobnik, S., Lappin, S., and Larsson, S. (2014). A probabilistic rich type theory for semantic interpretation. In *Proceedings of the EACL 2014 Type Theory and Natural Semantics Workshop (TTNLS)*. EACL.

Cooper, R., Engdahl, E., Larsson, S., and Ericsson, S. (2000). Accommodating questions and the nature of QUD. In *Proceedings of the 4th Workshop on the Semantics and Pragmatics of Dialogue—Full Papers*, pages 57–62. SEMDIAL.

Cooper, R. and Ginzburg, J. (2012). Negative inquisitiveness and based negation. In *Logic, Language and Meaning*, volume 7218 of *Lecture Notes in Computer Science*, pages 32–41. Springer, Berlin Heidelberg.

Cooper, R. and Ginzburg, J. (2015). Type theory with records for natural language semantics. In Lappin, S. and Fox, C., editors, *The Handbook of Contemporary Semantic Theory*, pages 375–407. Wiley Blackwell, Oxford.

Corbett, E.P.J. and Connors, R.J. (1999). *Classical Rhetoric for the Modern Student*. Oxford University Press, Oxford, 4 edition.

Couper-Kuhlen, E. and Selting, M. (2017). *Interactional linguistics: Studying language in social interaction*. Cambridge University Press, Cambridge.

Dreyfus, S.E. and Dreyfus, H.L. (1980). A five-stage model of the mental activities involved in direct skill aquisition. Technical Report 102, Operations research center, University of California, Berkeley.

Ducrot, O. (1980). *Les échelles argumentatives*. Minuit, Paris.

Ducrot, O. (1988). Topoï et formes topique. *Bulletin d'études de la linguistique française*, 22:1–14.

Eckert, P. (2012). Three waves of variation study: The emergence of meaning in the study of variation. *Annual Review of Anthropology*, 41:87–100.

Ericsson, S. (2005). *Information Enriched Constituents in Dialogue*. PhD thesis, University of Gothenburg.

Eshghi, A. and Lemon, O. (2014). How domain-general can we be? Learning incremental dialogue systems without dialogue acts. In *Proceedings of the 18th Workshop on the Semantics and Pragmatics of Dialogue—Full Papers*, pages 53–61. SEMDIAL.

Fernández, R. and Ginzburg, J. (2002). Non-sentential utterances: Grammar and dialogue dynamics in corpus annotation. In *Proceedings of the 19th international conference on Computational linguistics-Volume 1*, pages 1–7. ACL.

Fernández, R., Ginzburg, J., and Lappin, S. (2007). Classifying non-sentential utterances in dialogue: A machine learning approach. *Computational Linguistics*, 33(3):397–427.

Fernando, T. (2006). Situations as strings. *Electronic Notes in Theoretical Computer Science*, 165:23–36.

Fillmore, C. (1982). Frame semantics. In *Linguistics in the Morning Calm*, pages 111–137. Hanshin Publishing Company, Seoul, Korea.

Fine, K. (2012). A difficulty for the possible world analysis of counterfactuals. *Synthese*, 189(1):29–57.

Flower, L. and Hayes, J.R. (1980). The cognition of discovery: Defining a rhetorical problem. *College Composition and Communication*, 31(1):21–32.

Gibson, J.J. (1977). The theory of affordances. *Hilldale, USA*, 1:2.

Ginzburg, J. (1994). An update semantics for dialogue. In *Proceedings of the Tilburg International Workshop on Computational Semantics*. ITK Tilburg.

Ginzburg, J. (1996). Dynamics and the semantics of dialogue. In *Logic, language and computation*, volume 1. CSLI publications, Stanford, CA.

Ginzburg, J. (1998). Clarifying utterances. In *Proceedings of the 2nd Workshop on the Semantics and Pragmatics of Dialogue—Full Papers*. SEMDIAL.

Ginzburg, J. (2010). Relevance for dialogue. In *Proceedings of the 14th Workshop on the Semantics and Pragmatics of Dialogue—Full Papers*, pages 121–129. SEMDIAL.

Ginzburg, J. (2012). *The Interactive Stance: Meaning for Conversation*. Oxford University Press, Oxford.

Ginzburg, J., Breitholtz, E., Cooper, R., Hough, J., and Tian, Y. (2015). Understanding laughter. In *Proceedings of the Amsterdam Colloquium 2015*.

Ginzburg, J., Fernández, R., et al. (2010). Computational models of dialogue. In *Handbook of Computational Linguistics and Natural Language*. Blackwell, Oxford.

Goodwin, C. (1979). The interactive construction of a sentence in natural conversation. In Psathas, G., editor, *Everyday Language: Studies in Ethnomethodology*, pages 97–121. Irvington Publishers, New York.

Gregoromichelaki, E., Cann, R., and Kempson, R. (2012). Language as tools for interaction: Grammar and the dynamics of ellipsis resolution. *The Linguistic Review*, 29(4):563–584.

Gregoromichelaki, E. and Kempson, R. (2015). Joint utterances and the (split-)turn taking puzzle. In Mey, J.L. and Capone, A., editors, *Interdisciplinary studies in Pragmatics, Culture and Society*. Springer, Heidelberg.

Gregoromichelaki, E., Kempson, R., Purver, M., Mills, G.J., Cann, R., Meyer-Viol, W., and Healey, P.G. (2011). Incrementality and intention-recognition in utterance processing. *Dialogue & Discourse*, 2(1):199–233.

Grice, H.P. (1975). Logic and conversation. In Cole, P. and Morgan, J.L., editors, *Speech Acts*, volume 3 of *Syntax and Semantics*, pages 41–58. Academic Press, New York.

Groenendijk, J. and Stokhof, M. (1991). Dynamic predicate logic. *Linguistics and Philosophy*, 14:39–100.

Healey, P.G., Mills, G., Eshghi, A., and Howes, C. (2018). Running Repairs: Coordinating Meaning in Dialogue. *Topics in Cognitive Science*, 10(2):367–388.

Hebb, D.O. (1949). *The Organization of Behavior: A Neuropsychological Theory*. J. Wiley; Chapman & Hall, New York, NY.

Heim, I. (1983). File change semantics and the familiarity theory of definiteness. In

Béuerle, R.B., Schwarze, C., and v. Stechow, A., editors, *Meaning, Use and Interpretation of Language*, pages 164–189. de Gruyter, Berlin.

Heim, I. (1992). Presupposition projection and the semantics of attitude verbs. *Journal of Semantics*, 3(9):183–221.

Hopper, P.J. (2007). Linguistics and micro-rhetoric—a twenty first century encounter. *Journal of English Linguistics*, 35(3):236–252.

Horn, L. (1984). Toward a new taxonomy for pragmatic inference: Q-based and r-based implicature. *Meaning, form, and use in context*, 42.

Horty, J.F. (2012). *Reasons as Defaults*. Oxford University Press, Oxford.

Howes, C. (2012). *Coordinating in dialogue: Using compound contributions to join a party*. PhD thesis, Queen Mary, University of London.

Jackson, S. and Jacobs, S. (1980). Structure of conversational argument: Pragmatic bases for the enthymeme. *Quarterly Journal of Speech*, 66(3):251–265.

Kamp, H. (1981). A theory of truth and semantic representation. In Groenendijk, J.A., Janssen, T.M., and Stokhof, M.B., editors, *Formal methods in the study of language*, pages 277–322. Mathematisch Centrum, Amsterdam.

Kamp, H. and Reyle, U. (1993). *From Discourse to Logic: Introduction to Model-theoretic Semantics of Natural Language, Formal Logic and Discourse Representation Theory*. Kluwer Academic Publishers, Amsterdam.

Karttunen, L. (1974). Presupposition and linguistic context. *Theoretical Linguistics*, 1(1–3):181–194.

Kempson, R., Cann, R., Gregoromichelaki, E., and Chatzikyriakidis, S. (2016). Language as mechanisms for interaction. *Theoretical Linguistics*, 42(3–4):203–276.

Keyt, D. (2009). Deductive logic. In Anagnostopoulos, G., editor, *A Companion to Aristotle*, Blackwell Companions to Philosophy, chapter 3, pages 31–50. Blackwell, Oxford.

Kratzer, A. and Heim, I. (1998). *Semantics in Generative Grammar*. Blackwell, Oxford.

Lappin, S. (2013). Intensional semantics without possible worlds. Philosophy Colloquium King's College London.

Lappin, S. (2015). Curry typing, polymorphism, and fine-grained intensionality. In Lappin, S. and Fox, C., editors, *Handbook of Contemporary Semantic Theory*. Wiley-Blackwell, Oxford.

Larsson, S. (2002). *Issue Based Dialogue Management*. PhD thesis, University of Gothenburg.

Larsson, S. (2011). Do dialogues have content? In *Logical Aspects of Computational Linguistics*, volume 6736 of *Lecture Notes in Computer Science*, pages 145–158. Springer, Heidelberg.

Larsson, S. and Myrendal, J. (2017). Dialogue acts and updates for semantic coordination. In *Proceedings of the 21st Workshop on the Semantics and Pragmatics of Dialogue*, page 59.

Larsson, S. and Traum, D. (2000). Information state and dialogue management in trindi dialogue move engine tool kit. *Natural Language Engineering*, 6:323–240.

Lascarides, A. and Asher, N. (2008). Segmented discourse representation theory: Dynamic semantics with discourse structure. In *Computing meaning*, pages 87–124. Springer.

Lavelle, M., Healey, P.G., and McCabe, R. (2012). Is nonverbal communication disrupted in interactions involving patients with schizophrenia? *Schizophrenia bulletin*, 39(5):1150–1158.

Leth, P. (2011). *Paraphrase and Rhetorical Adjustment: An Essay on Contextualism and Cohesion*. PhD thesis, University of Gothenburg.

Levin, J.A. and Moore, J.A. (1977). Dialogue-games: Metacommunication structures for natural language interaction. *Cognitive Science*, 1(4):395–420.

Levinson, S.C. (2000). *Presumptive Meanings: The Theory of Generalized Conversational Implicature*. MIT Press, Cambridge, MA.

Lewis, D. (1979). Scorekeeping in a language game. *Journal of Philosophical Logic*, 8(1):339–359.

Linell, P. (1998). *Approaching Dialogue: Talk, Interaction and Contexts in Dialogical Perpective*. John Benjamins, Amsterdam.

Linell, P. (2009). *Rethinking Language, Mind, and World Dialogically: Interactional and Contextual Theories of Human Sense-Making*. Advances in Cultural Psychology: Constructing Human Development. Information Age Publishing.

Lücking, A. (2016). Modeling co-verbal gesture perception in type theory with records. In *2016 Federated Conference on Computer Science and Information Systems (FedCSIS)*, pages 383–392. IEEE.

Ludlow, P. (2014). *Living Words: Meaning Underdetermination and the Dynamic Lexicon*. Oxford University Press, Oxford.

Maguire, E. (2019). Enthymemetic conditionals: Topoi as a guide for acceptability. In *Proceedings of the IWCS 2019 Workshop on Computing Semantics with Types, Frames and Related Structures*, pages 65–74.

Mann, W.C. and Thompson, S.A. (1986). Rhetorical structure theory: Description and construction of text structures. Technical Report ISI/RS-86–174, Information Sciences Institute.

Mann, W.C. and Thompson, S.A. (1988). Rhetorical structure theory: Toward a functional theory of text organization. *Text*, 8(3):243–281.

Maraev, V., Breitholtz, E., and Howes, C. (2020). How do you make an AI get the joke? Here's what I found on the web. In *First AISB Symposium on Conversational AI (SoCAI)*.

McCarthy, J. (1980). Circumscription—a form of non-monotonic reasoning. *Artificial Intelligence*, 13(1–2):27–39.

McDermott, D. and Doyle, J. (1980). Non-monotonic logic I. *Artificial Intelligence*, 13(1): 41–72.

Meyer, B.J. and Freedle, R.O. (1984). Effects of discourse type on recall. *American Educational Research Journal*, 21(1):121–143.

Miller, C.R. (2003). Writing in a culture of simulation. In Nystrand, P.M., Nystrand, M., and Duffy, J., editors, *Towards a rhetoric of everyday life: new directions in research on writing, text, and discourse*, pages 58–82. University of Wisconsin Press, Madison.

Mills, G.J. and Gregoromichelaki, E. (2010). Establishing coherence in dialogue: sequentiality, intentions and negotiation. In *Proceedings of the 14th Workshop on the Semantics and Pragmatics of Dialogue—Full Papers*. SEMDIAL.

Montague, R. (1973). The proper treatment of quantification in ordinary english. In Hintikka, J., Moravcsik, J., and Suppes, P., editors, *Approaches to Natural Language*. D. Reidel, Dordrecht.

Mora-Márquez, A.M. (2017). Aristotle's fallacy of equivocation and its 13th century reception. In de Libera, A., Goubier, F., and Cesali, L., editors, *Formal Approaches and Natural Language in Medieval Logic: Proceedings of the XIXth European Symposium of Medieval Logic and Semantics, Geneva, 12–16 June 2012*, pages 217–238. Brepols, Turnhout.

Noble, W., Breitholz, E., and Cooper, R. (2020). Personae under uncertainty: The case of topoi. In Howes, C. and Chatzikyriakidis, S., editors, CLASP *Conference on Probability and Meaning*.

Perelman, C. and Olbrechts-Tycteca, L. (1969). *The New Rhetoric: A Treatise on Argumentation*. University of Notre Dame Press, Notre Dame, IN.

Pickering, M.J. and Garrod, S. (2004). Toward a mechanistic psychology of dialogue. *Behavioral and Brain Sciences*, 27(2):169–190.

Pustejovsky, J. (1998). *The Generative Lexicon*. MIT Press, Cambrige, MA.

Ranta, A. (1994). *Type-Theoretical Grammar*. Oxford University Press, Oxford.

Razuvayevskaya, O. and Teufel, S. (2017). Finding enthymemes in real-world texts: A feasibility study. *Argument & Computation*, 8(2):113–129.

Recanati, F. (2001). What is said. *Synthese*, 128(1):75–91.

Recanati, F. (2004). *Literal Meaning*. Cambridge University Press, Cambridge.

Recanati, F. (2012). *Mental Files*. Oxford University Press, Oxford.

Reiter, R. (1980). A logic for default reasoning. *Artificial Intelligence*, 13(1):81–132.

Reiter, R. and Criscuolo, G. (1981). On interacting defaults. In *International Joint Conference on Artificial Intelligence*, pages 270–276.

Rosengren, M. (2002). *Doxologi: en essä om kunskap*. Rhetor förlag.

Rumelhart, D.E. (1980). Schemata: The building blocks of cognition. In R. Spiro, B.B. and Brewer, W., editors, *Theoretical Issues in Reading Comprehension*, Perspectives from Cognitive Psychology, Linguistics, Artificial Intelligence and Education, pages 33–57. Lawrence Erlbaum Associates.

Sacks, H., Schegloff, E., and Jefferson, G. (1974). A simplest systematics for the organization of turn-taking for conversation. *Language*, 50(4):696–735.

Schegloff, E.A. (2007). *Sequence organization in interaction: A primer in conversation analysis I*, volume 1. Cambridge University Press, Cambridge.

Schlangen, D. (2005). Modelling dialogue: Challenges and approaches. *Künstliche Intelligenz*, 3.

Schlangen, D. and Lascarides, A. (2003). The interpretation of non-sentential utterances in dialogue. In *Proceedings of the 4th SIGdial Workshop on Discourse and Dialogue*.

Schlöder, J.J., Breitholtz, E., and Fernández, R. (2016). Why? In Julie Hunter, M.S. and Stone, M., editors, *Proceedings of the 20th Workshop on the Semantics and Pragmatics of Dialogue*.

Schulz, K. and Van Rooij, R. (2006). Pragmatic meaning and non-monotonic reasoning: The case of exhaustive interpretation. *Linguistics and philosophy*, 29(2):205–250.

Smith, R. (2012). Aristotle's logic. In Zalta, E.N., editor, *The Stanford Encyclopedia of Philosophy (Spring 2012 Edition)*. http://plato.stanford.edu/archives/spr2012/entries/aristotle-logic/.

Sperber, D. and Wilson, D. (1995). *Relevance: Communication and Cognition*. Blackwell, Oxford, 2 edition.

Stalnaker (1974). Pragmatic presuppositions. In Munitz, M.K. and Unger, P., editors, *Semantics and Philosophy*. New York University Press.

Stalnaker, R. (1978). Assertion. In Cole, P., editor, *Pragmatics*, volume 9 of *Syntax and Semantics*. New York Academic Press, New York, NY.

Stalnaker, R. (1998). On the representation of context. *Journal of Logic, Language, and Information*, 7(1):3–19.

Stenning, K. and van Lambalgen, M. (2008). *Human Reasoning and Cognitive Science*. MIT Press, Cambridge, MA.

Strasser, C. and Antonelli, G.A. (2019). Non-monotonic logic. In Zalta, E.N., editor, *The Stanford Encyclopedia of Philosophy*. Metaphysics Research Lab, Stanford University, summer 2019 edition.

Strawson, P.F. (1950). On referring. *Mind*, 59(235):320–344.

Sztencel, M. (2018). *Semantics, Pragmatics and Meaning Revisited: The Case of Conditionals*. Springer, Heidelberg.

van Dijk, T.A. (1979). Pragmatic connectives. *Journal of Pragmatics*, 3(5):447–456.

Villing, J. (2009). Dialogue behaviour under high cognitive load. In *Proceedings of the SIGDIAL 2009 Conference: The 10th Annual Meeting of the Special Interest Group on Discourse and Dialogue*, pages 322–325. ACL.

Walker, M.A. (1996). The effect of resource limits and task complexity on collaborative planning in dialogue. *Artificial Intelligence*, 85(1):181–243.

Wason, P.C. (1968). Reasoning about a rule. *Quarterly Journal of Experimental Psychology*, 20(3):273–281.

Wilson, D. and Sperber, D. (2004). Relevance Theory. In Horn, L. and Ward, G., editors, *Handbook of Pragmatics*, pages 607–632. Blackwell, Oxford.

Wittgenstein, L. (1953). *Philosophical investigations. Philosophische Untersuchungen.* Macmillan, London. Translated by G.E.M. Anscombe.

# Index of Authors

# Index of Subjects

Printed in the United States
By Bookmasters